The Entrepreneur

An Economic Theory, Second Edition

Mark Casson

Professor of Economics, University of Reading, UK

Edward Elgar
Cheltenham, UK • Northampton, MA, USA

Published by
Edward Elgar Publishing Limited
The Lypiatts
15 Lansdown Road
Cheltenham
Glos GL50 2JA
UK

Edward Elgar Publishing, Inc.
William Pratt House
9 Dewey Court
Northampton
Massachusetts 01060
USA

First published 1982
Second edition 2003
Paperback edition 2005
Cased edition reprinted 2004, 2005
Paperback edition reprinted 2006, 2008

A catalogue record for this book
is available from the British Library

Library of Congress Cataloguing in Publication Data
Casson, Mark, 1945–
    The entrepreneur : an economic theory / Mark Casson. — 2nd ed.
      p. cm.
    Includes bibliographical references and index.
    1.   Entrepreneurship. I. Title.

  HB615 .C37 2003
  338'.04 — dc21   2002037937

ISBN 978 1 85898 910 5 (cased)
     978 1 84542 193 9 (paperback)

Typeset by Manton Typesetters, Louth, Lincolnshire, UK.
Printed and bound in Great Britain by Biddles Ltd, King's Lynn, Norfolk.

Contents

Figures

Tables

Preface to the second edition

I am delighted that the continuing demand for this book warrants the publication of a new edition more than 20 years after it first appeared. Although the book has been in print almost continuously since it was first published, thanks to a reprint arranged by Gregg Revivals some twelve years ago, this is the first occasion on which the text has been revised.

I don't know if other authors have a 'favourite book' amongst those that they have written, but I do – and this is it. I like it in spite of its deficiencies, and to some extent because of them. It is the most ambitious book that I have ever attempted, and I freely admit that it does not entirely accomplish what it set out to achieve. Indeed, attempting to make good the deficiencies of this book has become a major preoccupation of my subsequent academic career.

It is sometimes said that authors 'give birth' to their books, and regard them as their 'children'. Authors are certainly very concerned for the survival of their books – in particular, keeping them in print – as publishers are only too well aware. Pursuing this metaphor, it may be said that writing this book was the most difficult pregnancy I have ever endured (even if it was nowhere near as difficult as the real thing). The reason for the difficulty is that I wrote the book to bring some order into my own thoughts, so that for much of the time during which I was writing the book I wasn't entirely sure what I was trying to say!

Ever since I had been an undergraduate at Bristol University I had been disturbed by the tension between the comparative static method of neoclassical economics and the real-world dynamics of market adjustment. For example, I could never understand why, when demand in an industry increased, it was sometimes firms from outside the industry that entered, whereas in other cases firms already inside the industry expanded existing capacity instead. Moreover, how could the firms that expanded capacity know how many other firms were expanding capacity at the same time, so that just the right amount of additional capacity was created in the industry as a whole? Our lecturers at Bristol were very good at directing us to relevant writers – such as George Richardson and Ronald Coase – but, as is often the case, the answers provided to one set of questions raised new questions too. I eventually came to the conclusion that it was access to information that determined the dynamics of market adjustment, and that entrepreneurship was crucial in understanding who obtained the relevant information first. This in turn led me to the work of Frank Knight, Friedrich von Hayek, Israel Kirzner and Joseph Schumpeter. Reading these classic writings on entrepreneurship proved immensely stimulating, but it also produced some intellectual 'indigestion'. The ideas of each author seemed quite different, and it was not clear how they all fitted together. I therefore wrote the first draft of this book simply to sort out my own ideas – to cure my indigestion, in other words.

Some authors claim that writing is a form of 'therapy', and from what has been said above it is clear that 'therapy' was a motive in the present case. The disadvantage of therapy as a motive for authorship, however, is that the book is written for the benefit of the author and not the reader. If the author has no clear concept of the intended audience, other than people like themselves, then the book is likely to fail in commercial terms. The first edition of this book almost fell into this trap – but not quite. The danger was averted because, through giving seminars to colleagues at Reading and elsewhere, I began to appreciate the wide variety of motives that stimulate interest in the entrepreneur. For many people the major motive for studying entrepreneurship is not pure intellectual curiosity, but rather an admiration for entrepreneurs as successful and wealthy people. In recognition of this, I began the book with a mythical biography of Jack Brash – the stereotypical entrepreneur. If there is one thing that readers of this book seem to remember, it is the story of Jack Brash, which is reassuring in some ways, but rather depressing in others.

The most enthusiastic reviewer of the first edition was Karen Vaughn, who was very supportive of the notion of building a bridge between conventional economic theory on the one hand and the study of real-world entrepreneurship and market processes on the other. Not all reviewers shared her enthusiasm, however. A mathematical economist considered my reliance on diagrams, supported by verbal argument, to be an 'old-fashioned' method of exposition. A specialist on small business economics considered the book 'too philosophical'. Another reviewer confessed that that they could find nothing at all of any substance that was original in the book.

The most perceptive criticisms of the book, in my view, were those which drew a parallel between entrepreneurship and leadership. As already noted, much of the popular appeal of the entrepreneur rests upon the entrepreneur as 'role model'. People admire the way that a successful entrepreneur inspires their employees to dedicate themselves to the business, and converts their customers into enthusiastic believers in the product. Entrepreneurs benefit society, from this perspective, not only in material terms, but in raising morale, and in doing so they benefit themselves as well. By focusing, as its sub-title suggests, on the strictly economic aspects of entrepreneurship, the book failed to address the social aspects of the subject in sufficient depth.

I was particular sympathetic to these criticisms because I had already come to the same conclusion myself, but only at the end of the book, and without appreciating the full implications of this view. The first edition of this book concluded by looking forward to the emergence of an integrated social science – a social science that could do justice to the social as well as the economic aspects of the entrepreneur. This has provided me with a research agenda which I have pursued steadily over the last 20 years. Readers who enjoyed the book, and are looking for a sequel, could consult *The Economics of Business Culture* (1991), *Entrepreneurship and Business Culture* (1995), *Information and Organization* (1997) and *Enterprise and Leadership* (2000). All of these books attempt to build upon the foundations set out in this book in order to generate a more balanced approach to leadership and to the role of the entrepreneur.

Within the field of entrepreneurship, the ideas presented in this book have been taken up quite widely. The concept of entrepreneurship set out in the opening chapters is the basis for the definition of the entrepreneur used in *The New Palgrave Dictionary of Economics*, *The International Encyclopaedia of Social Science*, the *Fortune Encyclopaedia of Business*, the *Penguin Dictionary of Economics* and the *Oxford Encyclopaedia of Economic History*.

However, the field of entrepreneurship still remains somewhat divorced from mainstream economics. Ever since this book was written, it has seemed 'obvious' to me that entrepreneurship is at the heart of the market process, which is, in turn, supposed to be at the heart of mainstream economics. Entrepreneurs are the personification of the market process: without them, the market system as we know it would barely exist. Some markets might operate as auctions, but the familiar market in which entrepreneurs advertise products they have developed, and quote prices at which they are committed to trade with the public, would not exist without them. It seems equally 'obvious' that flows of information, and not just flows of product, are crucial to economic activity, for without a flow of information no-one would know what products are for sale. Indeed, it could be argued that, in a metaphysical sense, flows of intangible information are more 'real', in the modern economy, than the tangible product flows which they coordinate. Yet mainstream economists continue to emphasize flows of product, and flows of payment, as if they were the core of the economic system.

It is not only mainstream economists that continue to ignore the economic theory of the entrepreneur. Ironically, some researchers on small business do so too. Considerable confusion has been generated over the last 20 years by the mistaken habit of regarding the owners of small businesses as the only true entrepreneurs. Entrepreneurship, as defined in this book, is concerned with the exercise of judgment in all sorts of different business situations, including large-scale technological innovations undertaken by multinational manufacturing firms and large-scale financial speculations undertaken by international banks. It also includes political entrepreneurship – such as the founding of a new political movement – and criminal entrepreneurship, such as drug-dealing. Some small firms are certainly very entrepreneurial, but others are not. The notion that entrepreneurship is only to be found in small business is a myth, although quite a useful myth for those who wish to subsidize small business, or to win the small business vote. It is unfortunate that this myth has been perpetuated because researchers have taken too little note of the economic theory of the entrepreneur.

When revising a book that is more than 20 years old, a number of issues arise regarding the changes that should be made. To begin with, should the book be thoroughly rewritten and updated? If it were a textbook that had been regularly updated before then it would certainly be sensible to update it again. Recently published work would be cited and discussed, and issues raised by the latest thinking on the subject would be addressed. This book is not a textbook, however, but is intended to be an original contribution to theory. Furthermore, there has been a phenomenal growth in the literature on entrepreneurship in the last 20 years – particularly on the empirical side – and two different edited collections of major writings on the subject have recently been published. To incorporate all of this literature into the new edition would have meant writing a new book rather than producing a new edition of an existing book. I have therefore decided to leave the literature review and references as they were. This will help the reader to appreciate the context in which the book was originally written, and in particular to appreciate the relatively limited re-sources available to students of entrepreneurship some 20 years ago.

Economic theory has advanced significantly in the last 20 years, notably in the analysis of asymmetric information, which has an important bearing on the theme of this book. However, these advances have been broadly in line with the developments anticipated in the first edition, and so it has not been necessary to amend or correct any of the text in the light of recent work. Because the concept of asymmetric information is now more widely under-stood, however, it has been possible to abbreviate or omit certain sections of the text in which these ideas were elaborated. Growing recognition of the coordination problems created by asymmetric information means that gen-eral equilibrium theory is no longer such a dominant force in conventional neoclassical economics as it was at the time this book was written. To reflect this change, criticisms of 'neoclassical theory' in the first edition have been replaced by criticisms of '*simple* neoclassical theory' in this new edition, since sophisticated neoclassical theory is now immune to some of the criti-cisms advanced in the first edition of this book.

In the light of these remarks, the main changes in this new edition are designed to clarify the arguments which were advanced in the original edition of the book. The final draft of the first edition was completed in some haste, over a summer vacation. There was no time to put the draft manuscript to one side and return to it later for a final revision. As a result, some rather turgid sections of prose remained in the final version, together with some peripheral material which distracted from the main argument of the book. These problems were recognized in the opening sentence of the original Preface, which began, rather ominously, 'Inside every long book there is a good short book trying to get out.' In response to this problem, the present draft has been slimmed down by one-third – mainly just by eliminating repetition and peripheral material. The benefit to the reader is considerable, as the chapters now 'hang together' much better than they did before.

There is one important part of the book where no changes need to be made, and that is in thanking those friends and colleagues who helped me with the first edition of this book. I should like to reiterate my thanks to Peter Buckley, Paul Geroski, Charles Sutcliffe and Mike Utton for their detailed criticisms of the manuscript, and to Phil Rosson for his advice on the economics of marketing. Nicole Collis typed the manuscript, and my wife Janet helped me to improve the style. Michael Hay (now of London Business School) and Sue Corbett saw the book through the press. Lauraine Newcombe provided secretarial support during the recent revision of the book.

There are two people I should like to thank in particular because they have been involved with both the first edition and the revised edition. The first is Edward Elgar, who originally commissioned this book some 24 years ago when he was an editor with Martin Robertson (a division of Blackwells). I am very pleased that this new edition is appearing under his own imprint. The second is Jill Turner, Executive Assistant in the School of Business at the University of Reading, who has always been on hand to provide advice and support throughout the time in which this book has been in print.

MARK CASSON
UNIVERSITY OF READING

Introduction

We all of us know someone who is an entrepreneur. He may be a property developer, a small businessman, or just someone who knows how to 'turn a fast buck'. Perhaps he buys secondhand Jaguar cars that are destined for the scrapheap, does them up and sells them to the Japanese. Or he buys unwanted books from publishers and sells them at 'unrepeatable' bargain prices from a high-street shop.

Nowadays it is quite fashionable to be an entrepreneur. Suburban front rooms are stacked high with pocket calculators to be sold through mail-order advertisements in the local paper. Commuters' wives run 'nearly new' boutiques in their local village. It was not always so. A French sociologist, challenged to give a definition of the entrepreneur, is reputed to have said 'The entrepreneur is a pig.' This book attempts to give a more balanced view, but in doing so it faces the same problem as did the French sociologist: the most difficult part of studying entrepreneurship is to define who or what is an entrepreneur.

Most studies of the entrepreneur make no attempt at definition. They rely instead on a stereotype, that of the swashbuckling business adventurer. Anyone who conforms loosely to this stereotype is dubbed an entrepreneur. An examination of the folklore of entrepreneurship enables us to sketch the following portrait.

JACK BRASH – ENTREPRENEUR

John Brash was born in Stepney, East London, in March 1912, the son of Oskar Brasch and Sarah Meadows. His father, a Polish immigrant, changed his name to Brash on arrival in England, and took British nationality. He was a former merchant seaman, and ran a small import agency, supplying traditional Polish products to the immigrant community. By the outset of the First World War he had built up a useful trade, but increasingly the profits of the business were spent on drink. When John was only two years old his father abandoned his mother, who was forced to take a job making fashion garments. She worked from home and, as he grew up, John helped his mother with the outwork in the evenings after school. They were paid on piece-rates;

1

an item for which their wage was tuppence was priced at two guineas or more in the West End shops.

John did not do well at school; he was quiet and withdrawn. Leaving school at the earliest opportunity, he became an errand boy and then shop-assistant, but was sacked on his eighteenth birthday when he became entitled to higher wages. Finding another steady job hard to obtain, he resolved to go into business on his own account.

He chose house clearance and secondhand furniture dealing. It was a time of high unemployment, and many of the unemployed were so poor that they financed themselves by selling off family heirlooms, and many choice items were 'going for a song'. Jack's experience with fashion garments had taught him that, while many people were poor, there were still those rich enough to afford expensive goods, if you knew where to find them. His idea was to buy in bulk from the local neighbourhood and sell to West End dealers. What the dealers would not take he stored in the front room at home and sold from a market stall at the weekend.

Before he could begin he needed to buy a handcart. He did not have the ready cash but, finding a cart locally that was rather overpriced, he offered to give the asking price if he could be allowed six months to pay. The owner was delighted to find a buyer, and the cart was Jack's.

Jack was selective in what he bought. He always promised his sellers that their effects would be disposed of discreetly. By this he meant that they would be sold on the other side of town for a high price instead of locally for a lower price. He often worked unusual hours, so that he could call when the husband was out of the house. Wives were more willing to sell old things that were 'just gathering dust'. If they thought their husbands would miss it they might buy a cheaper item to replace it with; Jack often had something handy that would do. He soon learnt by experience what sort of things the West End dealers were looking for, but eventually these became more scarce as potential supplies were depleted by his own activities, and by competitors moving in on his field.

Jack realized that supplies were so tight that he would have to stimulate them artificially. In particular there was a strong demand for fancy gilt-framed mirrors, and to satisfy this demand he entered the reproduction market. He obtained a couple of quotations in nearby Whitechapel for a batch of 50 reproduction items, and set the retail price by quadrupling his unit cost. He took the mirror which was to be copied and hawked it round the dealers he knew, offering a basic trade discount of 40 per cent, with an extra 10 per cent for an order of five or more, and a further 5 per cent for cash in advance. In this way he collected enough cash to finance production of the first batch of 50.

The business took off in a big way. The dealers sold out the first batch very quickly and re-ordered in bigger quantities. However, Jack's profit on the first batch only allowed him to finance another batch of 50 right away, though by the time the fourth batch was under way, ploughed back profits together with prepayments allowed the production run to increase to 250. Unit costs fell as batch size increased, and Jack found that he was doing very well indeed. He began to look around for something to do with the cash. He realized that what sold the mirror was the design of the frame, and that the same sort of frame could be used for pictures, prints and photographs as well, so these products were added to his range.

About this time it occurred to Jack that he could cut out some of the dealers and sell direct to the public. Without the dealers' margin he could set a lower price and sell more units. The logical place to sell was where the market was biggest, and so when the premises next to his largest trade customer became vacant he rented them, and set up in competition. By cutting his price he devalued his competitor's existing stock, and shortly the firm was forced into liquidation. However, Jack helped his old friend by taking over the lease and buying up the stock, on what Jack considered very generous terms.

When war broke out in 1939 Jack realized that, as a first-generation Briton, he was in a rather vulnerable position. As a youngster he had been aware of Cockney antipathy to the aliens who settled in East London. He sold his business while it was still doing well, and invested the proceeds in jewellery. This was the form in which he kept his savings throughout the war. Very patriotically he enlisted, and soon found his niche running the stores on an airfield. As a quartermaster his methods were somewhat unconventional, and the stores often contained some things they shouldn't and were short of a few things they should have held. However, Jack never made anything personally out of his deals, though by the end of the war quite a few people owed Jack a favour. After the war Jack kept in touch with them, and some of them repaid the favour by investing in his business ventures, or introducing Jack to useful contacts.

By the time he was demobilized Jack's experience in the stores had given him a good idea of the sort of surplus goods that would be coming onto the market, and for some years after the war he made a living buying up motor spares and selling them to people who were trying to keep their pre-war vehicles on the road. However, his big opportunity did not come until restrictions on the production of domestic furniture were lifted.

Immediately after the war the rate of household formation had been very high on account of marriages deferred because of the war. All these households had been furnished with utility items, built to government specification, but public provision had resulted in too low a degree of product differentiation for most consumers' tastes. As a wartime economy measure this was fully justified, but it was ill-adapted to the emerging post-war 'affluent society'. Jack decided to go back into fancy frames and mirrors, but to give his products a futuristic look.

He sunk his own savings in an initial batch of frames and was fortunate to sell them outright to a buyer for a chain of high-street stores. The frames sold well, but to Jack's surprise the buyer suggested that an antique-look frame might also sell, provided that the frames were in better taste than Jack's pre-war product. As the chain expanded so did Jack's own business; however, the store managers always insisted on putting the frames at the back of the store, instead of at the front, as Jack would have preferred.

Jack resolved to set up his own outlets in order to keep the chain store on its toes, and to improve his bargaining power. He rented a number of shops and sold prints, antique maps and mirrors as well as frames. However, although his sales were high, his costs were even higher, and very soon he was in financial difficulties. He approached his bank manager to ask for an overdraft to finance his working capital. The manager was sympathetic, but cautious. He introduced him to an accountant who drew up a proper balance sheet and made projections of income and expenditure. The accountant made a number of recommendations for 'turning round' the business.

1. The shops should sell a wider range of merchandise and not just Jack's own products.
2. Stock control should be improved, using more formal procedures.
3. Jack should stop trying to run everything himself, and managers should be given more discretion.
4. Higher wages should be paid to attract better-quality staff. He should stop recruiting 'yes men' and hire people with some flair of their own instead.
5. Jack should form a limited company and put some professional people on the board to advise him.

The bank manager indicated that the money would be available if these changes were made. It seemed to Jack that the 'establishment' had finally gained the upper hand. But he needed the money and so he agreed; and this is how the Flash Furniture Company was born.

Very soon Jack's stores were stocking a complete range of furniture and glossy household goods, and 'Flash Homes' were pictured in full-page advertisements in the women's weeklies. They could also be seen in the show houses on the big new estates. A special feature was that items were coordinated to form a complete range of room furnishing in a particular style. You could buy Tudor or Spanish as well as the budget-price Superluxe range. You chose the items you wanted using the special Adjustable Room Planner. Later a Nordic range was introduced, finished in brightly coloured plastic for easy cleaning, but this dated rather quickly. Much of it was sold off for office use; the remainder was lost when a mysterious fire gutted a warehouse, but fortunately it was fully insured.

About this time unpleasant rumours began to circulate about Jack's personal life. He featured in the gossip columns, particularly in the flat-racing season, when he hosted frequent parties for other racehorse owners. It was said, however, that he neglected his mother, who still lived in a flat in East London. Jack strenuously denied the charge, and said that his mother was given everything she wanted – including a television – and that she was too old to get about anyway.

In 1936, he had married Georgina, only daughter of Brigadier Mount of Monk's Court, Oxfordshire, and an heiress to a small fortune. They had no children, and after the war Jack had begun to groom his young cousin Robert to take over the business. Soon after Robert came of age Jack retired from active management of the business, and began devoting himself to the pursuits of a country gentleman. He became well known for his views on free education as the key to equality of opportunity. He lavishly endowed one of the newer universities, and re-equipped its common rooms in the Nordic style. The business began to go down hill, but Jack did not seem to notice, being preoccupied with the honours heaped upon him by the establishment. Shortly before his death he was knighted for his services to education and industry, and was awarded an honorary doctorate from one of the newer universities. At the degree congregation he was described as a 'great public benefactor' and a 'man of the people'. He always tried to 'give the public what it wants' and believed passionately in the housewife 'voting with the pennies in her purse'. It was generally agreed that, if there were a few more people like Jack Brash, then the country would not be in the state it is in today.

The existence of this stereotype has undoubtedly impeded the economic analysis of the entrepreneur. There is a tendency to evaluate theories solely on the basis of their ability to rationalize this preconceived view. This procedure is the very antithesis of proper research methodology. Many of the qualities with which the heroic stereotype is imbued are simply a reflection of contemporary cultural attitudes.

Nevertheless, the stereotype is useful in that it provides various hypotheses regarding the family background, personal qualities and the business methods of the entrepreneur. The fact that these hypotheses are value-loaded does not matter, so long as they are regarded only as working hypotheses and not as statements of empirical regularity. The stereotype is useful as an articulation of the view that there is a correlation between various personal characteristics and entrepreneurial activity. It serves to direct the theorist's attention to the need to derive, if possible, relations between observable personal characteristics and the level of entrepreneurial activity. It is one of the objects of this book to deduce from very simple assumptions testable hypotheses of this kind.

PART I

Theoretical Foundations

1. The significance of the entrepreneur

1.1 A GAP IN ECONOMIC THEORY

The stimulus for writing the first edition of this book was a perception that, at the time, there was no established economic theory of the entrepreneur. The subject area had been surrendered by economists to sociologists, psychologists and political scientists. Indeed, it seemed that all the social sciences, except economics, had a theory of the entrepreneur.

There were two main reasons why there was no economic theory of the entrepreneur. These were connected with the limitations of the two main schools of economic thought at the time. First, the neoclassical school of economics made very extreme assumptions about access to information. Simple neoclassical models assume that everyone has free access to all the information they require for taking decisions. This assumption reduces decision making to the mechanical application of mathematical rules for optimization. It trivializes decision making, and makes it impossible to analyse the role of entrepreneurs in taking decisions of a particular kind.

Secondly, the Austrian school of economics, which takes the entrepreneur more seriously, is committed to extreme subjectivism – a philosophical standpoint which makes a predictive theory of the entrepreneur impossible. Austrians argue that anyone who has the sort of information necessary to predict the behaviour of entrepreneurs has a strong incentive to stop theorizing and become an entrepreneur himself. They suggest, furthermore, that by entering the system himself, the theorist might well generate a behavioural response which would falsify his own prediction. This argument, however, really applies only to the prediction of entrepreneurial success; it may be much easier to predict entrepreneurial failures. The argument also fails to recognize that many economic laws refer to the aggregate behaviour of populations of individuals, and that it may be possible to predict the behaviour of a population of entrepreneurs even if it is impossible to predict the individual behaviour of any one of them. In any case, the inability to predict individual behaviour depends crucially on the absence of barriers to entry into entrepreneurship. As we shall see, there are often significant barriers and in this case the successful theorist has no opportunity to 'endogenize' his predictions. As a consequence it may even be possible to predict the exploitation of specific entrepreneurial opportunities. Finally, even where prediction is impossible, it may still be feasible to develop a retrodictive theory of entrepreneurship – that is, a theory that can be tested, with the benefit of hindsight, on historical data. Thus even if a predictive theory cannot be developed, it is still possible to have a testable one.

1.2   A REVIEW OF THE ISSUES

The prevalence of the negative attitudes outlined above might have reflected a situation in which there was little demand for a theory of the entrepreneur. But that was the very opposite of the truth. In many fields of economics, existing theories were demonstrably inadequate, and writers in these fields frequently pointed to the need for a theory of the entrepreneur.

This need was most apparent when analysing the reasons for economic success and failure. The problem of explaining why some succeed while others fail is crucial to the study of economic development, the growth of the firm and the distribution of income. The spread of subjects is so broad because success can be analysed at a number of different levels: the individual, the institution (for example the firm), the region, the nation-state and the empire.

Orthodox economic theory attributes success and failure almost entirely to material factors. For example, it attributes international differences in living standards to differences in national endowments of labour, capital and natural resources, which in turn stem from differences over time in rates of population growth, saving and natural resource depletion. Statistical evidence, however, indicates a significant 'residual factor' which is connected with differences in the quality rather than the quantity of resources, and also with differences in the efficiency with which these resources are utilized. In recent statistical analysis of growth, differences in the quality of labour and in the efficiency of resource use have been attributed to differences in the endowment of 'human capital'. Human capital is often assumed to reflect technical skills acquired through education and training, but it may also reflect the underlying entrepreneurial abilities of the population. In this case, to fully eliminate the 'residual' from the explanation it is necessary to have a theory of the entrepreneur.

When economic growth and development is considered in a historical perspective, the role of the entrepreneur comes into sharper focus. Entrepreneurship appears as a personal quality which enables certain individuals to make decisions with far-reaching consequences. With the benefit of hindsight the historian can see that certain people were right at a time when practically everyone else was wrong. By acting differently from other people, and achieving success in doing so, their example caused other people to change their mind, and thereby altered the course of history. The significance of the entrepreneur, on this view, lies in the fact, first, that he is atypical and, secondly, that though in a minority of one it is he that is right and the majority that is wrong. What is needed therefore is not so much a theory of the success of the entrepreneur as a theory of the failure of those around him. The essence of the theory of the entrepreneur is not so much the rationalization of success as the explanation of failure.

Returning to the issue of international disparities in development, what needs to be explained is why the unsuccessful nation cannot allocate resources as efficiently as the successful nation. An obvious hypothesis is that achieving efficiency in resource allocation is a difficult and costly business, and that there are barriers to communicating the information and the attitudes that underlie the most efficient allocation system. Entrepreneurial effort is required to develop an improved allocation of resources and to transfer the relevant know-how to other countries. If two countries differ in their endowments of entrepreneurship then there will be a tendency for improvements to originate in the country with the most abundant endowment of entrepreneurs. A corollary of this is that, where indigenous entrepreneurs are scarce, it will be left to foreign entrepreneurs from the economically successful country to enter the backward country and improve the allocation of resources. An 'efficiency gap' will emerge, with one country consistently allocating resources better than the other. One country moves further ahead just as the other one is catching up. Moreover, as the catching up process depends upon the efforts of foreign entrepreneurs, the dependency of the backward country upon the successful country increases all the time.

At the microeconomic level, the entrepreneur is obviously an important figure in the foundation and development of firms. Although economic theory has little to say on the matter, intuition suggests that there is a close connection between the personal qualities of the entrepreneur and the economic success of the firm, as measured by its growth and profitability. This highly personalized view of the firm is very common in the writing of business history, and has been pursued extensively in the sociological literature.

The personal qualities found within a society will be influenced by the latent abilities of the ethnic groups that comprise the population, their level of education and the prevailing culture and morality. The extent to which these qualities are exercised in business will be affected by the relative status of different occupations and careers, and the legal freedoms that are enjoyed in commerce. One of the most interesting features of successful entrepreneurs is that they are frequently drawn from minority groups in society – groups that find alternative avenues of social advancement closed to them. It is therefore apparent that society and its institutions have an important influence on the development and selection of entrepreneurs. Given that entrepreneurs are an important influence on national economic success, it is clearly desirable to know what sorts of social institution provide a favourable climate for developing qualities of entrepreneurship.

The theory of the entrepreneur has an important role in the field of economic dynamics. Orthodox theory provides an unsatisfactory account of the way in which individuals and economic systems adjust to change. Simple neoclassical theory is inherently static in its approach, and is usually rendered dynamic simply by introducing *ad hoc* assumptions about adjustment lags. It offers very little insight into the ways in which different economic systems adjust to change. It trivializes the comparison of market economies and centrally planned economies by focusing on the case of perfect information in which resources are reallocated simply by applying two different versions of the conditions for the same mathematical optimum.

This problem is a manifestation of a deeper problem, which is that neoclassical economics has no adequate theory of the competitive *process*. Competitive *equilibrium* is analysed in detail, but the *process* by which this equilibrium is reached is discussed in a highly artificial way. Neoclassical theory presents a view of the market which has no room for the entrepreneur. In neoclassical theory the closest parallel to the entrepreneur is the Walrasian auctioneer. The Walrasian auctioneer calls out trial prices, and adjusts these prices until supply is equal to demand. This process of calling out prices is similar to the role of entrepreneurs in announcing price quotations. In the artificial world of the Walrasian auctioneer, price setting costs nothing to carry out, and the auctioneer's services are provided free. In the real world of the entrepreneur, on the other hand, price setting is costly and the entrepreneur is rewarded for his effort by a margin between the price at which he buys and the price at which he sells. This margin covers the costs of the price setting and provides a profit to the entrepreneur as well. The entrepreneur requires a profit because, unlike the auctioneer, he undertakes to trade at the prices he quotes, whether there is an equilibrium or not. Thus entrepreneurs may trade at disequilibrium prices whereas the Walrasian auctioneer does not. Trading at disequilibrium prices exposes the entrepreneur to risks for which he must be compensated in the form of profit.

When explaining the trade cycle, the amplitude and frequency of fluctuations depends crucially on the lengths of the various adjustment lags. These lags depend partly upon the willingness of people to adjust by relinquishing habitual modes of behaviour, and also upon technological constraints on adjustment. Adjustment is much easier the longer the time allowed, and the time available is greater the sooner the need to adjust is foreseen. If a few individuals have the foresight to recognize the impending need for change, then their example may encourage others to adjust as well. In this way the existence of a few people with an entrepreneurial outlook may contribute to reducing adjustment lags and so help to improve the stability of the economy over the trade cycle. Thus, without a theory of the entrepreneur, it is impossible to provide a complete account of the lags which govern the dynamics of the trade cycle.

The basic problem is that as yet there is no satisfactory account of the economic *function* of the entrepreneur. It is apparent both to the historian and to the modern observer that entrepreneurs have an important role in the market economy. Yet orthodox theory provides no room for the entrepreneur, for all the economic functions that need to be performed are already performed by someone else. This gives a certain implausibility to the neoclassical account of economic behaviour. To remedy this problem it is necessary to make far-reaching changes in economic theory.

1.3 OUTLINE OF THE APPROACH

Criticisms of neoclassical theory are very common, but the theory remains influential because most of its critics can offer little to put in its place. Because they are unable to focus their criticisms properly, the problem of meeting their criticisms is quite unmanageable. It is therefore incumbent upon a new author to summarize concisely his main criticisms and to indicate how he intends to meet them.

At an intuitive level, the basic objection to neoclassical economics is that it depersonalizes the market process. Transactors are faceless economic agents; the only personal characteristics that really matter are their tastes for consumer goods. The transactors are linked by an equally impersonal mechanism – the invisible hand of Adam Smith, which neoclassical economics translates into an assumption of perfectly competitive market equilibrium. On the few occasions when market adjustment is personified it is in terms of the Walrasian auctioneer, as described above. It is essential to resolve the tension that exists between the invisible hand of Adam Smith and the all-too-visible hand of the entrepreneur, or alternatively between the very real entrepreneur and his fictional counterpart, the Walrasian auctioneer.

In this book the theoretical reconstruction proceeds on two fronts. The first is to recognize that individuals differ not only in their tastes but in their access to information. Individuals with similar tastes, acting under similar circumstances, but with different information at their disposal, may well make different decisions. The entrepreneur exhibits an extreme form of this. The entrepreneur believes that the totality of the information available to him, in respect of some decision, is unique. On account of this, he will decide one way when everyone else would decide another. The entrepreneur believes that he is right, while everyone else is wrong. Thus the essence of entrepreneurship is being different – being different because one has a different perception of the situation. It is this that makes the entrepreneur so important. Were he not present, things would have been done very differently. In this way the entrepreneur's perception of the situation exerts a material influence on the allocation of resources.

The entrepreneur hopes to profit from this difference in perception by 'taking a position' *vis-à-vis* other people. He may take up a position by contracting with them, or merely by adjusting his own behaviour in the light of his expectations about how they will behave. Suppose that the entrepreneur chooses the contractual route. Intuitively, he places bets with those who dissent from his view, in the hope that he will be rewarded when his beliefs turn out to be correct. Many of the predictions of the economic theory of entrepreneurship come from considering the tactical aspects of this strategy.

The most important tactical problem is that the entrepreneur can only contract with other people on favourable terms if he can protect the information on which (he believes) his superior judgment is based. If he fails to maintain secrecy then he will be faced with competition from other people who share his views, and the terms on which he can contract will become less favourable as a result. He must also recognize that the people with whom he contracts will require assurances that he can pay up if he is proved wrong – a constraint which may prove difficult, and quite irritating, for someone who has little wealth but is certain that he is right. The obvious strategy is to seek someone to underwrite the risk that he (the entrepreneur) is wrong. But since everyone else believes he is wrong, to whom can be turn? He can only obtain underwriting by persuading someone else that he is right. And therein lies the catch, for anyone else who believes the entrepreneur is right is *ipso facto* a potential competitor. As we shall see, it may be possible to establish special institutions to resolve this problem. But it should be apparent that, in the absence of such institutions, access to capital may prove a substantial barrier to entry into entrepreneurship.

The second area of reconstruction stems from recognition of the difficulties that are inherent in organizing a market. Simple neoclassical theory assumes that there are no costs of organizing a market, but in practice setting up a transaction involves a significant resource cost. The buyer has to be put in contact with the seller, price has to be negotiated, physical custody of the goods has to be exchanged, their quality checked and default penalized. Since it is the entrepreneur that first perceives the opportunity to contract, it is he that normally takes the initiative in approaching the other party. Consequently, it is he that incurs the cost of setting up the trade. In particular, the entrepreneur incurs the brokerage cost of making contact with the other party and communicating his offer to trade. The allocation of some of the other costs may be determined by the provisions of the contract. But at the time the contract is negotiated the brokerage costs are sunk costs, and so there is no guarantee that they can be recovered from the other party. The entrepreneur must allow for these costs before initiating the transaction, and rely on his bargaining skill to recover the costs from the negotiated price. Thus, once transaction costs are recognized, it is apparent that the entrepreneur's bargaining skills are crucial in enabling him to appropriate the profits of his superior judgment through the contractual route.

It is also important for the entrepreneur's success that he minimizes the transaction cost incurred in establishing any given volume of trade. This transaction cost embraces both the cost incurred directly by the entrepreneur and also any costs incurred by the other party that will be reflected in the negotiated price.

Transaction costs represent the opportunity costs of the market-making services that are required to overcome obstacles to trade. Most obstacles to trade stem from ignorance of one kind or another – that is, from a lack of information. As a result, market-making services typically involve information processing; this is certainly true of brokerage, negotiation, metering and quality control. We have seen that most market-making costs are incurred in the first instance by the entrepreneur, since he usually initiates the trade. In principle the entrepreneur could hire all the market-making services he requires, but in practice this is not always possible, for there are costs of making markets in market-making services and in many cases these costs are prohibitively high. This is because it is extremely difficult to check the quality of the market-making services supplied. The only effective way of checking quality is to supervise production of them, since only supervision gives access to the kind of information necessary for an absolute guarantee of quality. To effect this supervision it is necessary to create an institution in which the production of market-making services can be supervised. This institution is the market-making firm.

The rationale of the market-making firm is that it produces trade at minimum cost. Implicit in this is a much broader concept of production than is used in neoclassical theory. Unlike the neoclassical theory, production involves not just the transformation of material inputs into outputs, but also the creation of trade from inputs of market-making services. These services are in turn generated by the utilization of assets. Two types of asset are particularly important: human assets such as administrative workers, and purpose-built infrastructures, such as transport and communication systems.

Compared with the material-transforming firm, the market-making firm is of much greater economic significance. The process of material transformation may interest the scientist and engineer, but economists prefer to regard as a 'black box' whatever lies behind the production frontier. By contrast, the activity of making a market is of central interest to the economist. Indeed, we shall argue that the material-transforming firm is really of interest only in so far as its activities become integrated with market making, that is only in so far as it takes the initiative in hiring its own inputs and selling its own output. We suggest, furthermore, that the initiative for this integration normally comes from the market-making activities, and not from material transformation, which from an economic point of view is a quite trivial activity.

The activities of the market-making firm are probably best understood by considering the relations between the firm and the household. Households supply factor services to firms and buy consumer products from them. We are all familiar with the fact that in setting up these transactions it is usually the firm that takes the initiative in approaching the household. In consumer product markets, for example, the firm seeks out the household by advertising its product, displaying it in convenient locations (shops) and offering to supply the product on demand at a publicly quoted non-negotiable price. The firm guarantees the quality, and provides households with a sanction to ensure that this is enforced – namely a brand name with a valuable reputation which can be lost as a result of complaints. Similarly, in the labour market, firms typically advertise vacancies, quote wage rates and also take the initiative in evaluating 'product quality'; for example, they assess the worker's performance while he is in probationary employment. As a consequence, the worker needs to take only a fairly passive role in placing himself in employment.

The fact that the entrepreneur has often to create an institution to make markets between himself and other transactors extends the range of issues about which the entrepreneur has to make judgments. Although he does not have to perform all the activities within the institution himself, he is responsible for the structure of the institution and, in particular, for the way in which specific tasks are delegated, and the way that the delegates are supervised. As a consequence, the theory of the market-making firm feeds back upon the original conceptualization of the entrepreneur. It describes a specific range of issues with which many entrepreneurs are heavily preoccupied, and upon which entrepreneurial judgment has to be continuously exercised.

1.4   PLAN OF THE BOOK

The next chapter defines the role of the entrepreneur and introduces the basic concepts which are required to analyse it. One of the most important of these concepts is coordination. Chapters 3 to 5 are devoted exclusively to this concept. They show how the entrepreneur's assessment of a situation is crucial in affecting where, when and how coordination occurs.

Chapters 6 to 10 relate the theory of the entrepreneur to the theory of the firm. The firm is the institution through which the entrepreneur operates in a market economy; indeed, the entrepreneur is often identified as the founder, or as the owner or manager, of a firm. One of the main objects of this part of the book is to locate the entrepreneur within the firm, and in particular to identify the circumstances under which he is the employer and the circumstances under which he becomes an employee.

The final part of the book, comprising Chapters 11 to 15, weaves together the different threads of the argument which have appeared in the main body of the book. Entrepreneurship is related to wider issues such as social mobility and the distribution of income. The book ends where it begins, by using the theory to re-evaluate the stereotype of the entrepreneur.

SUMMARY

This chapter has identified one of the main issues in entrepreneurship to be the explanation of success and failure in individuals, organizations and nations. It has been argued that radical change is called for if the entrepreneur is to be integrated into mainstream economic theory.

NOTES AND REFERENCES

The psychological literature on entrepreneurship is organized very much around the concept of achievement. The most influential work has been by D.C. McClelland (1967) and McClelland and Winter (1969), and it has stimulated a good deal of subsequent work, both critical and confirmatory; see Durand and Shea (1974), Freeman (1976), Lessner and Knapp (1974), Pandey and Tewary (1979), Redlich (1963) and Vanneman (1973). Psychologists have also considered motivational determinants of risk taking (Atkinson, 1957) and the information-processing capabilities of entrepreneurs. The political and sociological literature will be referred to in detail throughout the book.

The subjectivist approach to economic theory is set out in a number of places, notably Buchanan (1973), Lachman (1969, 1976), Martin (1979) and Rizzo (1979). Subjectivism has radical implications not only for entrepreneurship, but also for the theory of cost and price in general, see Thirlby (1946, 1952) and Wiseman (1953, 1957). For a systematic exposition of the subjectivist view of 'purposeful human action', see Rothbard (1962) and von Mises (1949). An interesting recent attempt to present Austrian insights in a textbook format is Reekie (1979).

It is inevitable that the neoclassical theory that we are attacking should be something of a 'straw man'. The attack on 'orthodox theory' is chiefly an expository device, though if the reader wishes to identify a particular target, then Debreu (1959) will suffice. The classic statement of the 'gap' in economic theory is Baumol (1968). Theoretical interest in the entrepreneur has recently been renewed, both from the subjectivist standpoint, for example Buchanan and Pierro (1980), and the neoclassical one, for example Kihlstrom and Laffont (1979).

The 'gap' has proved particularly serious in the study of economic development. Denison has measured the 'residual component' in the economic growth of rich nations (Denison 1962, 1967), though the existence of this component was recognized long before (Cole, 1954); the entrepreneurial factor in the development of poorer countries is emphasized by Broehl (1978), Gerschenkron (1953), Hagen (1962), Harbison (1956) and Hirschman (1958). Recent progress in the study of entrepreneurship and economic development is reviewed by Leff (1979).

For an overview of the literature on entrepreneurship, see Cochran (1968), Cole (1959), Hoselitz (1951) and Schreier and Komives (1973); other useful references include Becker and Whisler (1967), Bruce (1976). Glade (1967), Gurzynski (1976), Kingston (1977), Miller (1962), Sawyer (1951) and Schultz (1975).

The seminal paper on market behaviour when individuals have limited access to information is Stigler (1961), though subsequent developments of Stigler's approach have been somewhat tangential to entrepreneurship; for a survey see Rothschild (1973). Somewhat similar issues are considered from a different perspective in a volume edited by Cox (1967). Richardson (1960) presents an interesting analysis of the allocation problems that are raised when information is restricted. Manne (1966) has considered the role of privileged access to information in the context of insider-trading on the stock market. Assumptions about the distribution of information between transactors underlie the stock market philosophies reported by Smith (1981). Finally, mention should be made of a very interesting study of access to information in cereals trading by Stewart (1970).

The most dramatic examples of success and failure are to be found in the histories of firms and their product innovations; 'high points' in the literature of success and failure include Brooks (1963), Bylinsky (1976) and Robertson (1974). For an interesting account of success and failure from a more academic perspective, see, for example Church (1969).

2. Basic concepts of the theory

2.1 TWO KINDS OF DEFINITION

As noted in the Introduction, the definition of the entrepreneur is one of the most crucial and difficult aspects of the theory. There are two main approaches to defining anything: the functional approach and the indicative approach. In the context of the entrepreneur, the functional approach says quite simply that 'an entrepreneur is what an entrepreneur does'. It specifies a certain function and deems anyone who performs this function to be an entrepreneur. The indicative approach provides a description of the entrepreneur by which he may be recognized. Unlike a functional definition, which may be quite abstract, an indicative definition is very down-to-earth. It describes an entrepreneur in terms of his legal status, his contractual relations with other parties, his position in society, and so on.

The term 'entrepreneur' seems to have been introduced into economics by Cantillon, but the entrepreneur was first accorded prominence by Say. The word was variously translated into English as merchant, adventurer and employer, though the precise meaning is the undertaker of a project. James Stuart Mill popularized the term in England, though by the turn of the century it had almost disappeared from the theoretical literature. The static approach of the emerging neoclassical school did not readily accommodate a concept with dynamic connotations, such as the entrepreneur. Alfred Marshall, for example, laid much more stress on the routine activities of management and superintendence than he did on the innovative activity of the entrepreneur.

By and large, economic theorists have adopted a functional approach and economic historians an indicative one. This is as it should be. Economic theory offers a set of concepts and techniques for analysing the allocation of scarce resources. Unless entrepreneurship ultimately derives from a scarce resource it is of little economic interest, even though it may be of social importance. To analyse the allocation of the resource, and to explain the valuation it commands, it is sensible to define the resource in terms of the use to which it is put. For the economic historian, however, the starting point is a set of concepts relevant to the recording and interpreting of events. Such concepts form a descriptive rather than an analytical framework. Their primary role is in the development of a taxonomy rather than a theory. It is therefore natural to work with definitions which relate directly to observables, and which distinguish the major types of economic agent observed in practice.

The problem with the theory of entrepreneurship is that these two approaches have never been integrated. The functional approach should predict the emergence of a particular group of people embodying a unique complex of characteristics – characteristics which enable them to carry out their function most efficiently. Given that at least some of the characteristics are observable, they could then form the basis for an indicative definition of the entrepreneur. It is one of the main objects of this book to achieve a convergence of the two approaches along these lines. Since this is a theoretical work, we begin with a functional definition, and then move towards an indicative one.

2.2   THE FUNCTION OF THE ENTREPRENEUR

The entire structure of the theory developed below rests upon the following definition: *an entrepreneur is someone who specializes in taking judgmental decisions about the coordination of scarce resources.* It is instructive to consider this definition as one would a text, almost word by word.

An entrepreneur is *someone*; in other words the entrepreneur is a person, not a team, or a committee, or an organization. Only individuals can take decisions; corporate bodies only arrive at decisions by aggregating votes. Individuals in committee make strategic decisions on how to influence other people's voting and on how to vote themselves; it is these decisions that are entrepreneurial, not the decision of the committee as a whole. This does not mean that the role of teams and committees is excluded; it means only that the definition commits us to a detailed examination of how such teams and committees operate internally.

who specializes; everyone is involved in taking judgmental decisions at one time or another, but this does not make them a specialist at it. A specialist carries out his function not only on his own behalf but on behalf of other people. In a market economy specialist services may be offered for hire, and individuals can decide which services to supply in accordance with their personal comparative advantage. Decision making may be hired out on this principle, as when consultants or managers act as delegates to take decisions on an owner's behalf. Alternatively, decision makers may prefer to hire in resources, so that while on hire to them these resources are effectively under their control. Though they do not own the resources (in any permanent sense) they have control over them (as least temporarily) and can therefore exercise decision making with regard to their utilization. Thus the market for decision making can operate in two ways, with the decision-making service being hired by the owners of resources, or with the decision makers hiring resources from their owners. In either case the market effects a separation between decision making and other activities, and so facilitates specialization in decision making according to comparative advantage.

in taking judgmental decisions; the concept of choice, and hence of decision making, is central to economic theory. A judgmental decision is one where different individuals, sharing the same objectives and acting under similar circumstances, would make different decisions. The difference arises because they have different perceptions of the situation arising from different access to information, or different interpretations of it. The difference between them is not only a quantitative one, in the sense that it takes a longer time, or involves a greater expenditure of resources, in making the same decision, but a qualitative one, namely that the decision made is actually different.

about the coordination; coordination may be defined as a beneficial reallocation of resources. Coordination is thus a dynamic concept, as opposed to allocation, which is a static one. The concept of coordination captures the fact that the entrepreneur is an agent of change: he is not concerned merely with the perpetuation of the existing allocation of resources, but with improving upon it.

of scarce resources; the restriction to scarce resources limits the field of study to that usually identified as economic.

It must be emphasized that this definition is institution-free. It makes no reference to the type of economic system within which the entrepreneur operates, or to the particular kind of organization or institution with which he is associated. The entrepreneurial function can be performed by very different kinds of people under different economic systems. In principle, the entrepreneur could be a planner in a socialist economy, or even a priest or king in a traditional society. In practice, though, entrepreneurship is closely identified with private enterprise in a market economy.

This book follows convention in confining the analysis to the operations of the private sector in a market economy. It is assumed, furthermore, that entrepreneurs are motivated by self-interest. Their objectives relate to their consumption of goods and leisure, and to their status, as reflected, for example, in the amount of deference and respect they receive from other people. Consumption and status can, however, be bought using the income generated by entrepreneurial activity. To simplify the theory it is assumed that entrepreneurs operate their business purely with a view to maximizing the profit they obtain from a given amount of effort. They rely on the profit to buy the consumption and the status they require; they do not seek to increase their status by methods which would reduce the profitability of the business.

Although these assumptions are clearly counterfactual, the resulting theory goes a long way towards explaining entrepreneurial behaviour. The relaxation of these very strict assumptions has been a major preoccupation of the author's own recent work since the publication of the first edition of this book.

2.3   THE DEMAND FOR ACTIVE DECISION MAKING

Having defined the function of the entrepreneur, it must now be established that this function is not completely trivial. This section shows that entrepreneurship is a continuing function rather than a once-for-all, or possibly intermittent, activity.

There will be a demand for entrepreneurial services so long as opportunities for coordination exist. Opportunities will exist as long as new information is becoming available, in the light of which the existing allocation of resources appears inefficient. The new information may be a net addition to the stock of knowledge, in the sense of a discovery of something about which people were previously ignorant, or a replacement for obsolete knowledge. The former case is exemplified by scientific breakthroughs, successful prospecting for minerals and so on. The latter case, which is far more common, is exemplified by the updating of knowledge in the light of a recent event, that is by information that the state of the world has changed.

It is unlikely that the number of new opportunities will run down over time. Discoveries will continue so long as people remain inquisitive. Updating of knowledge will occur so long as unpredictable disturbances affect the state of the world. It is not necessary to assume that the appearance of new opportunities is exogenous. The modeller may postulate various historical laws determining the occurrence of new opportunities. It is, however, important that the actual opportunities which occur should be unpredictable to the economic agents themselves. Otherwise agents could plan ahead with just as much certainty as if things were to remain unchanged. All coordination could be organized in the present to be implemented automatically in the future. Thus, while there would be intense entrepreneurial activity in the current period, there would be none at all in future periods.

In principle, even the exploitation of unpredictable opportunities can be organized in the present for execution in the future using contingent plans. Contingency planning is analytically a very powerful concept. It is familiar to most economists through the time-state theory of general equilibrium. It is familiar to management scientists through the concept of scenario planning. Contingency planning involves identifying all probable future states, devising plans now for each of them, and triggering the relevant plan automatically once the future state has been realized. If contingency planning were implemented over an infinite time horizon then decision making would become a once-for-all event. All decisions about the future would be telescoped into the present.

The reason why contingency planning is never fully implemented is that it is not efficient to do so. It is not efficient because information processing is so costly. Planning involves information processing, and the further ahead one plans the more the contingencies multiply, and the greater the information costs become. Because contingencies evolve through a branching process, the number of contingencies typically increases exponentially with respect to the planner's time horizon. Thus as the planning horizon moves forward in time, so information costs increase at an increasing rate.

Information costs are minimized by planning only for the current period. However, such a strategy forgoes altogether the benefits of planning ahead. The main benefit of planning ahead is that it enables adjustment to anticipated events to commence earlier and so reduces costs of adjustment. For example, using a two-period plan it is possible to maximize the expected value of the objective conditional upon subjective probabilities attaching to second-period states of the world. The solution to this problem gives an efficient strategy for the current period (and a provisional strategy for the future period) conditional upon these probabilities. The expected outcome of the two-period plan may be compared with the expected outcome of two sequential one-period plans, in which the decisions made in the first period constrain the options available in the second-period plan. The expected value of the objective under sequential planning will normally be lower by an amount which reflects the increased costs of adjusting at short notice to second-period conditions. This shows that the expected cost of adjustment is dependent upon the time horizon.

Total planning cost is given by the sum of information costs and adjustment costs. It is minimized by setting the planning horizon at the margin where the increase in information costs incurred by putting back the horizon is just equal to the expected reduction in adjustment costs that would be effected. Normally this point corresponds to a finite multi-period planning horizon.

When multi-period planning is used, a plan must be revised with a frequency at least as great as the term for which it has been drawn up. It is often advantageous, though, to 'roll over' a plan, that is to revise a plan before the existing plan has expired. The frequency with which a plan is revised will be strongly influenced by the rate at which new relevant information becomes available to the planner. Each period a decision has to be made whether to continue with the existing plan or to revise it. The first policy is essentially a passive one; it requires no initiative on the part of the planner. The second policy is an active one, and incurs information costs when it is initiated. The planner must assess whether the efficiency gains from a revised plan will outweigh the costs of revision. If they do so then the plan will be revised; if not then the provisional arrangements specified in the existing plan will be implemented.

To a certain extent this distinction between active and passive planning encapsulates an important difference between entrepreneurs and other people. Consider for example a simple type of plan in which the same strategy is repeated one period after the next; in other words the plan involves the adoption of a habit. In this case the passive decision not to revise the plan is equivalent to a conservative 'no change' strategy. An active decision, on the other hand, involves a reappraisal of the habit, which possibly (though not necessarily) leads to a change. An entrepreneur may be characterized as an active planner, and a non-entrepreneur as a passive planner. Because entrepreneurs are active planners they invest heavily in decision making, while passive planners allow their decisions to be taken by default.

As we have seen, the rationale for active planning is that new information has become available which leads entrepreneurs to question the efficiency of their existing plans. Also two kinds of information have been distinguished, namely discoveries and updates. The kind of information to which the entrepreneur responds will determine whether he is seen as an instigator of change, or as someone who reacts to it. An entrepreneur who revises his plans when there has been no change in the state of the world is not responding to an objective change in the state of the world, but to a subjective change in his state of knowledge. But as a result of his plan revision, the state of the world may well be changed. In objective terms, therefore, he is an initiator of change. On the other hand, the entrepreneur responding to an information update is responding, indirectly, to an objective change in the state of the world, which rendered his original information obsolete. In objective terms, therefore, he is reacting to change rather than initiating it. Although superficially it seems important to know whether entrepreneurs are initiators or reactors to change, it is apparent that for analytical purposes the distinction between these roles is of relatively little consequence.

2.4   RESOURCE COSTS OF DECISION MAKING

Decision-making services are scarce because decision making involves the use of resources which have a positive opportunity cost. This section analyses these costs and briefly considers the ways in which entrepreneurs can economize on them.

The logic of a decision suggests that there are three main stages of decision making, each involving several activities (see the left-hand column of Table 2.1). The first stage in any decision is to formulate the problem. This involves specifying the objective, the potential strategies and the constraints, and deriving from them a decision rule. The objective is defined upon a set of targets, or goals. When there is more than one target the objective indicates the way that different targets should be traded off against each other. Each potential strategy involves setting particular values for each of the available instruments, that is for the variables under the decision maker's control. Typically one of the strategies will be a null strategy, which involves preserving the *status quo*. In the context of entrepreneurship this means that the allocation of resources will remain unchanged. The other strategies represent alternative methods of exploiting an opportunity for coordination. The optimal strategy is the one that maximizes the value of the objective.

Table 2.1   Decision-making activities and the qualities they require

Activities	Qualities
First stage: formulation of the decision problem	
Specification of the objective	Self-knowledge (or knowledge of the principal's objectives)
Specification of the potential strategies	Imagination
Specification of the constraints	Practical knowledge
Derivation of the decision rule	Analytical ability
Second stage: generating the data	
Data collection	Search skill
Data estimation	Foresight
Third stage: execution of the decision	
Application of the data to the decision rule	Computational skill
Initiation of the implementation process	Communication skill (in formulating instructions)

The constraints restrict the degree of freedom available when choosing the instruments. The formulation of the constraints is derived, either implicitly or explicitly, from a theory about the way the world works (or the part of the world directly relevant to the decision problem). In some cases the theory may be expressed in terms of a formal model in which the constraints are derived mathematically.

Combining the objective, the strategies and the constraints makes it possible to derive a decision rule. This rule is obtained by solving the first-order marginal conditions for the maximum of the objective subject to the constraints. A well-behaved decision rule establishes a one-to-one relationship between the values of certain state variables and the set of optimal strategies. The state variables correspond to the variables which appear in the specification of the objectives and the constraints.

The next stage in the decision is to generate the data. The data establish numerical values for the state variables. The data may already be available from secondary sources, or they may have to be gathered from primary sources on the initiative of the entrepreneur. When all available data sources have been tapped, the data set may still remain incomplete. The decision maker must then supply his own estimates of the unknown variables. In doing so he may wish to exploit correlations between the unknown variables and the known values of other variables. As a result, he may need to tap more varied sources of information than those from which his direct observations were obtained.

The final stage is the execution of the decision. This involves the application of the decision rule to the completed data set, and the initiation of the implementation process.

It is evident that the decision-making function consists almost entirely of information processing of one kind or another. In this context information processing includes the collection, analysis, communication and storage of information. Mental labour (as opposed to physical labour) is an important input in each case. Considering the human being as an information-processing unit, the senses are used for data collection, the brain for analysis and storage, and the body (voice, hands and so on) for communication. However, in each case there is some possibility of substituting non-human assets for labour. Instrumentation can be used to monitor physical events and so generate updated information on states of the world. Documentary files can be substituted for human memory in the storage of information. Computers economize on labour in both the analysis and storage of information. Finally, transport and communication infrastructures economize on the labour used for communication: for example, post and telecommunications are a substitute for face-to-face communication.

The fact that mental labour is a key input to decision making indicates that decision making has an opportunity cost in terms of leisure or manual labour services forgone. The fact that there is substantial investment in assets designed specifically to economize on mental labour indicates that the opportunity costs of mental labour are quite substantial.

The entrepreneur can reduce the time he spends on each decision through delegation. However, some activities are much more easily delegated than others. In principle the specification of the objectives and the options cannot be delegated; they have to be communicated by the principal to the delegate so that the delegate understands the nature of the problem. In practice, though, only the outline may be specified by the principal; the delegate may be left to fill in the details for himself. The other activities can all be delegated; indeed, in principle each activity could be delegated to a different person.

There are two main obstacles to delegation. The first is the difficulty of communication between principal and delegate. Communication involves encoding a message, transmitting it and decoding it, all of which takes up time for each party. Moreover, language is never completely unambiguous, so that there is always a risk that misunderstanding may result. The second difficulty relates to the organization of delegation. A major problem in delegation is default. Default may occur either because the delegate is incompetent or because he deliberately pursues his own interests at the expense of those of his principal. The risk of incompetence is controlled mainly by screening delegates for ability. Deliberate default may be controlled both by screening for honesty and by devising an appropriate system of incentives.

The problem of default in decision making is greatest when the delegate is given discretion to exercise his own judgment. In this case the delegate himself is a potential entrepreneur. The most efficient criterion by which the delegate's performance can be assessed is whether in retrospect his decision was reasonable, given the information he could have been expected to have at the time. However, the application of this criterion is likely to be expensive as it involves a difficult subjective assessment of what might have been. Furthermore, the principal may have to wait a long time before deciding whether the delegate has been in default, and this diminishes the effectiveness of any incentives offered to him. On the other hand, assessing the decision prematurely is an unsatisfactory solution, at least in the long run, because if the delegate expects to be assessed arbitrarily he will take little account of the correctness of his decision. It may even bias his decision so that he chooses a strategy which appears favourable on a short-run assessment, but is unfavourable to his principal in the long run.

The risk of default can be reduced over time by repeatedly delegating to the same reliable people. The risk borne by the principal is partly subjective, reflecting his ignorance of the personal qualities of the delegate. Repeated delegation to the same person, if it is successful, reduces this ignorance and enables the delegate to establish a reputation with the principal. As a result, the principal recognizes that, by his continuing this strategy, the risk of default will be much lower than the risk he originally perceived.

The alternative is to delegate without discretion. This means that the delegate is given precise instructions on how to proceed; that is, which information to collect from where, what decision rule to apply, and so on. The question of default here reduces to whether the delegate obeyed orders: did he record the

information accurately, apply the decision rule correctly, and so on? This kind of question can be answered in two main ways: either by checking the work as it is done, through supervision, or checking it after it has been done by replicating the procedure. Supervision has the advantage that the work is only done once, but also has the disadvantage that the supervisor and delegate have to be close together, so that the supervisor can make spot checks on the delegate. This normally means that they must work at the same location.

If each decision occupies the delegate for only a short time, then the average cost per decision of setting up the supervisory arrangement may be quite high. However, given that decision making is a continuing process, average cost can be reduced by offering continuity of work to the delegate. This arrangement also has the advantage of establishing mutual confidence between principal (or supervisor) and delegate, in the manner described above.

The commitment to continuity of work is likely to be of far greater significance to both parties than the nature of the individual decisions to which the delegate is to be assigned. The costs of contractual specification and negotiation may therefore be reduced if the delegate is hired and paid, not for each separate decision, but simply by the time he spends in decision making. This arrangement also provides the principal with the flexibility to reassign the delegate to another decision should unforeseen circumstances require it, without having to renegotiate the price for the job. The delegate does not lose by this arrangement so long as he is indifferent between the various decision problems to which he may be assigned. Contractual costs may be further reduced by providing for automatic renewal of the contract each period, that is by negotiating a contract for an open term. The non-discretionary delegate decision maker may therefore be offered an open-term contract for continuous employment at a time rate in return for following specific decision procedures under supervision. In other words, the delegate acquires the contractual status of the typical employee.

Discretionary decision makers too may take open-term contracts on time rates, but because discretion is allowed the case for detailed supervision is much weaker. Although contractually they may still be employees, their employer will typically control the quality of decision making not by daily supervision but by longer-term retrospective assessments of performance.

2.5   DECISION MAKING BY TEAMS

A decision does not need to be delegated in its entirety to a single person. Different decision-making activities can be specialized with different people. Nor does each delegate need to stand in the same contractual relation to the principal. The choice of decision rule might be delegated to a consultant for a fixed fee, and the information to be fed into the decision rule might be purchased in the form of a reference book, while the remaining functions might be performed by employees.

When there is specialization among employees in different facets of decision making, it is important to structure the information flows between them appropriately. In theory each delegate might communicate only with the principal, but in practice it is normally efficient for the delegates to communicate directly with each other. Each delegate then needs to know from whom he will receive communications, and to whom he should send them. Where delegates communicate directly with each other in the service of the same principal they are said to operate as a team.

The rules governing the information flow determine the organization of the team. It is tempting to suggest that the team itself can function as an entrepreneur but, as noted earlier, this is not strictly correct. The team coordinates the activities of individual decision makers. In so far as individual team members have discretionary powers, they may themselves be entrepreneurs. Also it is likely that the person establishing the organization is an entrepreneur, in the sense that he has to take judgmental decisions about which is the most suitable form of organization. But the team itself is not an entrepreneur.

2.6 ENTREPRENEURIAL QUALITIES

The qualities essential for successful decision making are listed in the right-hand column of Table 2.1. The diversity of the qualities required suggests that the entrepreneur needs to be a generalist rather than a specialist. In other words, it is important for the entrepreneur to be reasonably proficient in all aspects of decision making, rather than very proficient in some aspects but inadequate in others.

However, the fact that all the qualities are normally necessary does not mean that they are all of equal economic significance. Some qualities are possessed by practically everyone, so that the possession of them is not necessarily peculiar to the entrepreneur. It is those qualities that are most scarce which are of the most economic significance.

A scarcity of personal qualities usually occurs, not because everyone has only a little of the quality, but because only a few people have the quality and many people do not have it all. In other words, scarcity is associated with skewness in the distribution of qualities between people. It is the possession of scarce qualities which confers an advantage on some people in becoming an entrepreneur.

It has already been established that functional specialization in decision making is possible. This implies that the entrepreneur who is deficient in

*Table 2.2   Additional activities required when there
is functional specialization within decision
making, and the qualities they require*

Activities	Qualities
Delegation	Delegation skill
Organizational design	Organizational skill

some qualities can in principle hire delegates who have these qualities. The entrepreneur and the delegate complement each other and can take decisions successfully as a unit. The difficulty with functional specialization is, firstly, that it is necessary to screen delegates and to devise appropriate incentives for them to pursue their principal's objectives, and secondly, that if the delegates operate as a team then it is necessary to devise an organizational structure too. This means that, in order to hire complementary qualities, the entrepreneur needs additional qualities of his own, namely delegation skills and organizational skills (see Table 2.2).

The difficulty of screening and devising incentives is far greater for some qualities than for others. Among the scarce qualities, the most difficult to screen for are imagination and foresight. It is doubtful if anyone without these qualities can succeed in recruiting people with them. It follows that these two qualities are essential to the successful entrepreneur. Besides these qualities, however, the entrepreneur also needs *either* to be himself a generalist, so that he can discharge his function without delegation, *or* to possess delegation and organizational skills.

All entrepreneurial qualities are to some extent innate. However, not all of them are entirely innate. Some can be enhanced by training, or simply by experience. For example, analytical ability and computational skill can be enhanced by education at school and university, while practical knowledge and search skills can be enhanced by general experience of everyday life. Entrepreneurial careers will be strongly influenced by the desire to enhance qualities which are scarce and difficult to acquire from delegates because of the problems involved in screening. Of the two indispensable qualities mentioned above, imagination is almost entirely innate, while foresight, though to some extent innate, can be enhanced by a varied experience. Delegation skill and organization skill, though not essential, are highly desirable whenever large-scale decision making is contemplated. These too are qualities which can be enhanced through experience.

The analysis is summarized in Table 2.3. It suggests that there are four main qualities which are crucial to the success of the entrepreneur. One of the

Table 2.3   *An analysis of entrepreneurial qualities*

Quality	Essential to all non-trivial decisions	Scarce and unequally distributed	Difficult to screen for	Capable of enhancement	Essential, scarce and difficult to screen for	Scarce, difficult to screen for and capable of enhancement
Self-knowledge	✓		✓			
Imagination	✓	✓	✓		✓	
Practical knowledge	✓	✓		✓		
Analytical ability	✓	✓	✓	✓		
Search skill	✓		✓	✓		
Foresight	✓	✓	✓	✓	✓	✓
Computational skill	✓	✓	✓			
Communication skill	✓		✓			
Delegation skill		✓	✓	✓		
Organizational skill		✓		✓		✓

qualities – imagination – is almost entirely innate. The other three qualities are all capable of enhancement. The problems encountered in screening for these qualities, and in enhancing the ones that are deficient, have a number of important implications for the development of a successful entrepreneurial career. The analysis of these implications constitutes one of the main themes of this book.

SUMMARY

This chapter has presented a functional definition of the entrepreneur and has considered why the entrepreneurial function is so valuable. It emphasizes that the demand for entrepreneurship stems from the need to adjust to change, and that the supply of entrepreneurship is limited, first by the scarcity of the requisite personal qualities, and secondly by the difficulty of identifying them when they are available.

NOTES AND REFERENCES

The history of the functional concept of the entrepreneur is reviewed in Redlich (1949) and Routh (1975). The most influential early works were Cantillon (1755), Say (1803) and Mill (1848), with the concept becoming relatively neglected following Marshall (1890).

The relation of the functional concept to historical study has led to a long and rather inconclusive discussion, in which various good intentions were announced but in which the relation was never properly clarified; see Aitken (1963), Basmann (1965), Clark, J.M. (1942), Cole (1942, 1962, 1965a, 1965b), Evans (1942, 1949, 1959), Galambos (1966), Holmes and Ruff (1975), Hughes (1966a), Hyde (1962), Redlich (1959), Schumpeter (1965), Tucker (1972) and Wohl (1949, 1954).

The historian's use of the concept of entrepreneurship is illustrated in Campbell and Wilson (1975), Carter, Forster and Moody (1976), Dahmen (1970), Gough (1969) and Soltow (1968).

The major functional theories of entrepreneurship are reviewed in Chapter 14. The key references are Kirzner (1973), Knight (1921), Leibenstein (1978) and Schumpeter (1934); see also Davenport (1913). There is also a literature on profit theory which has some relevance to the entrepreneur; see, for example, Bernstein (1953), Clark, J.B. (1894), Hawley (1907), Körner (1893), Lamberton (1965, 1972), Weston (1949, 1950, 1954) and Willett (1901).

The idea that information processing is a costly activity has been expressed in a number of different contexts, notably in consumer theory (Cox, 1967;

Nicosia, 1966), organization theory (Marschak, 1968, 1971, 1972; Marschak and Radner, 1972; Simon, 1959, 1976, 1980) and the theory of the firm (Loasby, 1976; Williamson, 1975).

Shackle (1961, 1970, 1979) has laid great stress on the role of imagination as part of his theme that decision making is a creative process. It is worth pointing out, however, that the concept of imagination used in this book is very mundane compared with the concept that Shackle seems at times to have in mind. Our imaginative entrepreneur is not a budding Leonardo or Newton, but is simply someone who is able to visualize the probable consequences of a fairly marginal change in resource allocation. The question of the innateness of entrepreneurial ability is considered by Kierulff (1975).

3. The entrepreneur as intermediator

3.1 INTRODUCTION

The entrepreneur has been defined as someone whose judgment differs from that of other people. He believes that, without his intervention, a wrong decision would be made. The decision may be wrong because it is made passively, with the appropriate policy not even being given active consideration. Or it may be wrong because the appropriate policy has been considered and dismissed because of misinformation or faulty logic. Because of this wrong decision, resources will not be allocated as efficiently as they might be. Thus an opportunity for coordination exists.

The entrepreneur intervenes in order to exploit his superior judgment. There are several ways in which the entrepreneur could intervene, and these are considered in detail later (see Chapter 8). For the moment it is assumed that the entrepreneur intervenes by buying up the resources that would have been misallocated. By becoming the owner of the resources he can ensure that they are put to better use.

It cannot be too strongly emphasized that this motive for acquiring ownership of resources is quite different from the motive usually assumed in economics. The usual reason given for the acquisition of resources is the desire to consume them. When everyone's judgment is the same, the desire to consume is the ultimate reason for owning resources.

When judgments differ, a second – and probably more powerful – reason for the acquisition of resources comes into play. Change of ownership is the first stage in the reallocation of a resource to an alternative use. The second stage is for the new owner to utilize the resource in a way its previous owner would not. This change of ownership becomes one of the elements in a two-stage process by which differences in judgment are translated into the reallocation of resources.

If the entrepreneur wishes to acquire ownership of resources from other people by voluntary means, then he is committed to the contractual route. He is obliged to trade the ownership of another resource for the one that he wishes to acquire. Any private reward that the entrepreneur obtains from his superior judgment will be the result of negotiating favourable terms for these trades. Thus so far as the entrepreneur is concerned, superior judgment is turned to good account only when the exercise of judgment is combined with the exercise of bargaining power.

To simplify the analysis, it is assumed in this chapter that the entrepreneur attempts to exploit his bargaining power to its absolute maximum, by obliging other people to trade with him on terms which leave them no better off than they would otherwise be. In practice, of course, he must allow them a perceptible increase in their welfare in order for his proposals to prove acceptable. Subject to this qualification, however, the entrepreneur adopts a hard-line approach in which he appropriates all the potential economic rents for himself.

3.2 THE CONCEPT OF COORDINATION

As noted earlier, coordination is a principal function of the entrepreneur. It is important, however, to distinguish between the private and social aspects of coordination. It is assumed that every individual is motivated to achieve private coordination. Private coordination occurs when the individual concerned is made better off as a result of a reallocation of resources.

Social coordination occurs when someone is made better off without anyone else being made worse off; in other words, when there is a Pareto-improvement in resource allocation. One of the key issues in economics, and in the study of entrepreneurship in particular, is the extent to which the pursuit of private coordination indirectly leads to social coordination as well. In this context it is useful to introduce a weaker concept of social coordination. This asserts that coordination occurs when those who benefit from a reallocation could in principle compensate those who lose. In other words, there is a potential for Pareto-improvement, although, because compensation is not actually paid, the improvement does not occur.

Coordination can be analysed from either a general or a partial point of view. A general analysis considers coordination within the context of the economy as a whole: it is concerned with a change in the economy-wide allocation of resources. A partial analysis considers coordination in the context of a small part of the economy. It is assumed that a change in resource allocation within a given sector will exert a negligible influence upon the rest of the economy, so that the feedback on that sector from the rest of the economy can be ignored.

General analysis has the advantage that it provides a completely self-contained view of coordination. Unlike partial analysis, it has no loose ends where the effects of the coordination spill over onto parts of the economy outside the model. On the other hand, the structure of a general model is far more complex than a partial one: for example, it involves many more different types of resource. To compensate for this it is necessary to simplify by making very strong behavioural assumptions. Because partial analysis has intrinsically a much simpler structure, there is scope to make much more realistic assumptions about individual behaviour.

This chapter focuses upon the general analysis of coordination. Although the model presented is highly abstract, it illustrates some important aspects of coordination which might not otherwise be apparent. It has an important place within the logical structure of the book because it provides the foundations for the transition to the more relevant partial analysis which begins in Chapter 5.

3.3   THE ENTREPRENEUR AS MIDDLEMAN

In conventional economics the most fundamental example of coordination is the process of exchange. Consider an economy with a fixed endowment of two goods, good 1 and good 2. The more of each good that is consumed by one individual the less there is available for the other. The initial allocation of the goods is such that each individual is endowed with relatively little of the good that he most prefers. Suppose, for example, that individual A likes good 1 much more than good 2, while individual B likes good 2 more than good 1. If individual A is initially allocated most of good 2, and B most of good 1, then each would be happy to sacrifice some of his own endowment for some of the other. Both individuals could be made better off by an exchange of goods.

Now suppose that there is a third party, C, who is an entrepreneur. In the absence of C, no exchange can take place. A and B either are unaware of each other's existence or misperceive one another's preferences. Another possibility is that they expect one another to default upon the contract, and so are unwilling to trade except through an intermediary. For the moment, ignorance or misperception is assumed; discussion of dishonesty is postponed until Chapter 6.

The entrepreneur C knows the preferences of both A and B, but his preferences are not known to them. C can offer to trade with A and B using any combination of price and quantity he desires. C does not have any endowments of his own. He can only offer A what he intends to buy from B, and vice versa.

This example can be analysed easily using an Edgeworth box. It is assumed that the economy has a fixed endowment of the two goods. The total endowments are represented by the dimensions of the box *KLMN* in Figure 3.1. The allocation of goods to individual A is measured from the origin *K* and the allocation of goods to individual B from the origin *M*. Individual A's

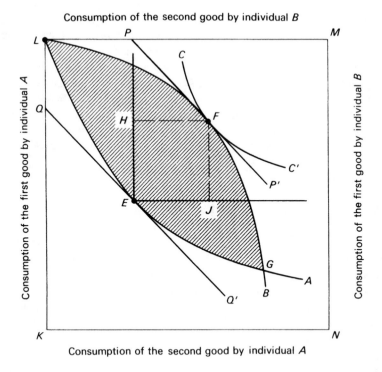

Figure 3.1   The Edgeworth box

consumption of good 1 is measured upwards along the left-hand vertical axis, whilst their consumption of good 2 is measured to the right along the lower horizontal axis. Individual B's consumption of good 1 is measured downwards along the right-hand vertical axis, whilst their consumption of good 2 is measured to the left along the upper horizontal axis. It is convenient to assume that initially each individual holds the entire endowment of one of the commodities. Thus the initial allocation of consumption is represented by a corner point in the figure, *L*, where all of good 1 is owned by A and all of good 2 is owned by B.

It is assumed that each individual regards the two goods as to some extent complementary in consumption. More precisely, if he is offered two equally desirable combinations of the goods, then he would rather consume some positively weighted average of the combinations – for example half of one and half of the other – than either of the combinations themselves. This property is indicated geometrically by the convexity of the indifference map to the origin. Individual A's indifference map emanates from the origin *K* and is exemplified by the indifference curve *LA*. Individual B's indifference map emanates from the origin *M* and is exemplified by the indifference curve *LB*. The two sample indifference curves have been chosen so that they each pass through the point representing the initial allocation, *L*.

In the absence of the entrepreneur, consumption will be confined to *L*. Yet any point within the shaded area *LEGF* between the indifference curves would place each individual upon a higher indifference curve. In other words, both individuals would be made better off by a movement to a point such as *H* in the interior of *LEGF*.

It is useful to distinguish two cases, in one of which the entrepreneur has full information about preferences, and in the other of which he has more limited information, which is actually collected as part of the negotiation process.

When the entrepreneur has full information about preferences he has no difficulty in mapping out the trading possibility set *LEGF*. Using hard-line negotiating tactics, he can move individual A along the indifference curve *LA* and at the same time move individual B along the indifference curve *LB*. It follows that the entrepreneur's own consumption possibilities lie on or within the boundaries of the trading possibility set. The entrepreneur's own preferences are indicated by the sample indifference curve *CC'* drawn with respect to the origin *E*. The entrepreneur's optimal strategy is determined by moving the origin *E* along the boundary *LEG* until the tangent *QQ'* is parallel to the tangent *PP'* which is common to both the upper boundary of the trading possibility set and the entrepreneur's indifference map. The entrepreneur offers individual A the bundle *E* and individual B the bundle *F*. As a result, the entrepreneur is able to appropriate a surplus, comprising *EH* units of the first good and *EJ* units of the second. This consumption represents the real profit of intermediation.

It is readily established that the new allocation of consumption is not only privately efficient for the entrepreneur, but socially efficient as well. This follows from the tangency conditions at *E* and *F*, which imply that the marginal rates of substitution in consumption for all three individuals are equalized. Since both A and B have been constrained to their original indifference curves, all the gains from trade are appropriated by the entrepreneur.

The tangents *PP'* and *QQ'* can be used to analyse the pricing strategy of the entrepreneur. The simplest strategy is for the entrepreneur to use a two-part tariff. A different tariff is offered to each party. The first part of each tariff is a lump sum payable for the right to trade with the entrepreneur; the second part consists of a fixed rate of exchange equal to the equilibrium marginal rate of substitution between the goods. The entrepreneur's reward for intermediation is obtained entirely from the lump sum payments. Individual A pays a lump sum equivalent to *QL* units of the first good and individual B pays a lump sum equivalent to *PL* units of the second good (as valued by the price set in the second part of the tariff). This indicates that, because of the entrepreneur's monopoly of the trading opportunity, his reward consists essentially of lump sum payments from transactors for the right to trade with him.

3.4 ENTREPRENEURSHIP WITH LIMITED INFORMATION

It is somewhat implausible to assume that the entrepreneur has the kind of information on preferences assumed above. He may still be able to spot a trading opportunity even though he has quite limited information. The key factor is that he has more information than the others – or at least a better combination of information; complete information is not necessary.

In the case above the entrepreneur could, in theory, obtain full information if he were prepared to ask the transactors about all the points on their current indifference curve. However, although individuals may behave as though they have indifference curves, they do not necessarily think in terms of them. The entrepreneur may therefore have to obtain the information he requires by presenting people with a series of binary choices between alternative consumption bundles. There are many problems with this, one of which is that the number of separate choices required to determine the form of the indifference curve could be enormous. A more practical alternative is to quote trial prices to consumers and monitor their quantity response. To control the number of different prices quoted it is desirable to use only a one-part tariff. By offering different trial prices to each transactor, and noting the quantity he is willing to trade, the entrepreneur maps out the transactor's offer curve. This is different from the individual's indifference curve, although the two are, of course, related.

Suppose, therefore, that the entrepreneur now has information not on indifference curves but on offer curves. The trading possibility set is represented in Figure 3.2 by the shaded area *LSPT* between the offer curves *LA'* and *LB'*. The new possibility set lies entirely within the old possibility set, indicating the reduced opportunities for the entrepreneur consequent upon his more limited information.

The entrepreneur's optimal strategy is determined by the points *S* and *T*, at which points the slopes of both the offer curves and of the entrepreneur's indifference map are equal. The slopes of the chords *LS* and *LT* indicate the relative prices at which the entrepreneur trades with the two parties. The angle *SLT* between the chords is related to the entrepreneur's margin, that is, to the difference between the buying price and the selling price for each commodity.

Theoretical foundations

Consumption of the second good by individual *B*

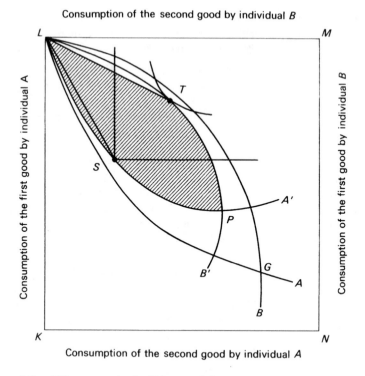

Figure 3.2   Offer curves in the Edgeworth box

It is readily established that the outcome of entrepreneurial intermediation using a one-part tariff is not socially efficient. The reason is that the slope of an offer curve does not represent a pure substitution effect in consumption, but a mixture of income and substitution effects. The entrepreneur creates trade with each individual up to the point where his own marginal rate of substitution between the two goods is equal to their marginal rate of transformation through trade. This marginal rate of transformation is measured by the slope of the trading partner's offer curve. It therefore differs from the trading partner's marginal rate of substitution, so that the two rates of substitution are not equalized.

It can be shown that social efficiency would be achieved by increasing the entrepreneur's volume of trade with each individual. The entrepreneur's exploitation of his monopoly using a one-part tariff produces too low a volume of trade. This does not, of course, imply that the entrepreneur's trading partners would be better off without him. Without the entrepreneur, no trade would occur. The allocation of resources produced by the entrepreneur is a Pareto-improvement on the no-trade situation, for it makes the entrepreneur better off without making either of his trading partners worse off; indeed, it makes his partners better off as well. It is just that it is possible to visualize an even better allocation. Even so, this better allocation is of purely academic interest, for no-one – including the entrepreneur – has the information required to achieve it.

3.5   THE ENTREPRENEUR'S BARGAINING TACTICS

The preceding analysis demonstrates just how crucial bargaining tactics are for entrepreneurial success. Success does not just depend upon the entrepreneur having superior judgment to other people. While superior judgment is a necessary condition for success, it is not a sufficient condition. It is also necessary that the entrepreneur be able to turn his judgment to good account by contracting with parties of inferior judgment on terms favourable to himself.

To negotiate favourable terms it is normally necessary to have information about the preferences and beliefs of the other party. Even more important, it is necessary to prevent one's superior judgment being communicated to the other party during the negotiation process.

To begin with, the entrepreneur must avoid the other party recognizing that he values a resource more highly than they do. He must create an expectation that he cannot afford to pay more than the amount currently offered. He does this using a hard-line bargaining strategy in which no concession is ever made to the other party. Consequently, no indication is ever given of what is the most that the entrepreneur would actually be willing to pay.

When intermediating an exchange, it is also important for the entrepreneur to prevent the two parties negotiating directly with each other. Once such negotiations have been established, the two parties are unlikely to need the entrepreneur. The main exception is when negotiations break down and the entrepreneur has to be called in as an arbitrator. It is very difficult, however, for the entrepreneur to appropriate a significant reward from such arbitration. To prevent the two parties making contact with each other, it is necessary to negotiate with each separately. Establishing round-the-table multilateral negotiations would *ipso facto* make the entrepreneur redundant. He would have performed a valuable social service in getting the other parties together, but, because he would no longer have a monopoly in bargaining with each of them, he would have no means of obtaining a private reward for this service.

SUMMARY

The chapter analyses the role of the entrepreneur in achieving coordination by promoting exchange. In each case the entrepreneur's superior judgment enables him to identify an opportunity for coordination which he exploits through intermediation. In order to protect his superior judgment he has to keep apart the people between whom he is intermediating. He also has to ensure that he does not weaken his bargaining position by giving away too much information in the course of negotiating with each party.

4. The competitive threat to the entrepreneur

4.1 INTRODUCTION

The preceding analysis of coordination has assumed that each opportunity is exploited by a single entrepreneur. It has been shown that the entrepreneur can appropriate a private reward which, under certain conditions, is equal to the value of the improvement in resource allocation which he effects. In some cases his reward exceeds this value and in other cases it is less.

In the long run, the existence of such potential rewards will bring entrepreneurs into competition with each other in seeking them out. This raises the possibility that a given opportunity could be discovered simultaneously by several entrepreneurs. There is no reason why any of the entrepreneurs should know that others have made the same discovery – at least not until they all seek to exploit the opportunity at the same time. At this point each entrepreneur will become aware of competition through his inability to negotiate a favourable price. He is unlikely to know from precisely where this competition originates. It is possible, of course, that he could identify the source of competition and arrange to eliminate it through collusion. In practice this is likely to prove difficult; for, even if the source of competition could be identified, a collusive agreement would prove difficult to enforce.

The simultaneous discovery of an opportunity for coordination is not, however, the only threat to the entrepreneur. A more serious threat comes from the presence of people seeking to acquire knowledge of opportunities at second hand from the entrepreneur. These people are not true entrepreneurs themselves for they rely upon the entrepreneur to provide their information for them. In effect they back the entrepreneur's judgment rather than their own by seeking to replicate whatever the entrepreneur does. They hope by doing so to obtain a 'free ride' upon the entrepreneur's judgment. Alternatively, they may be entrepreneurs, but misguided ones. They believe, erroneously, that the entrepreneur will fail to exploit the opportunity properly. As a result, they think that they can exploit the opportunity themselves without facing any effective competition from the entrepreneur from whom they have taken the idea. These imitators, of whatever sort, may be termed follower-entrepreneurs to distinguish them from the leader-entrepreneurs who discover opportunities at first hand.

The first part of this chapter examines the consequences for the entrepreneur of competition in the exploitation of a given opportunity. It shows that, not surprisingly, competition reduces the reward to entrepreneurship and – more significantly – that in most cases it completely eliminates it. The relation between leaders and followers is then examined and the conditions under which competition from followers can be eliminated are discussed. Finally, it is shown that, if followers can be deterred, then in the long run the leaders may be able to achieve an equilibrium in which each obtains a positive reward. Adjustment to equilibrium is, however, likely to be slow and uncertain even at the best of times.

4.2   COMPETITION IN EXPLOITATION

The main result is easily stated: if two or more entrepreneurs compete to exploit the same opportunity, then normally neither of them will obtain any reward. This result needs to be modified slightly when there is uncertainty about the situation. In this case, competition from the more risk-averse entrepreneur constrains the reward that the less risk-averse entrepreneur can obtain. Only when the degree of risk aversion is the same for both does neither obtain any reward.

The reason why competition eliminates rewards is that the information exploited by the entrepreneur is an indivisible good. Once the information has been acquired, the additional cost involved in its exploitation is zero. Thus, so long as a positive reward accrues to the information, it pays each entrepreneur to bid away from his competitor the resources required to exploit it. Consequently, competition between entrepreneurs bids down the reward for information to zero.

The operation of this principle may be illustrated by an example based upon the model of exchange presented in the previous chapter. Consider two entrepreneurs, C and D, attempting to intermediate an exchange between two consumers A and B. Suppose that C is the first to approach A and B. His optimal strategy in the absence of any constraints imposed by D is to negotiate with A and B separately and to move A and B along their indifference curves until the marginal rates of substitution of A, B and C have been equalized. The situation is illustrated in Figure 4.1, which is based upon Figure 3.1.

As before, individual A's consumption of the two goods is measured from the origin K and individual B's consumption from the origin M. The initial allocation of the goods is represented by L, with all of the first good being allocated to A and all of the second good to B. Individual A is on the indifference curve LA and individual B on the indifference curve LB. Entre-

Consumption of the second good by individual *B*

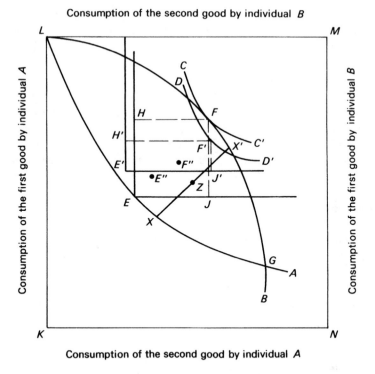

Figure 4.1   *Competition between two entrepreneurs in intermediating an exchange of goods using a multi-part tariff*

preneur C's consumption is measured from the origin *E* and his initial strategy is to consume at *F*, where his indifference curve *CC'* is tangent to B's indifference curve *LB*. *E* and *F* are jointly determined by this condition, together with the condition that the tangent to *LA* at *E* is parallel to the tangent to *LB* at *F*. It is planned to consume the profits of intermediation in the form of *EH* units of the first good and *EJ* units of the second good.

Suppose that entrepreneur D now enters the picture. To bid away trade from C he must offer both A and B an improvement in their welfare. For illustrative purposes it is useful to assume that the increment in welfare is fairly substantial in each case. Entrepreneur D's counter-offer to A is indicated by the point *E'* which lies on a higher indifference curve than *E*, and his offer to B by *F'*, which lies on a higher indifference curve than *F*. D's consumption is measured from the origin *E'* and his planned consumption is at *F'* on his indifference curve *DD'*. He plans to consume *E'H'* units of the first good and *E'J'* units of the second good.

To regain trade, entrepreneur C must now improve upon D's offer. For example, he may offer A consumption at E'', which lies on a higher indifference curve than E', and simultaneously offer B consumption at F'' which lies on a higher indifference curve than F'. It is apparent from the figure that C's profits from intermediation have shrunk considerably, as his own consumption of both goods is lower than before. As offer follows counter-offer so profits are squeezed further until the process terminates at a point such as Z. Z represents the common limit of the sequence $E, E', E'', \ldots$ and the sequence $F, F', F'', \ldots$ When referred to the origin K, it indicates individual A's consumption and when referred to the origin M it indicates B's consumption. Profits have been completely eliminated and so neither C nor D consumes anything.

The point Z cannot be uniquely determined unless the negotiation process is modelled more fully, which is beyond the scope of this chapter. The only restriction upon Z is that it lies upon the contract curve XX'. The contract curve is the locus of points within the trading possibility set $LEGF$ at which the indifference maps of individuals A and B are tangent to each other. Any point on the contract curve apportions the total stock of the two goods between the individuals A and B in a manner which equalizes their marginal rates of substitution. Because there is total apportionment of the stock between A and B, there is no margin of profit for C and D; and because the marginal rates of substitution are equal, there is no potential for profit from the intermediation of exchange.

There is no guarantee that a point such as Z, once attained, will be a stable equilibrium. For one entrepreneur can always undermine the other entrepreneur's offer, by proposing trade at another point on the contract curve. This offer is bound to seem preferable to one of the transactors, and worse to the other. If two such offers are 'on the table' at the same time, then neither offer will be acceptable to both of the parties and trade will be unable to proceed. To guarantee a stable outcome it is necessary to assume that, once the profit of intermediation has been eliminated, one of the entrepreneurs quits and leaves the other to settle the final allocation of consumption between the two individuals. This does not eliminate the constraint on the other entrepreneur so long as the threat of re-entry remains.

4.3   INTERMEDIATING EXCHANGE USING A ONE-PART TARIFF

Implicit in the preceding analysis is the assumption that both entrepreneurs have at their disposal a multi-part tariff. It is often more plausible to assume that they are both restricted to a one-part tariff. This case is also of particular

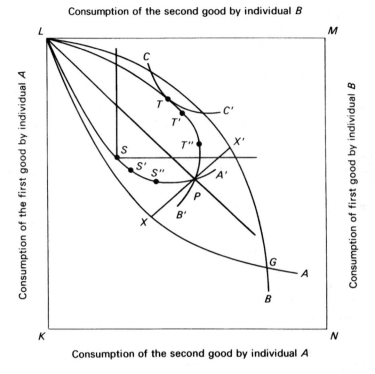

Figure 4.2   Competition between two entrepreneurs in intermediating an exchange of goods using a one-part tariff

theoretical interest as it leads to a very simple result which links the theory of entrepreneurship to the elementary theory of supply and demand.

With a one-part tariff, both entrepreneurs are restricted to trading possibilities determined by A's and B's offer curves. The trading possibility set is indicated in Figure 4.2 by the area *LSPT* lying between A's offer curve *LA'* and B's offer curve *LB'*. The analysis depends crucially upon two properties of the offer curves. The first is that they intersect at a point, such as *P*, on the contract curve *XX'*. The second is that each individual's welfare increases as he moves along his offer curve away from the no-trade position. Thus as individual A moves along *LA'* from *L* to *S* and then to *P* and *A'* his welfare increases, and similarly as B moves along *LB'* from *L* to *T* to *P* and *B'* his welfare increases too.

Suppose that entrepreneur C begins by ignoring competition from D. His optimal strategy is to set a price for A so that A consumes at *S* and to set a price for B so that B consumes at *T*. His own consumption is measured from the origin S and, given S, his optimal strategy is to consume at T where his indifference curve CC' is tangent to the frontier of the trading possibility set, as given by the offer curve LB'. S is determined by the condition that the tangent to LA' at S is parallel to the tangent to LB' at T.

When entrepreneur D enters the picture, he seeks to bid away trade from C. To do this he must offer both A and B a higher welfare than before. He must therefore move A to a point such as S' to the right of S and move B to a point such as T' to the right of T. Thus both individuals move further away from the no-trade position L.

To counter D, C must now offer to trade at points such as S'', to the right of S', and T'', to the right of T'. The process of offer and counter-offer continues until one of the entrepreneurs arrives at the intersection P. There is no point in continuing beyond P because the entrepreneur would then be incurring debts which will make him worse off than he would be by quitting the market and which, in any case, he would be unable to pay. Neither is there any point in the other entrepreneur challenging the allocation P, and so that is where equilibrium will be achieved.

The actual mechanism of adjustment is, of course, price competition. Another property of the offer curves is that the terms of trade improve as the individual moves along his offer curve away from the no-trade position. The terms of trade are the price at which the individual obtains his purchase, expressed in terms of the good in which he makes his payment. Competition takes the form of offering each individual trade at a more favourable price: for each good a lower price is quoted to the buyer and a higher price to the seller. The process ends when the margin between the buying price and selling price has been eliminated. Because of the nature of the process, at this price supply and demand for each good will be equal.

It is necessary to qualify this analysis in one respect. It has been assumed that the offer curves intersect only once, and there is no guarantee that this condition will be satisfied. Relaxing this condition leads to indeterminacy in the outcome. Equilibrium will still be achieved at an intersection and one of the intersections will still lie upon the contract curve. But the equilibrium itself is no longer unique and so the price and quantity traded cannot be predicted with certainty.

It is worth noting that, where entrepreneurial competition leads to an equilibrium on the contract curve, social efficiency is achieved. This applies whether a single- or multi-part tariff is used. When a multi-part tariff is used, social efficiency is achieved even in the absence of competition, as shown in Section 3.3. The most interesting result, therefore, is that competition is a sufficient condition for entrepreneurial intermediation to lead to social efficiency when a one-part tariff is used.

4.4 BARRIERS TO ENTRY

As we have seen, the essence of entrepreneurship is superior judgment, and the reward to this judgment depends critically upon the entrepreneur enjoying monopoly power. It is important, however, to distinguish between a monopoly of the information on which the judgment is based, and a monopoly of the situation to which the judgment relates.

To achieve a monopoly of information, two conditions must normally be satisfied. The information must be discovered before anyone else discovers it, and when it has been discovered other people must be excluded from it. The first condition involves getting to the source of the information before anyone else does. If several people arrive at the same source simultaneously, then no-one can gain a monopoly. Competition will be present right at the outset. The second condition is that the information, when discovered, is kept secret. Secrecy means that the information is not communicated to anyone else. But there is more to secrecy than just this. People must be prevented from independently gaining access to the source. The risk of subsequent discovery must be reduced by putting other people 'off the scent'. A basic requirement is that the discoverer of the information should act as though he has not discovered anything. A more sophisticated strategy is for him to make out that he has discovered something else, and so divert people's efforts to making contact with quite different sources instead.

It must be recognized, however, that as soon as privileged information is exploited for personal gain, the very act of exploitation is likely to draw people's attention to it. Secrecy is usually only a temporary expedient. This does not imply, though, that the entrepreneur's monopoly power must be dissipated. Although the monopoly of information may be lost, the monopoly of its exploitation may be retained. Even if the information becomes public knowledge, competition from other entrepreneurs can be prevented if there is a barrier which deters them from doing anything with it. Two possible situations can be envisaged. In the first case the discoverer can do nothing to prevent people who share the information from exploiting it. In the second case, the discoverer can use a temporary monopoly of the information to erect barriers to competition which confer a monopoly of exploitation. In this case secrecy becomes a means to an end. Secrecy buys the discoverer sufficient time for him to consolidate his advantage. He uses his temporary lead to erect a permanent barrier to competition.

Barriers to competition are only important where the exploitation of the opportunity is a continuous process. If the opportunity can be pre-empted entirely by a once-for-all initiative, then nothing remains for potential competitors to exploit. This indicates an important distinction between coordination involving stocks, and coordination involving flows. The reallocation of a stock is a once-for-all activity which appropriates the gains from coordination in perpetuity. The reallocation of a flow is a continuing activity; imitators who notice it once it has begun can move in and bid away the activity from the innovator.

In the latter case the innovator could, in principle, translate his activity from the flow to the stock dimension: he could 'capitalize' the flow by establishing long-term contracts with the other transactors involved. The existence of long-term contracts ties up the sources of supply and demand upon which a potential competitor would depend.

The difficulty with this strategy is twofold. First, for reasons explained in Chapter 7, long-term contracts are difficult to negotiate and to enforce. Secondly, they can only be negotiated on terms favourable to the entrepreneur if transactors believe that future competition is unlikely to occur anyway. If transactors expect prices to become more competitive, then they will be unwilling to trade now on terms which capitalize the entrepreneur's monopoly profit. The strategy will only work if the entrepreneur can use his negotiating skill to persuade transactors that competition is unlikely whether or not they contract with him on a long-term basis. This suggests that, while long-term contracts may be a useful adjunct to another barrier, they are unlikely to be an effective barrier in themselves unless the entrepreneur has exceptional negotiating skill.

Suppose then that the entrepreneur is coordinating in the flow dimension, that his activity cannot be kept secret, and that long-term contracts cannot be negotiated unless some independent barrier to competition exists. The entrepreneur has a choice of four main strategies to deter competition:

1. He can apply for a statutory monopoly, for example a licence, patent or charter.
2. He can identify a resource which is indispensable for the exploitation of his opportunity, and which is in inelastic supply. By buying up this resource he can monopolize exploitation indirectly by monopolizing an indispensable input.
3. He can commit himself at the outset to exploitation on such a scale that the entry of a competitor would lead to overexpansion, and so incur losses for the competitor as well as for the entrepreneur. This is particularly important if there is a substantial minimal scale on which the competitor must enter.
4. He can build up goodwill towards himself in the early stages of exploitation, and thereby hope to make his trading partners suspicious of any competitors who appear. In other words, he can increase customers' 'switching costs'.

The choice of strategy depends crucially upon the kind of activity in which the entrepreneur is involved. It is desirable to postpone further discussion until the partial analysis of coordination is introduced in the following chapter. Partial analysis provides practical examples of coordination at the industry level. Using these examples it is possible to identify the factors which influence the entrepreneur's choice of a barrier to competition in each particular case.

4.5   COMPETITIVE SEARCH FOR INFORMATION

The remainder of this chapter is concerned with long-run competition between entrepreneurs in identifying opportunities for coordination. This is analysed in terms of a competitive process of search for information.

It was suggested earlier that the successful entrepreneur requires a monopoly of some item of information. Strictly speaking, however, the only item that has to be monopolized is the information that a particular profit opportunity exists. Information about the existence of a profit opportunity may be called commercial information. It is shown in the following chapter that commercial information is typically a synthesis of other information, which may be called raw information. Items of raw information are like the pieces of a jigsaw that have to be fitted together to get the overall picture. This picture tells a story, and a story it tells is the commercial information.

It is assumed that each entrepreneur enters the search process with fairly wide-ranging background information, as a result of both incidental experiences and purposive search in the past. Not all entrepreneurs have the same background information by any means, but all are searching for the last few items of raw information – in other words, for the last few pieces of the jigsaw. Entrepreneurs have a choice as to where they direct their search. Information sources are localized and searching one area will lead to one type of commercial information, while searching in a different area will lead to another kind of commercial information. Here the jigsaw analogy rather breaks down. A better analogy would be searching for pieces of a Meccano set. Different types of synthesis can be effected with different combinations of pieces, and people with imagination may be able to achieve a synthesis with a given combination that other people would be unable to visualize. It is the imagination that dictates what kinds of synthesis are believed to be possible, and so lends direction to the search process.

By and large, entrepreneurs wish to avoid searching areas of information that other entrepreneurs are searching in too. Because of differences in background information, a considerable degree of overlap can be tolerated, but if too many people search in too narrow an area then the prospective reward to each is reduced. The greater the number of entrepreneurs searching in a given area, the lower the probability that any given one of them will be the first to make a discovery. If each entrepreneur is basically as well equipped for search as the others, then his probability of obtaining a reward from search varies inversely with the number of entrepreneurs in the field.

Suppose that there is a fixed number of different areas of search. An area is distinguished by the subject matter of the information, though it also has a geographical dimension to the extent that sources of information on particular subjects tend to be concentrated in particular locations. Suppose also that there is a fixed number of able entrepreneurs, each of whom has an actuarially fair chance of achieving priority in any area. This chance depends, of course, on the number of other entrepreneurs also searching in the area. All areas of search are freely accessible to any entrepreneur, but each entrepreneur can search in only one area at a time.

There are also some other entrepreneurs who are not so able. They do not realize that they are not as able as the other group, though they are in the process of finding out. They find out the hard way, by striving for success and not finding it. The less able entrepreneurs, when in competition with the more able entrepreneurs, stand no chance of achieving priority in discovery. In competition with each other they stand an actuarially fair chance of achieving priority. Their main chance of reward lies in areas which offer gains to priority, but provide too little opportunity to attract any of the more able entrepreneurs. Here less able entrepreneurs may be found sheltering under the lack of interest of the more able entrepreneurs. This possibility is ignored in the analysis below.

Each entrepreneur plans his search over a unit period and is confident that during this period there will be just one discovery in each area. All the able entrepreneurs share the same perception of the potential reward available in each area. Finally, all the entrepreneurs are risk-neutral, and there is no area offering pre-emption by priority which affords too small a reward to attract at least one able entrepreneur.

Under these conditions there exists an equilibrium in which the expected reward to search in each area is equalized across all areas. In fact the equality is only approximate because, by assumption, the entrepreneurs are indivisible in allocation, and so there has to be an integer number of entrepreneurs in each location. The equilibrium condition applies, of course, to the able entrepreneurs. The less able entrepreneurs also receive the same expected reward in each area but that is lower than the reward to the able entrepreneurs; indeed, it is zero. This zero reward applies independently of the allocation of less able entrepreneurs among the different areas. The allocation of the less able entrepreneurs depends upon their own – misguided – perceptions of the opportunities and rewards.

The equilibrium condition determines a unique allocation of able entrepreneurs between the different areas (except for possible problems at the margin caused by indivisibility). Under the equilibrium allocation, the number of able entrepreneurs in each area is directly proportional to the potential reward available. This means, of course, that in areas where preemption by priority is impossible, no able entrepreneurs will be found at all.

This simple result accords with the view that entrepreneurs are attracted to areas where the highest rewards are to be found. It also accords with the view that the ability to pre-empt by priority – a principle enshrined in the patent system, for example – is crucial in attracting entrepreneurial activity. Thus, other things being equal, able entrepreneurs will be attracted to areas where patent and other forms of barrier to entry are available, and will avoid areas where patent protection is not available or where, in general, followers can undermine a leader's position.

4.6 COORDINATION OF SEARCH BY CONJECTURE

The previous section described an equilibrium in entrepreneurial search, but it did not describe the process of adjustment to it. One possibility is that each entrepreneur is aware of the provisional plans of the other entrepreneurs and so can assess the number of entrepreneurs tentatively allocated to each area. Using this information each entrepreneur can assess the probability of his achieving priority of discovery in each area, and thereby allocate himself to the area which offers the greatest expected reward. But if all entrepreneurs are simultaneously reallocating themselves in the light of the others' provisional allocations, what guarantee is there that the process will converge upon the equilibrium allocation? More generally, what grounds are there for believing that entrepreneurs can know each other's provisional allocations when deciding upon their own strategy anyway?

The short answer is that no formal mechanism for harmonizing entrepreneurs' plans exists. Entrepreneurs must rely upon conjectures about the others' plans in order to coordinate their own strategy with those of others.

A possible alternative to coordination of search by conjecture is coordination by contract. Two variants may be considered. In the first, the entrepreneurs who are engaged in search contract directly with each other. However, a consistent economy-wide search plan could only be arrived at either by a multilateral negotiation bringing all the entrepreneurs simultaneously 'round the table', or by an extremely prolonged series of bilateral negotiations. Multilateral negotiations would be prohibitively costly to organize, while different bilateral negotiations would take so long to harmonize that unac-

ceptable delays would result. Moreover, even if the contracts could be negotiated, they would be extremely difficult to enforce.

An alternative is to establish a statutory body to license search in different
areas. The licensing body would not necessarily confer a monopoly of search
on particular entrepreneurs, but would merely regulate entry to avoid over-
crowding in particular areas. In effect the right to search would be transferred
from common ownership to public ownership, by virtue of the latent right of
state regulation being activated.

Under a regime of public ownership contracts would be established, not
between one entrepreneur and another, but between entrepreneurs on the one
hand and the state on the other. Since the state would be a party to all the
contracts, the contracts would tend to be easier to set up and to enforce.

The state could realize the competitive equilibrium described earlier by the
simple expedient of selling licences to entrepreneurs. It would issue a sufficient number of licences to achieve approximate equality in the price of
licences for each area. The state would of course have to fix the number of
licences of each type before auctioning them, as entrepreneurs would be
reluctant to bid for licences whose value could be subsequently diluted.

Since information is a public good with infinite capacity, social efficiency
requires that there be no replication of its production. It was assumed earlier
that there was only one discovery to be made in each area, and that this
discovery would be made even if there was just one entrepreneur searching in
the area. If interpreted literally, this implies that when entrepreneurial effort
has a positive opportunity cost only one entrepreneur should be allocated to
each area. Social efficiency also requires, of course, that the less able entrepreneurs should be excluded from search altogether. On this basis social
efficiency is achieved if the licensing authority establishes a single licence for
each area and then auctions each licence to the highest bidder.

In cases where the area of search can be identified fairly easily this principle has been applied with some success. In some cases the areas of search do
actually correspond with geographical areas, as when prospecting for mineral
deposits, for example, but it has to be admitted that there are many other
cases in which it is simply impossible to specify precisely what the subject of
the information is until you have it. For reasons which are fully explained in
Chapter 8, any form of coordination by contract is out of the question in such
cases. There is no alternative but to rely upon coordination by conjecture, and
the very vague tendency to converge to the competitive equilibrium described
in Section 4.5. The economy simply does not have the kind of information –
or the facility for exchanging it – which is necessary to provide proper
guidance to the entrepreneur who is deciding upon his area of search.

SUMMARY

This chapter has shown that the private reward to the exercise of entrepreneurial judgment depends crucially upon the absence of competition from like-minded individuals. Since the information on which judgment is based is a public good in common ownership, the successful entrepreneur is always vulnerable to threat of imitation. The erection of a barrier to entry is important in consolidating the entrepreneur's temporary lead over his competitors. If barriers to entry are difficult to erect, then entrepreneurial search for information will be deterred. It is difficult in any case for entrepreneurs to consolidate their search effort because the fact that information is in common ownership means that unintentional congestion in some areas of search is difficult to avoid.

NOTES AND REFERENCES

The advantages of disadvantages of placing the right to exploit information into private ownership are considered in the patent literature. See, for example, Arrow (1962a), Bennett (1943), Blankart (1975), Bowman (1973), Fox (1947) and Ravenshear (1908). An interesting empirical study of industrialization without patents, which is rather sceptical of the advantages of 'privatizing' information, is Schiff (1971). The impact of rivalry on the search for, and the exploitation of, entrepreneurial opportunities is analysed by Baldwin and Childs (1969), Kamien and Schwartz (1972, 1974, 1978) and Scherer (1965, 1967). The influence of market structure on innovation is surveyed in Kamien and Schwartz (1975). For an interesting empirical study of rivalry, see Grabowski and Baxter (1973).

The classic reference on barriers to entry as a whole is Bain (1956). Literature on this topic is surveyed in Koutsoyiannis (1979). The importance of rewarding entrepreneurs, and the implication of this for competition policy, are considered in two well-known critiques of anti-trust legislation, Armentano (1972) and Mason (1951).

5. Partial coordination: the case of innovation

5.1 INTRODUCTION

The preceding chapters have been concerned with very fundamental issues. Much of the discussion has been highly abstract. The main formal model employed was based upon an economy comprising just two people and two goods. To generate practical testable hypotheses it is necessary to recognize that the real world is much more complicated than this. In practice, entrepreneurship involves many millions of people interacting with each other, and for this purpose a range of institutions, such as firms, and trading mechanisms, such as markets, must be employed. These mechanisms and institutions emerge as a means of addressing the problems created by the complexity of real-world phenomena. This chapter examines some of the basic issues raised by the fact that many different entrepreneurs are at work in a particular economy at any given point in time.

In a market economy, individual entrepreneurs do not formulate proposals to reallocate all the resources in the economy as part of a single plan. They formulate partial proposals concerned with reallocation in some small sector: forming a new production plant, arbitraging between two segments of a market, and so on. The reason why proposals are partial is not difficult to see. To formulate a partial proposal the entrepreneur requires only very limited information which may be quite close to hand. A more wide-ranging proposal requires a great deal of extra information, much of which may only be obtainable from distant and diverse sources. Thus, as the scale of the proposal increases, the entrepreneur has to widen his area of search to tap additional sources which are much more costly to reach. As a result, information costs increase with the scale of the proposal at an increasing rate.

Even if the entrepreneur did formulate a far-reaching proposal it would be difficult to finance it. His own personal wealth would almost certainly prove inadequate. He would have to borrow the funds. But, as noted earlier, it is a characteristic of the entrepreneur that people are reluctant to lend to him because his assessment of the situation differs from their own. How much more reluctant they are likely to be if the proposal is a far-reaching one! To begin with, the larger the scale of the proposal, the more different backers the entrepreneur will require. Some potential backers will be naturally more optimistic than others. A small-scale proposal can attract sufficient funds just from the most optimistic backers, but a large-scale proposal must obtain funds from the less optimistic backers too. On these grounds alone, the large-scale proposals will prove more difficult to finance. But in addition, even the most optimistic backers are likely to be less optimistic about a large-scale proposal than they would be about a small-scale proposal made by the same entrepreneur. For, once they realize that the entrepreneur is extending his skill and competence to the limits by tapping distant and unfamiliar sources of information, their own perception of the risks is bound to increase. Both of these factors mean that as the scale of a proposal increases, so the cost of borrowed capital increases at an increasing rate.

5.2 THE CASE FOR SEQUENTIAL NEGOTIATION

In a large economy there will be a number of different proposals being made by different entrepreneurs at any one time. Each proposal will normally be formulated on the assumption of no change elsewhere in the economy. But because of the other proposals in hand this assumption will be incorrect. What guarantee, therefore, is there that the different proposals will be consistent with each other?

Suppose that two proposals place conflicting demands upon the same resource. In this case it is the owner's responsibility to avoid congestion in the use of the resource. He must sell a right of access to one entrepreneur and deny it to the other. This effectively vetoes the other entrepreneur's proposal; unless he can find a substitute resource he must abandon his proposal, and try to reformulate it so that it imposes no demand upon the resource concerned. In this way the exercise of the right of ownership ensures the compatibility of the demands upon the resource. If all resources with finite user capacity have owners, and all the rights of ownership are exercised, the proposals which are actually implemented are bound to be consistent with each other.

Given that inconsistencies are eliminated in this way, is there any guarantee that the best of the proposals are chosen and the worst abandoned? This condition could, in principle, be satisfied by simultaneous negotiations over all the proposals. Each entrepreneur would haggle simultaneously with all the owners of the resources that he required. Each resource owner would haggle simultaneously with all the entrepreneurs who demanded his resource. Haggling would continue until no-one thought that they could achieve a better outcome: no resource owner could expect to get a better offer from the entrepreneurs, and no entrepreneur could expect to obtain better terms from any of the resource owners. In the process, entrepreneurs with good proposals would bid away resources from entrepreneurs with worse proposals. As resource prices rose, so proposals which conflicted with better ones would become loss makers and their entrepreneurs would abandon them. At the end only the best proposals would remain.

Unfortunately, simultaneous negotiation of this kind is likely to prove prohibitively costly. It involves keeping open the channels of communication between everyone concerned for the duration of the negotiations. It puts people under psychological strain by obliging them to participate in several different negotiations at once. The alternative is sequential negotiation, in which each individual negotiates with only one person at a time.

The advantages of sequential negotiation are obvious. The main disadvantage is that no-one is sure whether, by accepting an offer now, it may become necessary to refuse a better offer later. This has two main implications for behaviour.

First, all negotiations have to be based upon expectations of what alternative future negotiations would yield. It is expectations of these future outcomes which determine what the outcome of the current negotiations will be. Unless the current negotiations break down, the alternative future outcome is completely hypothetical. Given this subjectivity of expectations, it is open to each negotiator to influence the other negotiator's expectations so that he will make concessions in his favour. This tactical aspect of bargaining was emphasized in Chapter 3 where bargaining tactics were shown to be an integral factor in successful entrepreneurship.

The second – and perhaps most significant – implication of sequential negotiation is that it encourages transactors to hold idle resources. If a transactor completely commits all his resources in a current negotiation then, as noted above, this negotiation is concluded at the expense of any alternative opportunity for negotiation which could present itself immediately afterwards. But if the transactor has a deliberate policy of undercommitting his resources now, then a future opportunity for trade can still be negotiated. Thus, to avoid the risk of having to forgo future trading opportunities, transactors may systematically undercommit themselves in current negotiations. Each transactor holds an uncommitted inventory of resources which he can draw upon when a future opportunity for negotiation arises at short notice.

The economy outlined above is very much like the economy as it really is. It is certainly a more realistic model of the economy than that of general equilibrium. It is this realistic model that provides the background to the following analysis of individual entrepreneurs' partial plans. Three examples of coordination are given: technological innovation, product innovation and arbitrage. The analysis is based upon the familiar supply and demand curves. As in conventional theory, these curves are drawn on the assumption that the coordinating activity to which they relate is only a small part of the total economy. As a result the activity exerts a negligible influence upon the rest of the economy, and so there is no feedback from the rest of the economy onto the entrepreneur. Reactions from the rest of the economy could easily be accommodated within our framework of analysis, but a discussion of this would involve digressing from the main line of the argument into the theory of, for example, oligopolistic reaction curves.

There is one important difference, however, between the demand and supply curves used below and those which appear in orthodox analysis. The demand and supply curves used in orthodox analysis are drawn conditional upon a state of general equilibrium in the rest of the economy. The curves below are drawn, instead, conditional upon current entrepreneurial activity in the rest of the economy. The individual entrepreneur is temporarily insulated from the spillover effects of entrepreneurial activity in the rest of the economy by the slack that is built into the system. This slack allows potential spillovers to be absorbed by unplanned inventory adjustment – that is, by variations in the quantity of uncommitted resources.

5.3 TECHNOLOGICAL INNOVATION

This section presents the first, and perhaps most influential, example of partial coordination, which is due to Schumpeter. Schumpeter emphasizes the role of the entrepreneur as a technological innovator. He distinguishes between invention, which is a scientific activity not necessarily motivated by economic advancement, and innovation. The inventor develops a technique which the innovator seeks to exploit for the creation of wealth. Innovation involves a judgmental decision whether to commit scarce resources to the application of the invention.

The introduction of a new technique often results in a new design and specification of the product. For example, new techniques often have important implications for product quality. For analytical purposes, however, it is often useful to separate these two aspects of innovation. In the present section it is assumed that the new technique merely reduces the cost of production, and leaves product quality unchanged. In the next section it is assumed that the technique facilitates the development of a new variant of the product which is regarded by buyers as a close substitute for the old variant.

It is assumed that the new technique is a proprietary technique, but that the old technique is not. The entrepreneur has a temporary monopoly of the new technique stemming from the superiority of his judgment. In certain cases he may be able to convert this temporary monopoly into a long-term monopoly. The old technique may at one time have been a proprietary technique too, but now there is free access to it. As a result there are now many producers using the old technique, and so product price is competitively determined.

It is assumed that production under both the old technique and the new one incurs constant long-run marginal cost. This is either because efficient production requires a single plant which exhibits constant returns to scale or because the optimum scale of each plant is very small relative to total output, so that production is adjusted by varying the number of plants in use, and not by varying production in each. If in addition all factor inputs are variable and in perfectly elastic supply to the firm, then the long-run marginal cost curve is horizontal.

The innovation of any technique incurs a set-up cost which is a fixed cost independent of firm output. For the old technique this set-up cost is a sunk cost incurred a long time ago by the innovator of the technique. Subsequently, other firms have entered the industry gaining a 'free ride' on the innovator by benefiting from his experience. For the innovator of the new technique, however, the set-up cost is an opportunity cost. It may be translated from a set-up cost into a recurrent cost by assuming that it is financed by a bond whose maturity equals the time span of the innovator's monopoly. Using this convention, the innovator's long-run average variable cost exceeds his long-run marginal cost, but approaches it asymptotically as firm output increases.

Product demand is a decreasing function of price, assuming incomes and all other prices to be constant. This is illustrated by the downward-sloping demand curve *DD'* in Figure 5.1, whose slope measures the degree of substitutability between the product and a composite bundle of all other goods. In the absence of any competition, *DD'* would be the demand curve facing the entrepreneur. However, the entrepreneur faces competition from other firms using the old high-cost technique. This competition will force industry price down to *OP*, the price which just covers the long-run marginal costs of existing producers, as indicated by the horizontal long-run marginal cost curve *PP'*. This price constitutes a limit price for the entrepreneur. If he charges above this price he is liable to be undercut by users of the old technique, and so will be unable to sell anything. If he charges below this price then users of the old technique will shut down to avoid losses and he will acquire a monopoly of the industry. Thus the firm demand curve is infinitely elastic at the price *OP* and coincides with the industry demand curve at below this price. It is indicated in the figure by the kinked demand curve *PED'*.

The profit-maximizing strategy for the entrepreneur is to produce where marginal revenue equals marginal cost. If the entrepreneur can charge discriminatory prices, such that each unit can be sold separately at the maximum that the market will bear, then the marginal revenue curve coincides with

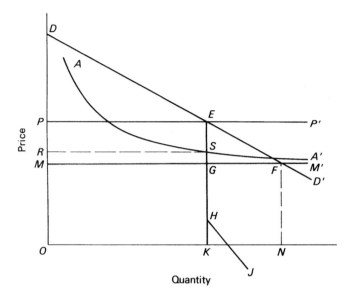

Figure 5.1   Technological innovation: a partial analysis

demand curve *PED′*. Equilibrium for the firm is at *F* where *PED′* intersects the marginal cost curve of the new technique *MM′*. It follows that firm and industry output is *ON*, all produced using the new technique, and the price of output varies between a minimum of *OM*, the marginal cost, and *OP*, the limit price.

It may however be difficult for the entrepreneur to discriminate in price. He may not have the requisite information on the demand curve (as suggested in Chapter 3) or he may not be able to prevent resale between buyers. If he is confined to uniform pricing, then his marginal revenue curve differs from the demand curve: it is shown in the figure by the curve *PEHJ* which has a discontinuity *EH* at the output *OK* at which the demand curve has a kink. The discontinuity is caused by the fact that below the output *OK* an additional unit of output can always be sold without any reduction in price, whilst above *OK* an additional unit of output can only be sold by reducing the price, thereby reducing the revenue obtained from the units which could have been sold anyway at the higher price. The marginal revenue and marginal cost curves intersect at *G*, giving an output *OK* and a price *OP*. Average cost of production is *OR* and so profit is given by the area of the rectangle *PESR*.

With a uniform price, price is on average higher and output is correspondingly lower (a trade-off indicated by the downward-sloping portion *ED′* of the demand curve). Profit is also lower under uniform pricing. It is readily established that the profit forgone is measured by the area of the triangle *EFG*.

The profitability of the innovation ensures that private coordination is achieved by the entrepreneur. It is readily established that innovation achieves social coordination as well. None of the original buyers of the product is any worse off, for no-one has to pay more than the price they were paying before. None of the original producers is any worse off, for under competition they were only operating at break-even point away, so the fact that they have to shut down does not mean a loss for them, so long as they shut down immediately the innovation occurs. None of the factor owners is any worse off, since by assumption the price of factors of production is unaffected by the innovation because the industry is so small a part of the entire economy. The entrepreneur, on the other hand, is better off on account of the profit he earns. Since the entrepreneur is better off and no-one else is worse off, social coordination has been achieved.

It does not follow that the allocation of resources is socially efficient. To demonstrate efficiency it is necessary to show that no further opportunities for social coordination exist. In this respect the pricing strategy of the entrepreneur is crucial. Under uniform pricing the entrepreneur refuses to supply output in excess of *OK* even though the value of this output to buyers (indicated by the height of the demand curve) exceeds the value of the inputs used to produce it. If the entrepreneur could sell the additional output at below the price of the rest of the output, then the buyers would be no worse off, while the entrepreneur would be better off. It follows that social coordination may be achieved by replacing uniform prices with discriminatory prices. Thus, while discriminatory pricing may lead to social efficiency in innovation, uniform pricing normally does not.

It should be emphasized that social coordination in the full sense is achieved by innovation only when there are no fixed factors involved in the exploitation of the old production technique. Since by assumption these factors have no alternative use, their value will be annihilated by the innovation. This is an aspect of what Schumpeter called 'creative destruction'. More generally, if the innovating industry were a large one, so that factors were in less than perfectly elastic supply, then innovation would tend to reduce the value of the factors used relatively intensively in the old technique, and increase the value of factors used relatively intensively in the new technique.

These possibilities were excluded by assumption from the discussion above. If the assumption is relaxed, then it is apparent that, because there is a group of factor owners adversely affected by the innovation, social coordination in the strong sense cannot occur. However, social coordination is still possible in the weak sense that those who benefit from the innovation could in principle compensate those who lose from it and still leave themselves better off.

5.4   PRODUCT INNOVATION

Consider the innovation of a new product which is a differentiated version of an existing product, and so is a close substitute for it. It is assumed that the market for the new variant is small compared to the market for the existing variant, so that the price of the existing variant remains fixed independently of the innovator's pricing and output strategies. Some buyers have a positive preference for the new variant and are willing to pay more for it than they are for the existing variant. Others prefer the existing variant and will buy the new variant only if its price stands at a discount to the existing one. Thus, notwithstanding the substitutability between the two variants, there is a demand for the new variant in its own right. Substitutability simply means that the demand for the new variant at any price is governed by the price of the existing variant.

In Figure 5.2 the price of the old variant is *OL* and demand for the new variant is indicated by the downward-sloping demand curve *DD′*. The entrepreneur monopolizes the supply of the new variant, so that *DD′* is his demand curve too. The cost structure of the innovator is assumed to be the same as before: production is under constant returns to scale, so that with factors of production in infinitely elastic supply, there is a constant long-run marginal cost. Innovation incurs a set-up cost which is independent of output, so that long-run average cost exceeds long-run marginal cost, but is asymptotic to it at high levels of output.

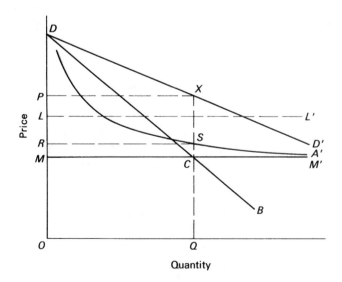

Figure 5.2   Product innovation: a partial analysis

The geometric analysis of profit maximization closely parallels that of the previous section. To avoid too much repetition, it is appropriate to consider just one of the possible pricing strategies, namely uniform pricing. With uniform pricing the marginal revenue curve is *DB*, which lies below the demand curve *DD'* for all positive levels of output. It intersects the horizontal marginal cost curve *MM'* at *C*, giving an equilibrium output *OQ* and an equilibrium price *OP*. As shown, *OP* > *OL* so that the new variant sells at a premium with respect to the old one. This outcome is probably typical, though it is by no means inevitable. Average cost is *OR*, and profit is given by the area of the rectangle *PXSR*.

To analyse social coordination it is necessary to specify the conditions under which the old variant of the product is produced. If the old variant is produced competitively by firms with no fixed factors, then the results parallel exactly those of the previous section. Producers of the old variant are no worse off because, although they have lost sales to the new variant, these sales afforded them no profit. Factor owners are no worse off because factor prices are unaffected. None of the buyers is any worse off, and most are much better off because they are able to buy the new product for less than they would actually be willing to pay. The entrepreneur is better off too, by an amount equal to his profit. Thus no-one is worse off, many people are better off and so social coordination has occurred.

The allocation of resources is not socially efficient, however, and for exactly the same reason as before. Both the entrepreneur and his customers could be made better off if additional units were produced for sale at discriminatory prices below the price of existing output. Thus while product innovation with discriminatory pricing may be socially efficient, product innovation with uniform pricing is not.

5.5   ARBITRAGE

Kirzner is the major modern exponent of the arbitrage theory of the entrepreneur. Kirzner takes his methodology from von Mises, and so places himself firmly within the Austrian tradition. This makes him sceptical of any attempt to create a positive theory of the entrepreneur based upon the neoclassical analysis of arbitrage. As noted in Chapter 1, and as emphasized again in Chapter 6, the neoclassical theory has weaknesses in analysing many aspects of market behaviour, including arbitrage. Equally, however, the Austrian methodological position has its weaknesses, since so much of it depends upon the absence of barriers to entry, which in entrepreneurship are very much a fact of life.

This book seeks to show that the insights of the neoclassical and Austrian theories can be synthesized within a broader framework, once the extreme methodological positions underlying the theories are abandoned. It is therefore entirely appropriate to examine to what extent the neoclassical theory of arbitrage can be used to elucidate an important special case of entrepreneurial activity.

Consider two perfectly competitive markets for the same product which are operating in isolation. For example, they may be two agricultural markets operating in different towns. Figure 5.3 illustrates a case in which the first market (on the left) has very limited demand and abundant supply, while the second market (in the middle) is in the opposite position with buoyant demand and relatively small supply. As a result the price in the second market is much higher than in the first. No-one perceives this apart from the entrepreneur. The Austrian economist Körner, pursuing the spatial analogy, supposes the entrepreneur to have built a watchtower which enables him to recognize a much wider market than anyone else. The man on the watchtower realizes that the two segments of the market can be integrated, and that integration affords profits of arbitrage.

Arbitrage behaviour is governed by the interplay of the excess demand schedule for the high-price market and the excess supply schedule for the low-price market. The excess demand schedule for a market shows the excess of demand over supply at any given price. The excess demand schedule for the high-price market is indicated by the schedule DD' in Figure 5.3(c). It is derived from the horizontal discrepancy between the demand schedule D_2D_2' and the supply schedule S_2S_2' in Figure 5.3(b). It shows the net demand in the high-price market that the entrepreneur can fill by redirecting supplies from the low-price market. The excess supply schedule for a market shows the excess of supply over demand at any given price. The excess supply schedule for the low-price market is indicated by the schedule SS' in Figure 5.3(c). It is derived from the horizontal discrepancy between the supply schedule S_1S_1' and the demand schedule D_1D_1' in Figure 5.3(a). It shows the net supply from the low-price market that the entrepreneur can requisition for resale in the high-price market.

The potential for arbitrage is indicated in Figure 5.3(c) by the intersection J of the excess demand and excess supply schedules DD' and SS'. The corresponding quantity OK indicates the amount of output forthcoming from the low-price market at a supply price less than or equal to its demand price in the high-price market. In the absence of transport costs this is the socially efficient volume of trade.

The effect of transport costs is to shift up the excess supply curve SS' to TT'. If transport services are competitively supplied under constant costs, then there will be a fixed charge per unit traded and the excess supply curve will shift up in parallel fashion, as indicated in the figure. In this case the socially efficient volume of trade is OQ, determined by the intersection E of DD' and TT'.

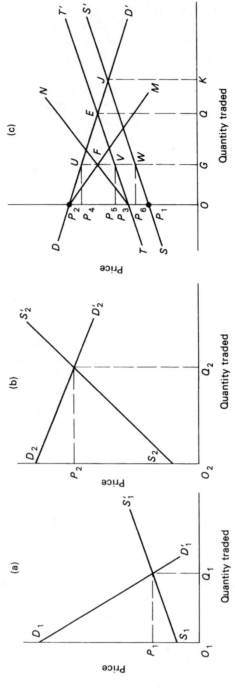

Figure 5.3 Arbitrage: a partial analysis

The imposition of a tariff would induce a similar shift in the excess supply curve. If the tariff were based upon quantity, the excess supply curve would shift upward in parallel fashion as before, but in the more likely case of an *ad valorem* tariff the shift would be an equiproportional one, so that the new excess supply curve TT' would be more steeply sloped than before. The introduction of a tariff does not of course change the efficient volume of trade, but it does change the actual volume traded. Assuming that there are no distortions elsewhere in the economy for which the tariff is designed to correct, the tariff will create social inefficiency by inhibiting trade.

In the case of arbitrage between two competitive markets the entrepreneur cannot normally impose price discrimination (though see Section 5.6 below). If the entrepreneur is unable to effect price discrimination in the high-price market, then his marginal revenue curve becomes P_2M. If he is unable to effect price discrimination in the low-price market, then his marginal cost curve becomes P_3N. If price discrimination is impossible in either market, then the entrepreneur's profit-maximizing strategy is to trade at F, importing OG units into the high-price market, which have been bought at a price OP_6 and are resold at a price OP_4. Payments for transport or tariffs are measured by the area of the rectangle P_5VWP_6. Profit is measured by the area of the rectangle P_4UVP_5.

Because the entrepreneur bids away supplies from the low-price market, buyers in this market now have to pay a higher price than before, and so are worse off. Similarly, because the entrepreneur increases supplies to the high-price market some sellers in this market receive a lower price than before, and so are worse off as well. Since some people are made worse off, arbitrage does not effect social coordination in the strong sense. However, it may be shown that it does effect social coordination in the weak sense, for the losses of the buyers in the low-price market and the sellers in the high-price market are exactly offset by the gains to buyers in the high-price market and sellers in the low-price market. Thus the buyers and sellers who gain are able to compensate the buyers and sellers who lose. The entrepreneur has to compensate no-one, and so his profit is a pure social gain.

Against this must be set the fact that the volume of trade is not socially efficient. The coordination that has been achieved does not go far enough because the volume of trade OG is below the socially efficient level, which is OQ when there are transport costs and OK when there are not. Thus, as before, uniform pricing leads to social inefficiency through the restriction of the volume of trade.

5.6   ARBITRAGING STOCKS INSTEAD OF FLOWS

It was noted above that an arbitrager cannot normally impose discriminatory prices. There is, however, one important case in which price discrimination may well be feasible. This is the case in which the entrepreneur is arbitraging stocks instead of flows.

Consider for example a fixed stock of some resource, say land. Suppose that there are two uses for this resource, say agriculture and housing, and that the market for agricultural land is organized separately from the market in housing land. An entrepreneur who specializes in reallocating land between agriculture and housing may be able to arbitrage between these two markets using price discrimination. Price discrimination is effected by transferring small units of land sequentially. In between each transfer both markets re-adjust to a new uniform price for the stock of land. Because each new transfer is effected only after the markets have adjusted to the previous transfer, each transfer takes place at different prices. Thus, by regulating the rate of flow of land between the two markets, the entrepreneur can achieve a maximum reward from the reallocation of the stock.

The situation is illustrated in Figure 5.4. The stock of land in use for housing is measured horizontally from the left-hand origin O_1, and the stock of land in agricultural use is measured from the right-hand origin O_2. Price is measured vertically: the price of housing is measured along the left-hand axis and the price of agricultural land along the right-hand axis. The total stock of land is measured by the length of the horizontal axis O_1O_2, with O_1K units

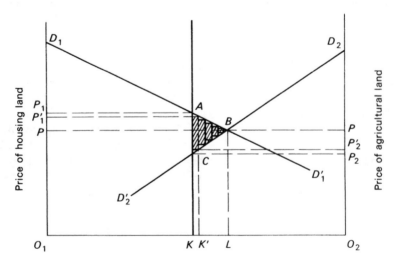

Figure 5.4   Arbitraging stocks: a partial analysis

being initially allocated to housing and O_2K to agriculture. The demand for housing land is measured from the origin O_1 and is given by the demand curve D_1D_1', while the demand for agricultural land is measured from the origin O_2 and is given by the demand curve D_2D_2'. Competition sets the initial price of housing land at O_1P_1 and the initial price of agricultural land at $O_2P_2 < O_1P_1$.

The entrepreneur spots the opportunity for transforming agricultural land into housing land. He begins by buying just one unit of agricultural land, forcing up the price marginally to O_2P_2', and reselling it for O_1P_1', marginally below the initial price of housing land. This reallocation provides $O_1K' > O_1K$ units of housing land and $O_2K' > O_2K$ units of agricultural land. The entrepreneur repeats this unit arbitrage until the price discrepancy in the two markets has been completely eliminated. This is achieved when KL units of land have been reallocated from agriculture to housing, and the prices of land have been equalized at $O_1P = O_2P$.

Because he never arbitrages more than one unit at a time, he is able to obtain each unit at its demand price in the low-price (agricultural) market and resell it at its demand price in the high-price (housing) market. His total profit is made up of the areas of rectangles of unit width, as indicated by the shaded area within the triangle ABC. As the indivisibility of the units is decreased, so this area tends towards the area of the triangle ABC. The profit earned by sequential unit arbitrage is thus equivalent to the profit obtained by price discrimination.

The initial users of intramarginal agricultural land lose as a result of the arbitrage, as do the owners of the initial stock of housing land. This is because the rise in the price of agricultural land transfers wealth from the users to the owners, while the fall in the price of housing land transfers wealth from the owners to the users. Those who gain are the owners of the land remaining in agricultural use, the initial users of housing land and, of course, the entrepreneur. It is readily established that those who gain can compensate those who lose and still have additional wealth left over. The owners of agricultural land can exactly compensate the users of it, and the users of housing land can exactly compensate the owners of it. The entrepreneur therefore has no need to compensate anyone. Thus the economy-wide increase in real wealth, measured by the area ABC, is equal to the profit of the entrepreneur and, although social coordination has not been achieved in the full sense, it has been achieved in the weak sense.

There is no scope for any further reallocation of land, and so the allocation is socially efficient.

5.7   THE SYNTHESIS OF INFORMATION

A feature common to all the previous examples is that the entrepreneur's recognition of an opportunity for coordination rests upon a synthesis of information. These examples therefore serve to highlight the point about the synthesis of information which has been made earlier in the book.

In the case of technological innovation, the entrepreneur needs to synthesize technical information on the new method of production with information about the scarcity of factors of production in order to assess whether the new technique, besides its technical virtues, will also reduce costs of production. In the case of product innovation, the entrepreneur needs to synthesize information about buyers' preferences for product quality with information about the production costs of the new design of good. In the case of arbitrage the entrepreneur needs to synthesize information about the balance of supply and demand at one location with information about the balance of supply and demand at the other location. This information must in turn be synthesized with information about the supply of transport services and about potential fiscal intervention in the flow of goods (for example tariffs). In the final example involving arbitrage in stocks, the entrepreneur needs to synthesize information about the balance of supply and demand in the market for one type of user service with information about the balance of supply and demand for another type of user service. The entrepreneur will also need to be aware of social and legal restrictions involving the reallocation of the stock from one use to the other.

In each of these cases the entrepreneur does not necessarily possess any single item of information that no-one else does. His advantage lies in the fact that some items of information are complementary, and that his combination of complementary items of information is different from everyone else's. This suggests that the key to successful entrepreneurship is not to have more specialized or detailed knowledge than anyone else, but simply to have the right sort of coverage of information.

Another point to emphasize is the diversity of the information synthesized by the entrepreneur. Many different types of information have to be synthesized, including information on preferences, technology, factor supply, transport services, tariffs and any other forms of restriction upon the reallocation of resources. This diversity of information means that the entrepreneur must be a generalist, capable of assimilating information of many different kinds. He must know enough about each subject area to know what it is he needs to know and to recognize and interpret relevant information when it is offered to him. He does not need to be a specialist at each of those subjects, but he needs to know enough to be able to delegate to specialists and to utilize them efficiently.

A further point is that primary sources of information are geographically dispersed. If channels of communication were perfect, then this would be of little consequence for the entrepreneur, for he could gather his information quite satisfactorily at second or third hand. In practice, however, channels of communication are imperfect and this suggest that there are at least two advantages to the entrepreneur in gathering information at first hand wherever possible. To begin with, the successful entrepreneur is the one who is first to achieve the synthesis of information, and so no entrepreneur can afford to be slow in gaining access to new information. Imperfections in communication cause lags to information filtering through to secondary and tertiary sources. To maintain his information up to date, the entrepreneur needs to be in contact with primary sources wherever possible.

The second advantage stems from quality control. As emphasized in Chapter 8, acting upon wrong information can lead to heavy losses. Information can often be distorted in communication. In particular, each communicator tends to be selective in what he passes on, and often stresses some aspects of information at the expense of others. In some cases information may even be concealed in order deliberately to mislead. Thus information obtained at second or third hand will not only be selective (which could in principle be a good thing), but will incorporate some of the attitudes and beliefs of the intermediators (which may well be a bad thing). To avoid distortion it is therefore best to go direct to the primary source.

In order to maintain contact with a diverse collection of primary sources, the entrepreneur needs to be geographically mobile. He must scan each of the key sources fairly regularly, which will tend to give him an itinerant lifestyle. Where he does rely upon intermediators, he needs to have some idea of the nature and the extent of the distortions they are liable to create: in particular, he needs to the able to check that they are not concealing anything important. In such cases there is no real substitute for face-to-face contact in communication. This imposes a further commitment to mobility on the entrepreneur unless of course he can organize things so that the intermediators visit him, instead of him having to visit them.

5.8   BARRIERS TO ENTRY IN PRACTICE

The examples discussed in this chapter also provide a convenient framework for analysing the kinds of barriers to entry that can be created in practice. Barriers to entry provide a *de facto* right of exclusion for the entrepreneur. Only so long as he holds this right can the entrepreneur normally obtain a private reward from the exploitation of information. As the previous chapter has shown, once entry becomes possible, competition from other entrepreneurs will reduce and eventually eliminate his profit.

Barriers to entry are sometimes regarded as exogenous industry character-istics, but it is more appropriate to regard them as being endogenously determined by the entrepreneur. The entrepreneur has a temporary monopoly of information about an opportunity for coordination and while this mon-opoly lasts he can invest in building barriers which will enable him to consolidate his monopoly position over a longer period.

So far as technological innovation is concerned, the most obvious barrier to competition is the patent. Historically, patents were developed to protect inventors from the predatory activities of innovators. However, to the extent that the innovator can exploit the inventor's ignorance of the market place to acquire patent rights cheaply, the innovator can profit as much, if not more, from the patent as the inventor. The patent system has a rather limited scope. It applies mainly to inventions embodied in machinery or some other durable form; it does not apply, for example, to management systems or to marketing techniques. It can be used to protect new designs of products such as con-sumer and producer durables, but cannot be used to protect new types of service such as vehicle hire or insurance. The patent system is also confined geographically to the developed market economies and the countries within their sphere of political influence.

The weaknesses of the patent system are to some extent made good by the application of similar principles to copyright in original literary and artistic work, and to the registration of trade marks. This means, for example, that while a management system may not be patentable, the documents describing it, and perhaps even the forms which are used when operating it, may be copyright. This, however, protects only against exact imitations; those who copy the principle, but make modifications in detail, can claim that no copy-right has been infringed. The same problem has arisen in the defence of patent rights themselves: the judiciary has tended to take the view that minor modifications of patented designs constitute new designs which are patent-able in their own right. Thus, while the innovator may be protected against the appearance of perfect substitutes, he is not protected against the develop-ment of very close substitutes which exploit the principles that he has pioneered himself.

A disadvantage of patenting anything is that it draws attention to it. Patent registrations are widely used as a source of information by entrepreneurs seeking new ideas. This has two disadvantages to the patentee: first, it in-creases the probability that close substitutes will be developed and, secondly, it encourages other people to 'spin off' derivative ideas before the innovator himself has had time to do so. If patent protection were perfect, of course, the first problem would not arise. The second problem would be avoided too because a perfect patent system would, in theory, require people who developed derivative ideas to pay a fee for each of the ideas that they drew upon.

An alternative to patenting is to try to perpetuate secrecy about the technology even when the innovation has occurred. There are two main threats to secrecy. One comes from imitation of the product design through 'reverse engineering'. Where the technology is entirely embodied in the design this threat is a very serious one. Some innovators have disguised their designs in order to deter reverse engineering (for example in the design of microelectronic circuits).

The other threat is that employees may 'steal' the technology for their own use. If the entrepreneur delegates the supervision of production, he places the supervisor in an ideal position to acquaint himself with the technology. One way round this difficulty is to spread out responsibilities so that each delegate is aware of only one aspect of the relevant technology. Thus, if any single delegate quits, he takes away very little information of commercial relevance with him. This principle applies to the structuring of any organization – for example a spy network – which handles confidential information and is vulnerable to defection. In effect, it puts the argument about the synthesis of information into reverse. Once the entrepreneur has achieved his synthesis of commercially relevant information, he delegates its implementation by breaking up the information again into its constituent parts. Another strategy is to 'lock in' the delegate by offering cheap mortgages and generous pension rights which he has to repay if he quits. This obligation may not prevent him from moving to another employer who has sufficient capital to offer similar perks, but it may be sufficient to deter him from becoming self-employed. Certainly, it increases the net capital requirement associated with going into business on his own account.

Another barrier to entry involves the entrepreneur acquiring a monopoly of some key resource which is in totally inelastic supply. This barrier to entry too mainly applies to technological innovation. A new technology may require intensive inputs of a raw material whose deposits are geographically concentrated in certain areas. The innovator can buy up mining rights in these areas and so secure future supplies for himself, while at the same time preventing other people gaining access to them except on his terms. In this way the innovator creates a barrier to entry by backward integration into the mining and extraction of raw materials. He defends his monopoly of the technology by acquiring a monopoly of the inputs required to exploit it.

In industries where the minimum efficient scale of production is fairly high, the initial scale of innovation may create a substantial barrier to entry. The minimum efficient scale of production is usually identified as the lowest level of output at which minimum average cost is attained. Suppose that minimum efficient scale is fairly large relative to the overall size of the market and the price elasticity of industry demand is fairly low. If the innovator commits himself to building sufficient capacity to almost saturate the market, then a potential competitor will perceive considerable risk in entering the industry and adding to its capacity. Assuming that the innovator does not voluntarily contract his output to accommodate his competitor, the additional supply from the entrant will lead to a lower industry price. The large scale of entry that is required, coupled with the inelasticity of demand, means that price may be very much lower than before. If the innovator chooses a suitable 'limit price' to begin with, he can ensure that the post-entry price will fail to cover average costs. Under these conditions the entrant can anticipate that his entry will eliminate all the profits that he is trying to share.

The deterrent effect depends crucially upon the entrant's expectations of how the innovator will react to his entry. It was assumed above that the entrant expected the innovator to react by cutting his price and leaving his output unchanged. It is possible, however, that the innovator may be able to influence the entrant's expectations by suggesting, for example, that the innovator would cut his price by even more than the entrant might expect. This effect on expectations could be achieved, for example, by the threat of a price war. If the threat is credible, then the expected costs of entry are increased further. Alternatively, the innovator may attempt to capitalize the value of the threat by setting a higher industry price in the first place.

Given that entrants often find the availability of capital a significant barrier, a particularly effective threat may be to bankrupt the entrant by making the price war particularly 'short and sharp'. In effect the innovator, who is assumed to be already adequately capitalized, threatens the entrant, who is potentially undercapitalized, with the loss of all his capital. This increases the risks perceived by the entrant's potential backers. The innovator hopes that as a result the entrant's cost of capital will become prohibitively high.

A final barrier is for the innovator to build up goodwill among his customers, and perhaps among key members of his labour force as well. Goodwill may be defined as a propensity to trade repeatedly with the same firm. It is particularly relevant to the innovator of a new product. Advertising is often cited as a method of building up goodwill in the form of brand loyalty; this is considered further in Chapter 11. There are many other devices which can be employed by an entrepreneur with marketing expertise. He can sell his product with a coupon giving a discount on the next item purchased. Of course, if the entrepreneur's revenue is not to be impaired, then the cost of the discount must be included in the price of the current purchase. The potential entrant can only compete with the coupon by launching his own product at the discounted price. But if customers suffer from 'coupon illusion' and assume that it must be advantageous to use the coupon, then they may not even attempt to evaluate the entrant's price. Another device for building up goodwill is to provide regular customers with privileges. The innovator has a head start in recruiting regulars so that, by the time the entrant appears, the innovator and his customers may have established a close working relationship. Customers will be reluctant to incur the set-up costs of establishing a similar relationship with another firm. The entrant must offer a substantial subsidy to new customers to compensate them for these costs. He may even have to sell his product at a loss in order to build up his demand. This not only reduces the profitability of entry generally, but increases the capital requirements because of the need to fund initial losses.

SUMMARY

This chapter has sought to explain why the coordination effected by entrepreneurs is partial, in the sense of being concerned with only a small sector of the economy, rather than general, in the sense of reallocating all resources according to some economy-wide plan. The answer lies in the increasing cost of synthesizing knowledge from very diverse sources. It is shown that partial coordination is a continuous process and that as a result the overall consistency of the different partial plans being implemented at any one time cannot be guaranteed. Slack has to be built into the system by holding idle inventories to accommodate unforeseen excess demands for resources. Inventories are economized by applying the principles of banking.

Three examples of partial coordination are given. Two of these examples integrate the theory of the entrepreneur with the conventional theory of industrial organization, whilst the third integrates the theory of the entrepreneur with the theory of arbitrage.

NOTES AND REFERENCES

The disequilibrium view of the coordination process has received little attention in the microeconomic literature; most attention has been given to its macroeconomic implications: see Hutt (1939) for example. The relation between partial coordination, disequilibrium and inventory adjustment is considered in, for example, Clower (1967) and Kornai (1971); see also Casson (1981).

The first two examples of partial coordination – technological innovation and quality innovation – are analysed using Chamberlin's techniques (Chamberlin, 1962); some of the wider issues concerned with these forms of innovation are considered in Freeman (1974) and Johnson (1975). The third example is an attempt to translate Kirzner's subjectivist theory of arbitrage (Kirzner, 1973) into a positivist framework.

PART II

The Market-making Firm

6.   Making a market

6.1   INTRODUCTION

It is appropriate at this point to take stock of the development of the theory. The analysis so far has been based upon a rejection of the simple neoclassical view that everyone has access to the same information. It has been shown that the relaxation of this assumption provides an economic rationale for the entrepreneur. Essentially, the rationale is that the entrepreneur has better – or at least more relevant – information than other people. It must be admitted, however, that in modelling the entrepreneur's behaviour certain assumptions have been made which in themselves are decidedly neoclassical.

In particular, it has been assumed that, while other people are disadvantaged in terms of access to information, the entrepreneur has all the information that he requires to set up a transaction. Because information about the market is freely available to the entrepreneur, the opportunity cost to him of setting up a trade is zero.

It is this assumption of zero opportunity cost that makes the preceding analysis of the entrepreneur so neoclassical. In neoclassical theory no-one incurs any costs in setting up a trade. In the theory of entrepreneurship developed above, everyone except the entrepreneur encounters prohibitive costs of setting up a trade. The entrepreneur encounters costs which are not only lower, but are actually zero. That is why the entrepreneur's behaviour is so neoclassical. Other people's costs make for a non-neoclassical environment, but the absence of costs for the entrepreneur make his response to that environment thoroughly neoclassical.

The assumption that setting up a trade is a costless activity stems ultimately from the neoclassical view about the way that markets work. Because of the way that markets are supposed to work, transactors require very little information in order to set up a trade. Most of the information they require is provided in an impersonal way by the market itself. It is for this reason that the introduction of the entrepreneur into a basically neoclassical economy often seems implausible. Given the very limited information that is required to establish trade, it is difficult to believe that transactors may not have this information and so may have to rely upon the entrepreneur instead.

In fact, however, the neoclassical view of the way that markets work is quite implausible. Some of the problems with the neoclassical views were indicated in the discussion of partial coordination in Chapter 5. A more extensive critique is given in Section 6.2 below. Markets work quite differently from the way that neoclassical theory suggests. Transactors require a great deal of information in order to effect a trade. This information is very costly to the average transactor and somewhat less costly to the entrepreneur. The entrepreneur requires information not only about the contract of trade itself, but about the specification of the product and the personal characteristics of those with whom he trades. Even with this information he may have to provide additional services to his trading partners so that trade can proceed. The entrepreneur therefore encounters significant costs of his own. It is the entrepreneur's efforts to minimize these costs that determine the characteristic way in which he behaves.

6.2   A CRITIQUE OF PERFECT COMPETITION

The neoclassical view of market behaviour is closely identified with the theory of perfect competition. This theory asserts that in each market there prevails a uniform parametric equilibrium price. The price is uniform in three respects. It is uniform across all units bought (or sold) by the same individual; in other words, each transactor faces a one-part tariff. It is uniform across all individuals on the same side of the market. In other words there is no price discrimination: all buyers pay the same price and all sellers pay the same price. Finally, there is no margin for intermediation: buying price and selling price are equal.

A parametric price is one that is taken as a datum: no-one believes that they can influence it. It is assumed that, given the parametric price, each individual can freely determine the quantity he demands or supplies; there is no rationing by quantity, only rationing by price.

Equilibrium is achieved when there is equality between total supply and total demand. The economy is in general equilibrium when there is simultaneous equilibrium in each market. Under certain conditions there exists a unique equilibrium set of relative prices for all goods in the economy, and a unique equilibrium quantity traded in each market.

As it stands, however, the theory merely describes the state of the market at a representative moment in time. It does not actually explain the process by which markets work. The crucial issue is about what connects the state of the market at one moment of time to the state of the market at another moment of time. There are two alternative accounts of this market process.

The first account is due to Walras. Walras invokes a mythical figure: the auctioneer. The auctioneer is in communication with all transactors. He announces a trial price in each market and aggregates the quantity responses that the transactors provide. In markets where demand exceeds supply, he raises the price and in markets where supply exceeds demand he reduces the price. If supply and demand are equal he leaves the price unchanged. Under suitable conditions this process converges to a general equilibrium across all markets.

The logic of the Walrasian process is unassailable, but equally, its practical irrelevance is undeniable. The pattern of behaviour which it describes is hardly ever observed in practice. According to Walras, price is uniform simply because the auctioneer says that it will be so. It is parametric to transactors because only the auctioneer can conduct trade. It is an equilibrium price because all the computation of demand and supply balances is centralized with the auctioneer, and he does not allow trade to proceed until his computations are complete and economy-wide balance has been achieved. The Walrasian process could possibly be advanced as a theory of decentralized planning within a state-controlled economy or within a firm, but it cannot be used to model a private ownership market economy.

The Walrasian process applies to any number of transactors: even to as few as two. However, there is a tradition in economics that seeks a rationale for perfect competition in the existence of a very large number of transactors. It is assumed that many traders participate in each market, and each wishes to trade an amount that is small relative to the overall size of the market.

It is argued that, because there are a large number of different traders, it is difficult to identify individual people and to prevent resale between them. Any attempt to charge different prices for different units will create an incentive for arbitrage. Suppose, for example, that sellers attempt to discriminate between buyers. Buyers who can purchase at the lowest price will increase their demand in order to resell to buyers faced with a higher price. As a result, all demand will eventually be concentrated on the low-price units and demand for the high-price units will be eliminated. Competition between arbitragers will eliminate any margin between buying and selling prices. Thus throughout the market the 'law of one price' will prevail.

Given that no transactor constitutes a significant part of the market for any good, a threat by him to withdraw from the market will have negligible consequences for the overall balance of supply and demand. It is likely that only a negligible variation in price will be required to restore the balance by inducing someone else to enter the market to take his place. Consequently, no-one can reasonably expect that their own quantity response to price can have any significant influence at all upon the prevailing price.

Price adjusts to equilibrium in each market through the response of frustrated buyers or sellers to a shortage or surplus of goods. If there is a shortage of supply, then buyers attempt to bid away supplies from other people by raising the price. The higher price causes some buyers to withdraw from the market, and encourages some suppliers to enter it. This reduces demand, increases supply and so adjusts the market to equilibrium. Conversely, if there is a surplus of goods, then suppliers bid down the price; this stimulates demand, discourages supply and so restores equilibrium.

In this model, price is uniform on each side of the market because of the threat of arbitrage, it is parametric because there are many insignificant traders, and it is maintained in equilibrium because transactors react instantaneously to any frustration of their trading plans.

On closer examination, however, these propositions rest upon three important implicit assumptions. First, it is assumed that there are no barriers to entry into markets and, in particular, that there are no barriers to entry into arbitrage activities within a market. The idea that there are no barriers to entry is implicit in the view that markets will involve a large number of traders. It is still more evident in the view that profit opportunities from arbitrage will be competed away.

Secondly, it makes very strict assumptions about the availability, and the relevance, of non-price information. It assumes, for example, that everyone has perfect knowledge of the specification of each product. Thus no buyer is ever in any doubt about whether or not the product will meet his requirements. Anything that people do not know is assumed to be irrelevant to their needs. Thus if transactors do not know one another's names and addresses, then it is only because such information is irrelevant. It is irrelevant because the economy has no spatial dimension: all transactors reside at the same place where simultaneous auctions are held perpetually. If transactors do not know one another's personal characteristics, then it is because such characteristics are common to everyone; for example, everyone is totally honest and as a result there is no chance of default. The only personal information which is really relevant is about preferences. In the perfect competition model, all relevant information about preferences is communicated to other transactors through the price mechanism. Thus the only relevant information is price information; non-price information about personal characteristics is of no value at all.

Finally, neoclassical theory assumes not only that markets adjust quickly, but that they adjust completely before any trade at all takes place. This is recognized explicitly in the Walrasian model, where no trade is permitted by the auctioneer until all markets are in equilibrium. In the absence of an auctioneer it implies that buyers and sellers whose trading plans are frustrated can initiate a complete renegotiation of contracts before anyone else can go ahead with their trades. Furthermore this recontracting between transactors will continue until all plans are fully harmonized, and only then will trade occur. The same assumption is implicit in monopolistic competition theory and in the preceding analysis of the entrepreneur. The monopolistic competitor is always in equilibrium in the sense that he always produces exactly what he can sell, and no more. The intermediating entrepreneur is always in equilibrium because he only buys what he knows he can sell, and only sells what he knows he can buy. Neither of them is ever left with unsold inventory, or is forced to default owing to shortage of supply, for trade is never allowed to proceed until all such potential discrepancies have been eliminated.

If interpreted literally, this assumption implies that, every time a market is subjected to disturbance, trading is suspended until recontracting has been completed, and only then is the market activated again. In an economy continuously subjected to change, it is doubtful if trading would ever be able to occur!

The analysis of entrepreneurship in the preceding chapters has been chiefly concerned with relaxing the first assumption about barriers to entry. It has assumed barriers to entry where neoclassical competition theory supposes none to exist. The entrepreneur is modelled as a monopolist enjoying privileged access to commercial information. Only once this monopoly is destroyed by the entry of another entrepreneur does the market tend towards the competitive equilibrium.

The second implicit assumption of neoclassical theory is that the organization of transactions is a costless activity. This assumption is not applied only to competitive markets; it is also a feature of the analysis of monopolistic competition, in which the monopolist always has complete information about the environment in which he operates, and transactors can easily familiarize themselves with the price and quality of the product. It is also implicit in the earlier analysis of entrepreneurial coordination, in which the entrepreneur has no difficulty in identifying and making contact with his trading partners because he has perfect information about them.

As noted above, the acquisition of information, and the other activities involved in setting up a transaction, incur a positive opportunity cost. This cost may be considered as analogous to a tax upon the transaction. Taxes on transactions, for example tariffs, lead to a separation of buying price and selling price. *Prima facie* transaction costs may be expected to have a similar consequence. The implications of transaction costs are analysed in detail in this chapter and the next.

The counterfactual nature of the third assumption has already been noted in Chapter 5. Recontracting involves economy-wide multilateral negotiation, and it is prohibitively time-consuming to carry out. The alternative to recontracting is to use sequential negotiation and to contain the spillovers between negotiations by holding inventories of idle resources. As a result, entrepreneurs need to hold inventories in order to facilitate the setting up of transactions. The consequences of inventory management for entrepreneurship are quite complex, and so discussion of this is deferred until Chapter 9.

6.3   OBSTACLES TO TRADE AND TRANSACTION COSTS

Transaction costs are costs incurred in overcoming obstacles to trade. It is sometimes asserted that transaction costs are a cause of market failure, but this is not strictly correct. The existence of transaction costs necessitates a modification of the perfect competition model. In this sense transaction costs appear as the immediate cause of the failure of the model. But it is obstacles to trade that are the ultimate cause of the failure of the market. A rational individual only incurs transaction costs in order to avoid a breakdown of trade. From this point of view transaction costs improve the efficiency of the market, they do not reduce it.

Six main obstacles to trade may be distinguished: they are summarized in the left-hand column of Table 6.1. This column should be studied in detail. Following the discussion above, the entries may be interpreted in two different ways. The conventional interpretation is that of an inventory of possible deviations from perfect competition. On this view it is appropriate to analyse

Table 6.1   Classification of obstacles to trade, and the corresponding market-making activities

Obstacle to Trade	Market-making activity
No contact between buyer and seller	Contact making via search or advertisment
No knowledge of reciprocal wants	Specification of the trade and communication of the details to each party
No agreement over price	Negotiation
Need to exchange custody of goods and pay any taxes or tariffs due on the transaction	Transport and administration
No confidence that goods correspond to specification	Monitoring, that is screening of quality, metering of quantity, timing of instalments, observation of contingent events
No confidence that restitution will be made for default	Enforcement

each obstacle to trade as though it were the only deviation present. The objections to this are twofold. First, it is unrealistic, for in practice many markets exhibit several simultaneous obstacles to trade. Secondly, and much more fundamental, is that the effectiveness of a policy designed to overcome one obstacle may be strongly influenced by the presence of other obstacles. For example, if each buyer finds it difficult to make contact with more than one seller, and vice versa, then the market will become fragmented, transactors will tend to be bilateral monopolists, and so it may be difficult to obtain agreement over price. Thus the existence of one obstacle – to making contact – gives rise to another obstacle – in obtaining agreement on price.

A more satisfactory interpretation of the table is that the entries describe the logical sequence of steps necessary to take transactors from mutual isolation, through anarchy (for example, a Hobbesian state of nature) by way of strategic haggling towards successful completion of a trade. Logically, the first step in a trade is for transactors to make contact, and then to communicate reciprocal wants which are embodied in the contractual specification. It is assumed that they exchange two types of good, one of which may be designated 'the product' and the other 'the payment'. The contractual specification may allow for product supply and/or payment to take place in various instalments at different dates, for the arrangements to be contingent upon particular events on or before these dates, and for various penalties or compensations to be paid in the event of default. After negotiating a price, the two parties exchange custody of the goods and pay any taxes or tariffs due on the transaction. Each party monitors the exchange: he screens the quality and meters the quantity of the good he offers, and checks that the other party's screening and metering of the good he receives is correct. (In certain cases it may be possible to eliminate this duplication of screening and metering: see Chapter 9 below.) Failure of the quantity or quality to comply with the specification constitutes default. In the final stage the penalties and compensations due in respect of default are enforced.

6.4 INFORMATION COSTS IN MARKET MAKING

To overcome each of the obstacles to trade, market-making activities are required; these are listed in the right-hand column of the table. The cost structure of these market-making activities is a major influence upon the prices and the quantities traded in different kinds of market, and upon the role of intermediation within them.

When analysing cost structure it is important to distinguish between set-up costs and recurrent costs, and between fixed costs and variable costs. A set-up cost is essentially a once-for-all cost; it represents an investment which is normally justified on the grounds that it reduces subsequent recurrent costs. A variable cost is a cost related to the number of transactions effected by the market maker, or to some other relevant factor. A fixed cost is a cost independent of these factors. A fixed cost usually reflects an indivisibility in a resource: cost is independent of the rate of utilization of the resource until its capacity limit is reached; thereafter a further indivisible unit has to be used. It should be emphasized, however, that the use of indivisible resources generates fixed costs of market making only if use of the resource cannot be shared by different market-making activities or by the makers of different markets.

Most, though not all, market-making activities involve handling considerable amounts of information. The properties of information are an important influence on the structure of market-making costs.

An item of information is an indivisible asset. It is also a potentially durable asset. So far as an individual is concerned, information once received can be memorized: it is therefore durable in the sense that it effects a once-for-all change in his state of mind. So far as an organization is concerned, information can be stored in files to which members of the organization – both present and future – can gain access. Since the lifetime of an organization can exceed the lifetime of an individual, the potential durability of information is even greater from the organization's point of view.

Many assets are indivisible, but information is unusual in being one of the few assets which is totally indivisible in demand. No-one ever demands more than one unit of an item of information. While it is possible to replicate the supply of an item of information, an individual or organization gains nothing from being supplied with an additional unit. Moreover, since an item of information is durable, demand is restricted not just to one unit at a time but to one unit in a lifetime. It appears, therefore, that an item of information is an indivisible good for which each customer only ever demands one unit. This may be summarized by saying that information is a satiation good.

The information required by a transactor may be classified by the object to which it pertains, namely the product, the trading partner, or the contract itself. The transactor needs to acquire knowledge of relevant characteristics of these objects in order to complete a trade successfully. The relevant characteristics of a product constitute its specification. Products can be specified both functionally and indicatively. A functional specification describes what the product does, while an indicative specification describes what it is and how it can be recognized. So far as the buyer is concerned, the functional specification is of paramount interest. For example, a person who buys a motor car expects to acquire a vehicle for the transport of passengers and irrespective of what the product looks like, if it does not perform this function then it does not qualify as a motor car. Given this functional approach, the relevant characteristics of the motor car include carrying capacity for passengers and their luggage, speed, fuel consumption, and so on. Once the functional characteristics have been assessed, the indicative characteristics come into play; these are mainly concerned with the appearance of the car: styling, colour, trim, and so on.

The relevant characteristics of a transactor include his name and address, his honesty, competence and his liquidity, and also his attitude to negotiations. Name and address are important for making contact (or for maintaining a contact made by chance). His address may also provide an indication of how easy it will be to enforce a contract with him; for example, the social sanctions and the legal system to which he is subject will depend upon his normal place of residence. If he lives in an area where social sanctions are severe, and in a country where the legal system is comprehensive and cheap to use, then costs of enforcement will tend to be low.

The need for enforcement only arises, of course, in the event of default. The supplier of a product can default on either quantity, or quality, or both. Default on quantity involves short supply (or possibly delay in supply, if time is of the essence in the contract). Default on quality signifies a failure to meet the specification. As noted above, the functional aspect of the specification is the most crucial, and it is here that default is most likely to arise. The product may not be fit for the purpose intended, or it may fail to achieve the standard of performance specified. Default in the indicative aspect is usually fairly easy to detect, and for this reason the supplier is much less likely to perpetrate it.

Default may be unintentional or deliberate. The risk of deliberate default is governed by the honesty of the person concerned. Unintentional default on quantity is liable to occur if the supplier holds inadequate stocks of the product. Default on quantity is usually considered with respect to payment rather than the supply of the product, though the principle is the same in either case: holding too little stock of the item that one is committed to provide. This may be identified as a liquidity problem, where liquidity is understood in its broadest sense. Unintentional default on quality is liable to occur if the supplier is incompetent in the manufacture of the product, or if there are inherent natural variations in the production process. Default arises when checks are too costly to carry out, or when the supplier lacks the skill to carry them out properly.

To some extent there is a 'grey area' between unintentional and deliberate default in which the supplier is simply negligent. Default due to negligence is deliberate in the sense that the decision to be negligent is deliberate and the eventual consequences of negligence are foreseeable. On the other hand, it is unintentional in the sense that none of the defaults that follow is specifically willed. Where negligence is important, the preceding remarks need to be modified slightly, though the principles remain the same.

Finally, the trading partner's attitude to negotiation is important because it influences the amount of time that needs to be spent on reaching agreement. There are three main aspects to the time costs of negotiation. The first is that, if the trading partner uses very subtle tactics, then considerable time may need to be spent planning for each round of the negotiations. The second is that, if the trading partner is willing to make concessions, but will only make very small concessions at one time, then many rounds of negotiations may be involved before a satisfactory price is obtained. Both of these factors increase the amount of mental labour used in negotiation. The third aspect is concerned with the speed with which agreement is reached. This is clearly related to the first two factors: the amount of preparation needed for each round of the negotiations and the number of rounds involved. However, it is not uniquely determined by them because there is usually a certain amount of slack in the timetable of negotiations to allow the two parties to do other jobs at the same time (to participate in other negotiations, perhaps). It is often the case that one of the parties is anxious to complete the negotiations because further delay to the transaction will 'spill over' and disrupt other plans. In this case slack in the other party's negotiation schedule may impose heavy costs on the impatient transactor. To a certain extent this 'externality' can be internalized by offering the other party more favourable terms conditional upon a quick completion of the transaction, but, given the tactical nature of negotiation and the fact that agreement is uncertain anyway, there is no guarantee of success. A simpler strategy is to make a preliminary assessment of whether the other party is himself interested in swift completion, and only to initiate negotiations if he is. It is in this context that the trading partner's attitude to negotiations is important.

The most important characteristics of a contract are quite simply the price and the quantity traded. Also relevant are the penalties stipulated for default and the arrangements made for the settlement of disputes. The latter are usually standing arrangements dictated by social convention and law, and are not explicitly stated in the contract.

Each of the three types of information distinguished above (product information, transactor information and contract information) qualifies as a satiation good. When entering a market for the first time, an individual needs product information: he needs to know exactly what is on offer. Once he has acquired this information he can trade as little or as much as he likes. It follows that the acquisition of product information is a fixed cost independent of the number of subsequent transactions and their value. Having acquired product information, the individual needs to find someone with whom to trade. Once he has acquired information about a trading partner he can, in principle, trade with them as much or as little as he likes. However, if he decides to investigate another trading partner, then additional information is required before trade can take place. It follows that the acquisition of transactor information is a fixed cost independent of the number and value of subsequent transactions with that person, though it varies directly with the number of alternative transactors investigated. Provisional contract information is made available through the negotiation process, though definite information is available only once agreement has been reached. Contract information is necessary whatever the final price and quantity agreed. It is therefore a fixed cost independent of the value of the transaction, though obviously it varies directly with the number of transactions effected.

The existence of fixed costs of entering a market, taking on a new trading partner and negotiating a contract have important implications for the behaviour of rational transactors. Other things being equal, it is better for a transactor to continue trading in a market with which he is already familiar than to enter a new market where there is a different product specification and in all probability a new trading partner must be sought out. Once he has found a satisfactory partner with whom to trade, there is a strong incentive for him to continue trading with the same partner rather than to seek out a new one. If his trade in the product is just a once-for-all event, then this is of little significance, but if he plans to trade repeatedly in the same product it will be advantageous to repeat-trade with the same partner. Finally, when repeat-trading is involved it may be cheaper to make occasional bulk transactions than to make frequent small transactions. This is because, each time a new contract is negotiated, a fixed cost is incurred, so that the average cost per unit amount traded is reduced if the average size of the transaction is increased in order to keep the frequency of transaction low. These consequences of fixed costs, together with others, are examined in greater detail below. The main line of argument is taken up again in Section 6.9.

6.5   FACTORS AFFECTING MARKET-MAKING COSTS

This section considers some of the factors which may explain why market-making costs vary between different markets.

Six main factors are isolated: the complexity of the product specification, the time elapsing between making and completing the contract, the synchronization (or lack of it) between payment and supply, and the ease with which custody of the product can be exchanged, its quantity metered and its quality checked. It is suggested that markets can be rated on each of these grounds without too much difficulty, and that markets with low overall scores will normally have prohibitive costs of operation.

When discussing the first factor – product specification – the term 'product' is used in its broadest sense, to refer not necessarily to a commodity but to a service or indeed to any kind of transferable property right. The more complex the specification, the more difficult it is for transactors to familiarize themselves with it. Someone has to devise the specification, and the greater the complexity the more time this will take. Messages about the specification will be long and therefore expensive to transmit between trading partners. Furthermore, it will take the recipient a long time to digest the content of the message. Thus a complex specification is not only expensive to devise, but increases the cost of informing people about the product.

The longer the time elapsing between making and completing the contract, the longer the contract has to be kept on file. If the final delivery of the product (or the final payment for it) occurs a long time after the contract is made, then there is a risk that the commitment may be forgotten. Both parties must remember the commitment: one to honour it, and the other to guard against default. Memorizing commitments ties up mental resources (or filing space) and so has a positive opportunity cost. The cost is greater the longer is the time span involved. In this way a time lag in completion of a contract increases memory costs.

The existence of a time lag also increases the risk that one or other of the parties will default by going bankrupt in the meantime. Bankruptcy is usually signalled by default in some other market. The law of bankruptcy allows this default to spill over into the remaining markets, and provides an easy way for those who have overcommitted themselves to renege on a large number of commitments simultaneously. The law of bankruptcy poses a serious hazard to those who rely upon deferred completion of a contract.

The existence of a time lag also means that circumstances may change in the meantime, so that the trade is no longer as attractive as it was. In principle this risk can be avoided using a contingent contract, though as shown in the following section this solution is often unsatisfactory on other grounds. In fact there is a double risk, for if the trade appears more attractive than it did, then it probably appears less attractive to the other party, and this provides the other party with an incentive to default. Thus deferred completion offers the worst of both worlds: the possibility of either trading on unfavourable terms or having the other party default.

The incentive for a person to default on a contract depends crucially upon whether the other party has already discharged his reciprocal obligations. The incentive to default on the supply of a product is much greater for someone who has already been paid than for someone who has not, for, in the first case, default effects a unilateral transfer of the payment, while in the second case the defaulter can expect the other party to repudiate the contract, so that his prospective payment is lost. It follows that the incentive to default is much greater when there is a failure to synchronize payment and supply. This is a quite separate issue from that of time lags in completion. A contract may take a long time to complete, and possibly involve many instalments as well; but so long as payment and supply are synchronized on all instalments throughout the contract period, the opportunity to effect a unilateral transfer does not exist.

Underlying this analysis of default is the idea that physical possession is a more important factor than legal title in determining who has the benefit of the product. The crucial aspect of supply and payment is not usually the transfer of a title but the transfer of physical custody of the product (or in some cases the resource from which the product is obtained). The transfer of custody is therefore an essential part of most transactions. However, the ease with which it can be effected varies considerably between products. Furthermore, where the product is cumbersome or unwieldy, it may be very difficult to achieve complete synchronization between the transfer of custody over the payment and the transfer of custody over the product. In this context the physical attributes of the product – its dimensions, weight, and so on, as given in its indicative specification – may crucially affect both the cost of exchanging custody and the consequent risk of default on the transaction.

Where the product is a straightforward commodity, the metering of quantity is unlikely to pose serious problems, though the costs may be non-trivial where gases, liquids, electric currents and so on are concerned. The metering of services may be more problematic, particularly if the source of the services tends to be somewhat unreliable, as with labour services. Some of the problems involved are considerable, as shown in Chapter 10 below.

Screening for quality is usually much more difficult. As noted earlier, quality is defined relative to product specification. Where natural variations in quality are inevitable, quality control is usually effected by grading. Where variations are avoidable, a simple dichotomy between perfect and faulty items is most often used. However, the dichotomous view is compatible with grading if it is assumed that the market being studied is for a specific grade and that any item of a lower grade is faulty while any item of the specified grade or above is perfect.

Where quality control is concerned, there is a crucial distinction between inspection goods and experience goods. An inspection good is a good whose quality can be assessed before use, while an experience good is a good whose quality can only be assessed by use. The distinction, of course, is not necessarily an absolute one, but may be a relative one, based upon whether the cost of inspection is low, or prohibitively high. Inspection before use does not avoid the disruption caused by having to find a replacement item, but it does avoid the costs associated with the possibly permanent damage that can be caused by utilization of a faulty item. Of all the product characteristics discussed above, it is probably ease of inspection that is the most significant influence on market-making costs.

6.6 CONTINGENT FORWARD CLAIMS AND THEIR SPECIAL PROBLEMS

This section considers one particular type of market and demonstrates the extreme difficulties encountered in organizing it. This is the market in contingent forward claims. As noted earlier, a contingent claim is a claim which has to be honoured if and only if a particular state of the world materializes. A forward claim is a claim which matures at a future date; it must be distinguished from a spot claim which is a claim that has to be honoured immediately.

Although contingent forward markets exist in practice, there are remarkably few instances of them. Relative to other types of market, the number actually in operation is minute compared to the number which would, in theory, exist if there were no market-making costs.

The cost of specifying a contingent claim is bound to be greater than the cost of specifying a corresponding unconditional claim because of the need to describe the event upon which the claim is contingent. To reduce the scope for disagreement it is necessary to specify the event very accurately. The need to devise the specification and to communicate it to all potential transactors adds to the fixed cost of creating the market. Moreover, when contracts have been exchanged, it is necessary for the parties to monitor the state of the world to check whether the event has occurred.

Particular difficulty will be encountered with events which are partially subjective. For example, a trader who believes his preferences are liable to change may wish to express a demand for future consumption which is contingent upon the state of his preferences at the time of consumption. But unless some objective method of ascertaining preferences is available, there is no way in which such a claim can be translated into operational terms. If the consumer knew that there was some objective event which would induce the change in his preferences, then the claim could be made contingent upon that event instead, but there is no guarantee that the consumer does know what the event would be.

There is a further difficulty if the claim is contingent upon an endogenous event, for then there is the possibility that one or other of the parties could influence the event to make it turn out in his favour. Such tactical manipulation of events could be considered as a form of default on the spirit (if not the letter) of the contract. This aspect of moral hazard is well known to insurers and is a major reason why in practice more forms of insurance are not available.

Most contingent claims are also forward claims, for most uncertain events lie in the future. Forward claims have problems of their own, whether or not they are contingent. By definition, forward claims involve a lag between contract and completion and so incur memory costs. These costs are greater the more remote is the date at which the claim matures. Moreover, if the forward claim is purchased with a spot payment, then the lack of synchronization provides the issuer of the claim with a major incentive to default. On the other hand, if payment is synchronized with supply, then the nature of the reciprocal claims is so tentative, given that either party may be bankrupted in the meantime, that neither is likely to have much confidence in the contract. Thus, unless the issuer of the claim has a first-class reputation, it is highly unlikely that the claim will be acceptable to anyone. It is because of this that very few forward markets operate, and many of those that do so involve claims either issued by governments or underwritten by them.

6.7 GENERAL METHODS OF REDUCING MARKET-MAKING COSTS

This section considers some strategies of a general nature for reducing market-making costs in a given market. They are general in the sense that they contribute to surmounting several different obstacles to trade at once, rather than being designed to overcome just one particular obstacle. They are also general in the sense of being applicable, in some degree, to almost every market.

Bulk trading affords three main advantages. First, it exploits the fact that contact making is a fixed cost independent of the size or value of the transaction. This means that infrequent bulk trades incur fewer contact-making costs per unit traded than frequent small trades. Secondly, it exploits the fact that, while negotiation costs may increase with respect to the value of a transaction, they normally increase less than proportionately. Consequently, infrequent bulk trades incur fewer negotiation costs than frequent small trades. Finally, bulk trading exploits the fact that there are often significant economies of scale in the physical distribution of goods, that is in the transport of the good from the seller's custody to the buyer's custody.

It should be noted, however, that as the size of a bulk trade increases, certain disadvantages become apparent. To begin with, bulk distribution of a good makes sense only if either there is a major geographical concentration of demand at one point and a major geographical concentration of supply at another, or the product is durable, so that bulk consignments can be accumulated at the point of supply, transported to the point of demand, and then gradually decumulated through use. Thus, to exploit bulk distribution, it may be necessary to agglomerate demanders and suppliers spatially and/or invest in substantial storage facilities. Beyond a certain point, the additional costs incurred by this strategy may outweigh the saving in distribution costs, and so a limit to bulk distribution will be set.

However, a limit on bulk distribution does not limit the bulk of the transaction in so far as the transaction may provide for distribution in a number of different instalments spread over a specified period of time. Savings in the administrative costs of contact making and negotiation can still be achieved provided contracts are made long-term. In fact, long-term contracts have the additional advantage that they offer the supplier security of demand, and the buyer security of supply. However, as the term of the contract is extended, what is secure in the short or medium term may become risky in the long term. Changes in tastes, technology and resource endowments may call for substantial changes in the pattern of trade, which may be inhibited by a long-term contract. To take account of this, the contract needs to be made contingent on future states of the world, but, for reasons explained above, it is only when transactors have an exceptional degree of confidence in each other that contingent long-term contracts are likely to be feasible.

The implication of this is that, while bulk trading does indeed offer scope for reducing transaction costs, the scope is limited because of the need for geographic agglomeration and additional investment in storage, and because of the costs associated with organizing multiple-instalment transactions.

Repeat-trading involves transacting time and again with the same person. It differs from multiple-instalment trading in that contact is renewed each time. The advantage of repeat-trading is threefold. First, the cost of renewing a contact is less than the cost of making a contact for the first time, since each transactor already knows where to find his trading partner. Secondly, experience of earlier trades will have given the transactor information about his trading partner's personal characteristics. Provided the overall experience was satisfactory, he can place reasonable confidence in his partner's competence and integrity, so that the subjective risk of default which he perceives is lower. In those respects where previous experience was unsatisfactory (for example, supply of an occasional faulty item) he knows more about the kind of problem likely to be encountered, so that he can prepare in advance to deal with it. Finally, repeat-trading affords an opportunity for improving the quality of service. A history of satisfactory repeat-trading may encourage each party to extend certain privileges to the other which will lead to a mutual reduction of transaction costs. For example, negotiation costs could be reduced by an informal agreement not to initiate renegotiation unless market conditions have changed significantly. Alternatively, one of the parties might offer some element of service (for example, very prompt replacement of a faulty unit) which is strictly outside the provisions of the contract, but could be deemed a reasonable expectation given the unforeseen circumstances that prevail. The prospect of further trades, coupled with confidence in the integrity of the other party, creates an expectation that the other party will feel obliged to reciprocate with a similar kind of gesture when the occasion arises. Thus an 'implicit contract' is created which avoids the specification costs which would be incurred by taking account of these contingencies in a formal manner.

Establishment of a reputation affects the status that a transactor enjoys among those with whom he trades. A transactor has a reputation when many of his potential trading partners believe they are well-informed about his personal characteristics. Only a good reputation reduces transaction costs – a bad reputation actually increases them.

From the trading partner's point of view, the important characteristics of a transactor are ease of contact, negotiating skill, screening ability and dependability. Ease of contact means that it is cheap to communicate with the transactor, for example because he has retail premises open long hours and reasonably close at hand, a telephone number which is easy to remember, a 24-hour answering service, and so on. Negotiating skill means that the transactor is easy to bargain with; either he quotes a realistic price which he sticks to, or he adapts his price readily if his initial quotation is out of line with the market. Screening ability ensures that the quality of the product he offers is reliable, and dependability means that there is little risk of default on quantity or timing.

A reputation for any of these personal qualities reduces the cost that other transactors perceive in trading with the party concerned. Reputation benefits the trading partners, because they are able to make trades which might otherwise seem to be too risky, and it also benefits the reputable party, for he is able to trade at a more favourable price than his less reputable competitors (indeed, his potential competitors may not even be able to trade at all).

The gains from reputation are analogous to the gains from repeat trading, to the extent that both are achieved by increasing transactors' confidence. However, there are some important differences. First, repeat trading generates mutual confidence, whereas reputation refers to a unidirectional confidence, because the reputable person does not necessarily reciprocate the confidence that other people place in him. Secondly, reputation involves a transactor having the confidence of many people rather than just the confidence of those with whom he trades regularly. Reputation is particularly important in attracting new trading partners, or those who trade only intermittently or on a casual basis. Finally, reputation does not need to be based solely upon past trading experience; it can also be built up by advertising, that is by publicizing claims on one's own behalf about one's personal qualities (or those of the product).

6.8   MONITORS AND SANCTIONS

This section considers two strategies specifically designed to reduce the risk of default – or at least to eliminate any exaggerated perception of this risk by the parties involved.

External monitoring occurs when one party allows his trading partner to monitor his own activity. For example, a seller may allow the buyer to monitor production of the good he intends to buy, or the buyer of a good may allow the seller to monitor the way he uses it. The monitoring of production by the buyer reduces the buyer's screening costs: intuitively, the buyer can see how the product is made, and so he does not need to take it apart when he has bought it to see that it is made properly. The rationale for the monitoring of use by the seller is at first sight not so obvious. It applies when the seller is parting with custody of a product in order that the buyer can utilize it, before returning it to the seller, that is it applies to a service supplied by the seller but rendered, as it were, on the buyer's premises. Monitoring by the seller may be important where the buyer hires a very valuable and fragile piece of equipment, or where the buyer is hiring the use of know-how which is the seller's property. In each case the seller may be afraid that the value of his asset may be impaired by the buyer's improper use of it.

Additional sanctions can be brought into play when the sanctions available through the legal system are believed to be inadequate. In fact it is not so much the sanctions themselves, but the threat of the sanctions, that is important in discouraging default. The typical extralegal sanction involves doing something which is harmful to all the parties involved – not just to the defaulter but to oneself as well.

The fact that it is harmful to oneself explains why it will only be done as a last resort. It also means that there may be a credibility problem with the threat to apply the sanction. However, if the sanction is applied just once, it may be worthwhile if it raises the other party's expectation that it will also be applied in subsequent trades. Furthermore, if the application of the sanction is publicized it may also reduce the risk of default in subsequent trades with other parties. So long as the other party perceives this, the sanction itself will be perfectly credible.

The acquisition of a sanction can be effected by extending the range of possible transactions with the other party. The outcome of one transaction is made contingent upon the successful completion of the other. The system works so long as there is always another transaction 'in the pipeline', for default on one transaction then means that the potential gains from the next transaction are lost. This provides a powerful argument for repeat-trading, in addition to those already presented above. More precisely, it provides an argument for offering the prospect of repeat trades to a party so that one is less likely to be treated as a 'one-off' partner who can make no reprisal in case of default.

The argument extends, of course, beyond repeat trades to any subsequent transaction between the two parties, whether in the same market or not. It also applies to any outstanding transaction negotiated earlier but not yet completed. A classic type of sanction involves extending short-term credit to a trading partner (usually a supplier) which can be withdrawn at short notice should he default on a transaction. While default on the transaction may be difficult to penalize legally, default on payment may be much easier to punish in law. In this case the legal sanction available in one market (for credit) is used to substitute for an ineffective legal sanction in another market (for the product).

The power of sanctions also extends to diminishing the defaulter's standing with other transactors by publicizing his default. The partners who are most vulnerable in this respect are those who have the greatest reputation for probity to begin with. This illustrates the fact that reputation provides assurance to trading partners in two quite different ways. First, it reduces the risks that they perceive to begin with, and secondly it increases the sanction that they have should the risk materialize and default occur.

It is apparent that sanctions can take many forms and, given sufficient ingenuity, they are not difficult to invent and to apply. The simplest sanctions are refusal to repeat the trade and to damage the defaulter's reputation. The important thing is not that the sanctions should be feasible (though that is desirable) but merely that they should be credible to the other party.

6.9   THE FIRM AS A MARKET-MAKING ORGANIZATION

It was emphasized in Section 6.4 that market making involves processing a considerable amount of information. The ease with which information can be handled depends crucially upon how well the information flow is structured. Two of the main influences upon information flow are social convention and organization (see Chapter 11). For information flows as complex as those required for the operation of a market, social convention is usually unable to provide the degree of structure required. Greater sophistication is called for and this necessitates the use of purpose-built organizations. Among these purpose-built organizations are market-making firms. These firms act as specialized intermediaries. Their principal function is to reduce obstacles to trade by improving information flow. The efficient market-making firm overcomes these obstacles with minimum transaction cost.

Because of the complexity of the information flows involved in a market, the determination of an optimal structure of information flow is a difficult task. Many different structures are possible and the factors governing a rational choice are not always measurable, or even properly understood. The choice of structure is therefore a judgmental decision and is liable to occupy skilled mental labour for some considerable time. Once the structure has been determined, however, few judgmental decisions of similar importance are called for. Subsequent decisions can therefore be delegated to people with more limited powers of judgment. Furthermore, an efficient structure will ensure that these decision makers are provided with much of the information they need through routine procedures which involve no exercise of judgment at all. The implementation of these procedures can be delegated to unskilled mental labour (that is, clerical workers) or to computers.

The logical structure of information flow has its adjunct in the layout of the physical infrastructure for communication. The infrastructure comprises resources for encoding, transmitting, receiving and decoding messages and for filing records; it also includes the channels required for face-to-face communication, and for telecommunication as well. To minimize communication costs, these elements all need to be brought into the appropriate spatial relation with each other. Assembling the elements in this way may involve considerable manual labour; if some of the elements have to be relocated from a considerable distance, then a significant input of transport services may be required as well.

The direct consequence of all this is that the set-up cost of a market organization is likely to be quite high compared with its recurrent costs. The initial decision on structure involves intensive use of a scarce input – skilled mental labour – while subsequent operation uses much more abundant inputs, such as semi-skilled and unskilled mental labour. The communication infrastructure also involves a set-up cost, though, because it involves more abundant inputs, it is unlikely to be as large. Both set-up costs are largely fixed costs independent of the number of transactions subsequently effected. This is because the organization and its infrastructure are essentially indivisible assets with a large capacity.

Some of the recurrent costs are also fixed costs. Information handling relies heavily on the use of labour and of specialized office machinery, both of which tend to be supplied in indivisible units. This means that, where small variations in utilization are concerned, many recurrent costs are fixed costs. Only where large variations are concerned do recurrent costs vary a great deal, and then in 'lumpy' amounts.

A further consequence of the indivisibility of inputs into information handling is that the minimum efficient scale on which a market-making activity can be conducted may be quite high. This relies upon a well-known argument that, where an activity involves the use of several indivisible inputs, all of the inputs are used to capacity only when the scale of the activity is equal to the lowest common multiple of the capacities of the separate inputs. When this condition is satisfied the activity can be conducted using an integer number of units of each of the inputs and all of the units are fully utilized. It follows that, even if the degree of indivisibility in the individual inputs is quite small, the minimum efficient scale of the activity may be quite large, particularly where many different inputs are involved.

The inescapable conclusion is that the fixed costs of an information-based market-making activity are likely to be very high. If the organization and the infrastructure both specialize in performing a particular activity in a particular market, then it follows that the level of transactions which warrants the operation of that market may be quite high. The implications of market-making costs for the volume of trade are examined in detail in the following section.

6.10   PRICE AND QUANTITY DETERMINATION WITH MARKET-MAKING COSTS

There have been two main schools of thought regarding the impact of market-making costs on market price and the volume of trade. The first takes the very negative view that market-making costs complicate the analysis of markets so much that nothing very definite can be said: in other words, once the neoclassical paradigm is abandoned, anything goes. The second exploits an analogy between market-making costs and tariffs (or transport costs) to argue that a determinate price and volume of trade will still exist, characterized in the usual way by marginal conditions. It is predicted that, when there are market-making costs buying price will be higher, selling price lower, and the quantity traded will be lower too.

The analysis below follows the second approach, though it differs from the conventional formulation in one important respect. It is assumed that each market is organized by a single entrepreneur who specializes in providing market-making services. Thus market-making costs are incurred in the first instance by the entrepreneur and not by the transactors themselves. However, the costs are ultimately borne by the transactors because the entrepreneur recovers his costs by setting a margin between his buying price and his selling price. This margin is equivalent to a tax upon transactions imposed by the entrepreneur.

The assumption that there is only one entrepreneur may seem very strict, but it merely reflects the fact that, when information is costly, markets tend to be segmented, and each segment tends to be formed around a particular entrepreneur. Thus the concept of a market used here involves not merely trade in a single good, but trade in a single good in a single geographical area between a given group of transactors who are in contact with the same entrepreneur.

The analysis begins with the derivation of the market-making cost function. It is assumed for simplicity that there are just two market-making activities which incur positive opportunity costs. These may be visualized as contact making (activity 1) and quality control (activity 2). For each activity there are two possible techniques. Without loss of generality it may be assumed that one technique has a higher fixed cost and a lower variable cost than the other (if both fixed cost and variable cost were higher it would never be efficient to use the technique concerned). In deriving variable cost as a function of quantity traded, it is assumed that variable cost is directly proportional to the number of transactions and that the average volume per transaction is fixed. It follows that with each technique the market-making cost, C, is a linear function of the quantity traded, Q. The cost function C_{ij} for the ith activity and the jth technique $(i, j = 1, 2)$ is illustrated in Figures 6.1(a) and (b). The quantity traded is measured horizontally and the cost vertically.

A profit-maximizing entrepreneur necessarily minimizes the market-making cost of establishing any given volume of trade. This determines the cost function for each activity as the envelope, taken from below, of the cost functions for the two alternative techniques. The slope of each cost function is discontinuous at the point where the costs of the two techniques are equal. This point, A_1 in Figure 6.1(a), A_2 in Figure 6.1(b), is a switch point. Below the corresponding volume of trade, Q_1 in Figure 6.1(a), Q_2 in Figure 6.1(b), it is efficient to use the first technique, which has the lower fixed cost. This may be visualized as a primitive technique, such as making contact by attending a public market place, or testing quality by examining every item purchased. Above the critical volume of trade it is efficient to use the second technique which has the higher fixed cost. This may be visualized as a sophisticated technique such as making contact through media advertising or the operation of permanent retail premises. In the context of quality control, it could be a formalized test procedure, implemented on a sample basis. It is readily deduced from the figures that market making exhibits decreasing average and marginal cost with respect to the quantity traded: in other words, there are increasing returns to scale in market making. It can also be deduced that returns to scale increase because of a switch from primitive techniques of market making to more sophisticated ones as the volume of trade increases. When the results for the two activities are aggregated, the result is a cost function which is similar in all respects to its component functions, except that it no longer has just one switch point, but two. In a sense, therefore, the aggregate cost function is slightly smoother than the functions from which it is constructed – see Figure 6.1(c).

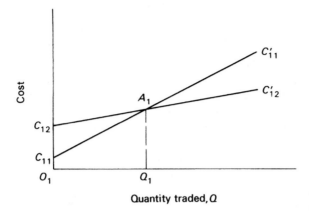

Figure 6.1(a)   Total cost functions for the first market-making activity

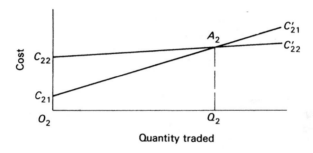

Figure 6.1(b)   Total cost functions for the second market-making activity

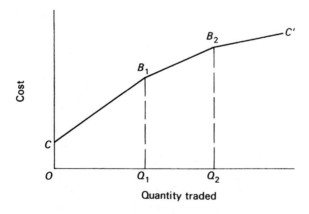

Figure 6.1(c)   Total cost function for market making

The impact of market-making costs upon price and quantity is illustrated in Figure 6.2, which presents a partial equilibrium of a single market created by a single entrepreneur. Two cases are distinguished, according to whether or not the entrepreneur can implement price discrimination. The familiar supply and demand curves DD', SS' are shown in the top half of the figure. With price discrimination – see Figure 6.2(a) – these also correspond to the entrepreneur's marginal revenue and marginal supply cost schedules. From these schedules it is possible to derive the entrepreneur's gross profit function OH_1 in Figure 6.2(b). This shows how the entrepreneur's profit varies with respect to the volume of trade in the absence of market-making costs. It reaches a maximum at Z_1, where the quantity traded is OK, which is the perfectly competitive volume of trade, corresponding to the point J in Figure 6.2(a).

Introducing the aggregate market-making cost function CC' into Figure 6.2(b) shows that net profit is maximized at X_1 where the slope of the net profit function OH_1 – indicated by the slope of the tangent V_1V_1' – is equal to the slope of the cost function. The relevant segment of the cost function is B_1B_2, indicating that the volume of trade is above the critical level Q_1 but below the critical level Q_2. It follows that the entrepreneur will operate a sophisticated system of contact making, but only a primitive system of quality control.

Equilibrium output is OY_1, which is less than the competitive output OK. Maximum buying price and minimum selling price are read off from the demand and supply schedules DD' and SS'. The entrepreneur buys at a maximum price OP_1 and sells at a minimum price OP_1', earning a gross profit X_1Y_1 and a net profit X_1X_1'. The maximum buying price is higher than it would be without market-making costs, and the minimum selling price is lower. Gross profit, as well as net profit, is lower too.

When the entrepreneur is restricted to uniform pricing, then his marginal revenue is given by DM, below DD', and his marginal supply cost by SN above SS': see Figure 6.2(c). The entrepreneur's gross profit is now given by the curve OK in Figure 6.2(d). This curve peaks at the output OG, which corresponds to the profit-maximizing output in the absence of market-making costs. Apart from this, the analysis exactly parallels the analysis of discriminatory pricing. Net profit is maximized at X_2 in Figure 6.2(d). At X_2 the slope of the gross profit function OZ_2K, as measured by the slope of the tangent V_2V_2', is equal to the slope of the aggregate market-making cost function CC'. The volume of trade OY_2 is much lower than before. In particular it is now below OQ_1, so that contact making as well as quality control is effected using a primitive technique. Buying price is OP_2, below the maximum buying price before, and selling price is OP_2', above the minimum selling price before, gross profit is reduced to X_2Y_2, and net profit is down to only X_2X_2'. The

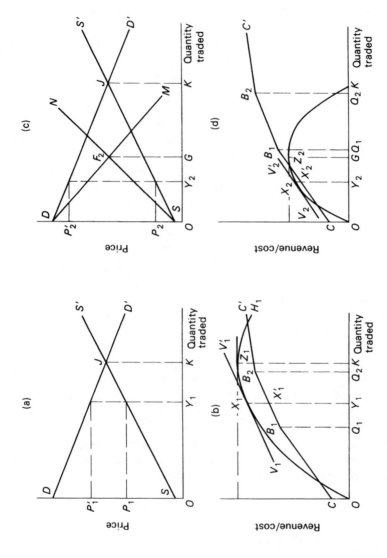

Figure 6.2   Determination of the quantity of trade with market-making costs

impact of market-making costs on the volume of trade is to reduce it from OG, which corresponds to the intersection F_2 of DM and SN, to OY_2. As a result, the entrepreneur's buying price is reduced, and his selling price increased.

It should be obvious that this analysis can be extended in many different ways. By imposing various restrictions upon the demand, supply and market-making cost functions, it is possible to predict not just the price and quantity traded in the presence of market-making costs, but also to predict how the choice of market-making technique will respond to parametric changes in demand and supply conditions through their impact on the equilibrium volume of trade. By extending the number of market-making activities included in the aggregate cost function, it is possible to provide still more detail about the way in which the entrepreneur will organize his market-making activities. The theory has tremendous potential and so far very little of that potential has been realized. The following chapter provides some more hints about the direction in which the theory of market making can be developed.

SUMMARY

This chapter has emphasized that intermediation, or 'making a market' is not the relatively trivial exercise that the analysis in Part I might suggest. It is shown that significant transaction costs are incurred in overcoming obstacles to trade. Many of these obstacles are due to ignorance and so the market-making activities required to overcome them involve the acquisition and processing of information. The rational entrepreneur will endeavour to minimize the transaction cost of conducting any given volume of trade, and will trade up to the margin where the private gain from an additional trade is just equal to the additional cost involved. Market-making information relates to product characteristics and transactor characteristics as well as to the terms of the contract itself. Most information costs are fixed costs, independent of the volume of trade, and this exerts a major influence upon the strategies pursued by entrepreneurs to minimize transaction costs. The most important strategies are reviewed, but discussion of their implications is deferred until later chapters.

NOTES AND REFERENCES

The relative neglect of transaction costs is one of the consequences of adhering to the perfect competition model. The reasons why this model evolved in the way it did, and why it acquired such ascendancy in economics, are considered by McNulty (1967, 1968) and Stigler (1957). Many writers have emphasized that the perfect competition model is not really about the process of competition at all: see, for example, Andrews (1964), Clark, J.M. (1955, 1961) and Hayek (1949). On the other hand, it has to be recognized that some of the predictions of the perfect competition model still apply even if a much more general concept of competition is used, see, for example, Alchian (1950).

The seminal paper on transaction costs is Demsetz (1968). Very little has been written by economists on the actual structure of transaction costs and upon the mechanisms for reducing them; most of the relevant material is to be found in the marketing literature, as reviewed by Kotler (1976). The conceptual framework, however, is already well established and in this respect the analysis above relies heavily upon Williamson (1975).

7.   Internal and external markets

7.1   INTRODUCTION

The previous chapter discussed, amongst other things, the methods available to an entrepreneur for reducing his market-making costs. The focus was on methods of improving the organization of trade within a particular market. This chapter analyses a quite different approach to the reduction of market-making costs. The focus is on achieving a reduction of market-making costs within the economy as a whole through a reduction in the number of markets that operate.

Because of the fixed costs incurred in making a market, conducting a roughly similar volume of trade through fewer markets reduces aggregate market-making costs. But how exactly is the number of markets reduced? And what are the criteria which determine which markets should be eliminated and which preserved?

The basic strategy is to absorb several different markets into a single market by devising a single composite good (or property right) to replace several distinct goods (or property rights) which would otherwise be traded separately. The principles underlying this approach are examined in Section 7.2 below. Efficiency demands that it should be relatively easy to make a market in the composite good. *Ceteris paribus*, goods which have low market-making costs should be chosen as composite goods, and the goods displaced should be those with high market-making costs. The economic forces which induce this result are examined in Section 7.3.

But what is the effect of the disappearance of some particular market on the freedom of the individual to allocate resources in the way he wants? The individual can respond in one of two ways. He can decide to abandon any attempt to influence the allocation of goods in the way that would have been possible had all markets been in operation. Alternatively, he can develop his own – internal – market to allocate the composite good to a use to which the more specific good would have been exclusively dedicated. To illustrate with a trivial example: if the market in purpose-made taxi cabs were to disappear, a taxi driver could respond either by switching to alternative work or by purchasing an ordinary motor car and using it as a taxi when required. In the first case the allocation of goods is constrained because taxi services are no longer supplied; in the second case an internal market is established by which a motor car is allocated to use as a taxi. The institutional structure of markets is different, but the allocation of resources is very similar to what it was before.

The internal market is not, however, merely a last resort for people who cannot obtain what they want in an external market. If the costs of gaining access to an external market are high, then some individuals may positively prefer to use an internal market even though the external one is available. This does not mean that they do not make use of an external market at all. It means that they use a different external market from the one that they would otherwise have used. They gain access to the market for a composite good instead of the market for the specific – or purpose-dedicated – good; they then deploy the composite good for the purpose they require. They gain to the extent that the net cost of the composite good (after allowing for the cost of access to the market) is lower than the net cost of the purpose-dedicated good (after allowing, also, for the cost of access to the market). If these gains outweigh the cost of operating the internal market, then internalization is positively preferred.

The coexistence of internal and external markets indicates that in practice coordination is a two-stage process. It is by no means the simple matter of market intermediation that was suggested earlier. The first step for an entrepreneur who believes that resources are misallocated is to acquire control of the goods concerned. The second step is for him to reallocate the goods to their appropriate use. Market intermediation is important because it allows these two steps to be performed by different people. For example an entrepreneur, C, may believe that individual B would make better use of a given resource than individual A. If he is correct, then he can profit by intermediating trade between A and B. This is true even if he does not know to what use B will put the resource. B himself performs the second stage of the coordination by buying the resource from C and allocating it to its proper use. In this example two different people perform the two different stages of coordination; the first stage involving intermediation in an external market is carried out by C and the second stage involving allocation through an internal market is carried out by B.

7.2 STRATEGIES FOR COMBINING MARKETS

This section considers ways of reducing market-making costs in the aggregate by reducing the number of different markets. The basic principle is to package different goods together to form a single composite good. The fixed cost of the market for the composite good need be no greater than the fixed cost of any one of the markets for a constituent good. Two separate cases need to be distinguished according to whether the constituent goods are complements or substitutes.

Packaging complements works best when the constituent goods are complementary in both supply and demand. The main application of the principle is to durable assets. A durable asset may be regarded as the equivalent of a bundle of dated services. Each service consists of the right to utilize the asset at a particular time. The different services are strictly complementary in supply because, when the durable is produced, each dated service is produced in a one-to-one relation with all the other services that can be rendered throughout the asset's life. The services are usually complementary in demand, though they are not necessarily so. Because of the fixed cost of exchanging custody of a good in order to utilize it, few people will wish to acquire just a single dated service. They will normally demand several consecutive dated services in order to recover the fixed cost of acquiring custody. In many cases they will demand all the dated services throughout the asset's life.

In principle, each dated service could be sold separately through a contract of hire. The owner of the asset would offer for sale all the services rendered on the different dates spanned by the life of the asset. He would be responsible for organizing the hiring so that the good is never double-booked (or, in the case of a public good, for ensuring that the number of simultaneous bookings does not exceed capacity). If there were no market-making costs, an efficient allocation of asset use could be achieved using only the markets for dated durable services, and without recourse to the market for the durable good itself.

There are two problems with this strategy. The first concerns the multiplicity of different markets that would have to be operated, and the consequent difficulty of covering the aggregate fixed cost of market-making. The second concerns the peculiar problems of enforcing claims on future supplies, which were noted earlier (Section 6.6).

Because the different dated services are joint products of the process which produces the durable commodity, and there are often economies of continuity in the process which utilizes the durable services, the principle of complementarity indicates that it is appropriate to package the dated services into a right of ownership of the durable asset itself. The durable asset is then traded in a spot market. The owner of the asset has physical custody of it and thereby ensures his own supplies of whatever future services of the asset he requires.

The minority demand for individual dated services can be satisfied by the purchase and resale of the asset. Instead of hiring the asset for a specific period, the user buys the asset at the beginning of the period and resells it at the end of the period. Although this involves two transactions where one would do, it is still efficient, given that the market for hire is so small that the total saving to hirers would be less than the fixed cost of operating the market.

Packaging substitutes is decidedly the most significant way of reducing aggregate market-making costs. It works best when the constituent goods are substitutes in both supply and demand. The embodiment of the principle is the multi-purpose good: the good is capable of being put to a number of alternative uses (so that the uses are substitutes in supply) and it is unlikely that more than one of these uses will be required at any one time (so that the uses are substitutes in demand). It would be possible to establish a market for each of the separate user services that the good is capable of producing. The owner of the good would sell specific user rights, and so would allocate the good to whatever kind of use commanded the highest price. In the absence of market-making costs, an efficient allocation of each good between alternative uses could be achieved using only the markets for specific user services; the existence of a separate market in the good itself would contribute nothing to efficiency. In practice, however, there are so many different user services that the number of different markets required would be enormous. Trading in many of these markets would be very thin and it would be difficult to recover the fixed cost of market making from each of them. Thus when market-making costs exist, it is normally efficient to suppress the markets for specific user services and to operate just the market for the multi-purpose good instead.

7.3 THE INNOVATION OF A MULTI-PURPOSE GOOD

This section analyses the role of the entrepreneur in promoting the development of a multi-purpose good. It is assumed that the entrepreneur recognizes the high market-making costs that are being incurred in the provision of specialized products to people with specialized requirements. These costs are incurred in the first instance by intermediators who are making the markets in these specialized products. But the costs are being passed on to the customers in the form of a high selling price. Some of the costs are also passed on to the producers because the intermediator sets a low buying price as well. Each specialist market therefore operates with a large margin between buying price and selling price and a small volume of trade. Each market can continue operating only so long as the total margin earned is sufficient to meet the (mainly fixed) costs of operating it.

The entrepreneur seeks to introduce a multi-purpose good which will meet a number of different specialized needs. The typical multi-purpose good is formed by assembling a mixture of components. By activating one subset of these components, the good can be put to one specialized use; by activating another subset of components it can be put to a different specialized use. A good example of a multi-purpose good is a 'music centre' which can be used as radio, tape-recorder, record-player, CD player, and so on. The user simply presses a button to select the preferred mode of operation. A personal computer may also be regarded as a multi-purpose good, in so far as it can run different types of software – games, word-processing, mathematical computing, and so on.

It is sometimes suggested that products can be identified in terms of characteristics over which consumer preferences are defined. In the present context, it could be suggested that the characteristics of a multi-purpose good correspond to the different functions that it can perform, while the different functions are generated from different permutations of the components that comprise the good. One of the objectives of the entrepreneur is to find the combination of components which gives as many different desirable characteristics (that is, specialized uses) for a given total component cost.

The multi-purpose good substitutes for all the specialist goods which previously performed these separate functions. However, being designed as a versatile good, it may not be able to achieve, in all cases, the same standard of performance as the specialist good it substitutes for. Demand for the specialist good may shrink, but not be eliminated. However, the fixed costs of market making may mean that the specialist markets can no longer operate profitably at a reduced level of demand. As a result, the specialist products may disappear from the market place altogether. The limited markets in high-performance specialized goods are superseded by a larger market in a versatile good offering a mediocre standard of performance instead.

It must be recognized that the introduction of multi-purpose goods does not reduce every single component of market cost. For example, the specification cost of a multi-purpose good may be no less than the total specification costs of the specialized goods it displaces. This is because goods are normally specified by function rather than appearance (as noted earlier). The versatility of the multi-purpose good makes for a very complex functional specification. Furthermore, the different functions of the good may not be immediately apparent from its appearance, unlike its more specialized counterparts. For this reason, verbal communication of the functional specification may be very important in attracting customers. Furthermore, the complexity of the specification means that diffusion of information about the specification must be carefully controlled: messages passed on at second or third hand may easily get distorted. All of this obliges the entrepreneur to invest heavily in advertising his product specification to customers, to the extent that advertising may become by far the largest cost in making a market for a multi-purpose product.

The burden of advertising costs may, however, be offset by economies in production which can be achieved in component manufacture. If the product is built up from components, then production switches from a low-volume output of specialized goods to high-volume outputs of components. There may even be more different components than there were specialized goods; this simply means that the average value of a component is relatively low. It is still true that each component has a high-volume output so that the producer can fully exploit economies of scale. It does mean, however, that additional markets have to be created for the components. The more components there are, the more markets are required, and the lower are the potential gains from introducing the multi-component good.

Fortunately for the entrepreneur, it is much easier to organize markets between a component producer and the producer of a multi-purpose good than it is to organize a market between the producer of a specialized good and the final users of it. One obvious reason is that fewer transactors are involved in buying the component than are involved in buying the final product. But perhaps the main reason is that it is far easier to internalize a market in a component than in a final product. Internalization significantly reduces the cost of operating a component market and means that, even if the number of components is large relative to the number of specialized goods that are displaced, the introduction of a multi-purpose good may still, overall, achieve significant economies in market-making costs.

7.4   INTERNALIZATION

Internalization of a market occurs when a transactor buys a good from himself or sells a good to himself. Internalization involves limiting the field of trading partners so narrowly that the only trading partner is oneself. The advantages of this are fairly obvious. There is no problem in making contact, there is no need to haggle over price (since payment effects a purely notional transfer of income), there is no need to exchange custody, there is no incentive deliberately to default on either quantity or quality – and while unintentional default cannot entirely be ruled out, at least the transactor has a good knowledge of his trading partner's capabilities! Moreover, by internalizing a transaction it is often possible to keep the details of it secret and so bypass fiscal intervention and avoid paying taxes or tariffs.

The disadvantages are equally obvious. In fact there is really only one: narrowing the field of trading partners reduces the opportunity to benefit from specialization. It means that in effect the buyer (or seller) cannot get as good a price for the good as he might. Internalization is only justified if the reduction in the gains from trade as reflected in the poorer price is more than offset by the saving of market-making costs.

The principle of internalization at its most basic is illustrated by the 'do-it-yourself' system of supplying household services. The gains from specialization forgone are measured by the additional time it takes the householder to perform the task relative to the time it would take the specialist (assuming both have the same opportunity cost of time). The reduction in market-making cost is measured by the saving of the specialist's charges for operating the market in his own services. The rational householder supplies do-it-yourself services if the saving of the specialist's market-making charges exceed the gains from specialization forgone.

The most important aspect of internalization, however, is concerned not with households but with firms. Specialization in production induced, for example, by the division of labour leads to a large volume of intermediate product trade. Intermediate products are goods produced in one plant which are passed on to another plant for further processing. Components used in the production of a multi-purpose good are intermediate products. Economies of specialization encourage the production of a component in one plant and the assembly of the multi-purpose good in another plant. Internalization of the intermediate product market means that both the component-producing plant and the assembly plant are brought under common ownership. The intermediate product can then be transferred from one plant to the other without any change of ownership, and therefore without any haggling or risk of default.

Internalization of intermediate product markets increases the scale and diversity of a firm's operations. The more markets that are internalized by a given firm, the greater is the number of activities that are brought under its control. This increases the extent to which coordination is effected through operations internal to the firm. The firm is still involved in external markets. To set up the firm to begin with, it is necessary for the entrepreneur to acquire the different plants through external markets. He can acquire the plants second hand by purchasing them from their previous owners; this is equivalent to creating the internal market through a takeover or merger of hitherto independent firms. Alternatively, he can acquire plants by commissioning their construction. In either case the external market is used in order to establish the internal market. Even when the internal market is set up, the firm is still involved in external markets, hiring labour and other factor services for the plants and selling the final product they produce. Internalization merely reduces the firm's dependence on external markets; it does not eliminate the use of external markets altogether.

It is apparent, therefore, that internalization is a major influence on the size and structure of the firm. The scope of the internal markets relative to the external markets determines the boundary between coordination by negotiation and coordination by control. The implications of internalization for the entrepreneur are examined in greater detail in Chapters 8 and 10. The different strands of the discussion are brought together in Chapter 11, which shows, amongst other things, how internalization influences the dynamics of the growth of the firm.

This chapter concludes with some observations upon the way that the peculiar problems of the external market in labour create a form of dual internalization. The problems of organizing external markets in specific labour services lead to these markets being internalized through a contract of employment in which the entrepreneurs acquire rights of control and supervision over employees. Secondly, the problems of recruiting and retaining employees encourage the entrepreneur to internalize his supply of labour within the family, or within any other kind of economic grouping to which he belongs. The consequences of this dual internalization of the labour market will become apparent as the argument proceeds.

7.5 THE INTERNALIZATION OF LABOUR SERVICES THROUGH THE EMPLOYMENT CONTRACT

Labour is probably the most versatile multi-purpose good, particularly when mental as well as manual labour services are taken into account. Within the labour market as a whole, various submarkets exist for particular skills. However, the allocation of labour to specific tasks is hardly ever effected by the labour market alone. Typically, the labour market allocates people to employers, or more precisely to a particular post with a particular employer. Each post has a job specification, which may be explicit in some cases, but less than explicit in others. The job specification determines the kind of tasks that the employee can be expected to perform. It also states who will issue the instructions about which task is to be performed at any given time. In some cases the instructor will be named (for example, if it is the employer himself), while in other cases the instructor will be identified by the post that he holds. If the post is with the same employer, then the employee is effectively operating within the hierarchy of an employing organization.

It is characteristic of employment that the employer has control of the employee within the terms of the contract of employment: that is, within the scope of the agreed job specification. It is the employer that determines the precise task to which an employee is allocated. In principle, though, the allocation of labour to specific tasks need not be effected in this way. In theory there could be a market for every labour service required for the performance of every possible task. Once a contract had been made in the labour market, the buyer of the labour service would have no need to give the seller further information about the task that he was to perform. The seller would know exactly what he was required to do as soon as the contract was agreed. Thus the buyer would have no control over the seller. He would be bound by a contract which specified exactly what the seller was to do. Under a regime of this kind there would be no employers as such: only buyers and sellers of specific labour services.

The rationale of the employment contract is that labour is a multi-purpose good and that, because of the fixed cost of making a market in each specific labour service, it is more efficient to work with fewer markets in more general labour services. Each of these general markets has a larger volume of trade and it is therefore easier to recoup the fixed cost of making the market.

Although workers are endowed with particular skills, even a specialist or craftsman may find that there are a number of different tasks in which his comparative advantage is roughly the same and between which he is largely indifferent as regards the non-income attributes of the work to be done. A worker in this position has nothing to lose from contracting to supply general labour services within his area of specialism rather than a single specific service. The costs of market making are significantly reduced if the complexity of the specification that has to be announced to potential suppliers of the labour service is kept as low as possible. This is achieved if a market in general labour services is created and all demands for specific labour services are channelled into this market. The market for specific labour services does not disappear altogether: it is merely internalized by the employer. Thus employers hire general labour services and instruct the person they hire about the specific services to be supplied. This does not, of course, reduce the cost of communication between employer and employee, but it does reduce the cost of communication between the employer and all those potential suppliers of labour services who do not finally work for him.

In common with many other multi-purpose goods, labour is a durable asset. The durability of labour is also an influence upon the employment contract. There are set-up costs associated with switching labour from one place of work to another. The cost of travel to and from the job means that it is efficient for the worker to work at just a single place each day. Travel to work is an important part of daily routine. Economies of habit formation make it desirable to work at the same place day after day. Also where labour is concerned the roles of transactor and resource are unified. Economies of repeat-trading, which relate to the advantage of trading with the same transactor, imply that there are economies of repeatedly using the same labour resource. This provides an argument for continuity of employment in the longer term, that is, over several months or years.

In principle the allocation of labour over time could be determined through forward markets in dated labour services. However, the difficulty of enforcing forward contracts suggests that the market-making costs would be prohibitive. Logic dictates that the employer should make an outright purchase of the resource: that is, he should buy out the employee.

It is one of the peculiarities of the labour market that an outright purchase of this kind is unenforceable, because of constraints imposed by social convention. The result is that the employer finds it difficult to secure a future supply of labour and the employee finds it difficult to secure a future supply of work. In an attempt to resolve this problem, a fairly complex system of customs has developed within the spot market for labour services. One of these customs is the open-ended labour contract. This provides for the automatic renewal of daily employment until one or other of the parties takes active steps to separate, by giving notice of either quitting or redundancy. This eliminates the need for each party actively to confirm renewal of the contract on a day-to-day basis. Negotiation costs are reduced by restricting the frequency of negotiation: convention dictates that wage rates are normally renegotiated not more than once a year.

Given the economics of repeat-trading, each party can impose a substantial cost upon the other by initiating a premature separation. The cost of separation is normally greater the shorter the notice that is given. Premature separation is deterred by incentives embodied in implicit contracts.

An implicit contract is a contract which is not enforceable in law, but is backed by sanctions of a more general nature, such as those described in Section 6.8. The terms of an implicit contract are not always precisely defined, so it is the spirit of the contract, rather than the letter, that is enforced. Implicit contracts have many roles besides deterring separation (see, for example, Section 9.3). In the context of separation, employers may threaten to give bad references to premature quitters, or to foreclose on personal loans advanced to them. Employees may deter redundancy by threatening to strike (backed by colleagues) or to instigate political action hostile to the employer.

7.6   SELF-EMPLOYMENT AND THE FAMILY FIRM

It is well known that the costs of organizing the labour market are very high. This partly reflects the heterogeneity of both workers and jobs and the consequent difficulties of matching the worker to the job. Partly it is due to social convention which imposes constraints on the contract of employment and the sanctions that can be applied to enforce it. The problem is exacerbated by the fact that it is difficult to organize private intermediation which, if it could be effected, would help to reduce transaction costs. For reasons already explained, an intermediator cannot buy and sell labour just like any other commodity. It is true that in some sectors of the labour market there are private agencies who employ labour specifically for rehire to other firms, but, because the agencies cannot enforce long-term contracts with their employees, they are always vulnerable to being bypassed. Once the agency has placed the worker with a firm, the firm can offer the worker a job directly, and so both firm and worker will terminate their contract with the agency.

The difficulties of intermediation in the labour market create an incentive to internalize the supply of labour services to firms. The most basic form of labour market internalization is self-employment. Instead of selling his labour services to an employer, the worker integrates forward and establishes a firm to employ himself. If he works in a service industry, he may be doing no more than marketing his own labour services to the public instead of relying upon an employer to do the marketing for him. But if he works in a manufacturing industry then he bypasses the market for labour services altogether, and becomes involved directly in the product market. He may rely upon an intermediator in the product market to put him in contact with his customers, or he may integrate further forward into market making, and market his own product directly to the customers.

Self-employment is, on the face of it, a very attractive way of bypassing labour market imperfections. The main constraint is that, if the self-employed person is successful, then he will need to take on extra labour and, in order to recruit it, he will be forced back into the market that he has tried to avoid. The only difference is that he will now enter the market as an employer rather than as an employee.

A possible solution to this problem is suggested by an extension of the concept of internalization from the individual worker to his family, and perhaps even to his friends. Instead of internalizing the labour market around an individual it is internalized around a social unit instead. Social ties are normally closest within the family (though exceptions have been noted in certain cultures). A self-employed person may expand his business by first taking on other members of his household, then non-resident members of his family, and then members of his extended family – for example those related at once or twice remove by marriage. Within the family, he may prefer to take on first those who are most dependent upon him, for example his children, as sanctions against them are relatively easy to enforce. The last to be taken on will be those who because of their family status hold sanctions over him.

It is worth noting that the family is capable of internalizing not only the labour market, but the capital market too. The family may even internalize the product market, in the manner explained earlier (Section 7.4), but this has little direct relevance to the entrepreneur.

A self-employed person who needs risk capital will often go to his family first. Ostensibly, he is hoping to exploit the goodwill of his family towards him. But goodwill often runs out when people are asked to part with their money – even within families. There is, however, an economic rationale to this strategy. First, the borrower can have confidence that his relatives – though they might refuse him a loan – would not stoop to stealing his ideas and putting them into practice on their own account instead. Second, the borrower is already well-known to the lenders; if the lenders are of an older generation they may have known him from his birth. They are therefore in a good position to assess his relevant personal qualities such as integrity and competence. Third, as members of his family, they are in a good position to monitor the way he uses their capital and to bring pressure to bear upon him should things not turn out as well as expected. Finally, if the borrower stands to inherit the lender's estate, then he is in effect being given no more than a mortgage upon his own inheritance. The lender is in a privileged position to provide the mortgage, because a third party might be unwilling to accept the prospect of an inheritance as security for a loan.

It has been suggested that some families actually operate an internal capital market in which financial resources are pooled under the management of the head of the family and are then allocated among family entrepreneurs on the basis of a strictly economic assessment of their prospects. Individual projects are screened by the head of the family, in much the same way as they would be screened by the board of a large company, or by the management of a merchant bank. The advantage of the family organization is that it captures all the information that family members have about each other and puts it to an economic use. Firms enjoy a similar advantage but to a much more limited extent. They can use the information gained from monitoring individual employees to assess the projects they present for consideration by the board, but they do not enjoy the same depth of information as does the family firm which draws upon personal knowledge that is not available to the typical employer.

SUMMARY

This chapter has stressed the role of internalization in the reduction of transaction costs. It is shown that internalization is intimately connected with control over the utilization of multi-purpose goods. Internal and external markets typically exist side by side, with coordination being achieved by a two-stage process in which multipurpose goods are first allocated through external markets to people who believe they can put them to a better use, and are then allocated internally by their new owners to their appropriate use. The cost advantages of internal markets constitute the basic rationale for the firm. They explain why it is that entrepreneurs seeking to intermediate transactions need to establish a unit of control within which the assets required to generate market-making services can be brought together. This unit of control is examined in greater detail in Chapter 10.

NOTES AND REFERENCES

The seminal paper on internalization is Coase (1937). The relation between transaction costs, internalization and theory of the firm has been explored by a number of writers, especially Williamson (1975). The analysis of the firm in the remainder of Part II relies heavily upon Williamson's work and also upon the author's own work with Peter Buckley (Buckley and Casson, 1976; Casson, 1979). Key references on internal markets and the theory of the firm include Alchian (1969), Alchian and Demsetz (1972), Kaldor (1934), Papandreou (1952), Robinson (1934), Ross (1952) and Williamson (1970). An important special application is to vertical integration: see Oi and Hurter (1965) and Williamson (1971).

The idea that property rights are traded in bundles, and that some individuals have a comparative advantage in owning and controlling certain bundles, is considered in a seminal paper by Alchian (1965).

8. The market for information

8.1 INTRODUCTION

An important application of the theory of market-making costs is to the market for information. It can be shown that there is a strong incentive for an entrepreneur to internalize the exploitation of the commercial information upon which his superior judgment is based. It is the internalization of commercial information that leads the entrepreneur to acquire control of assets, and hence links the entrepreneur to the management of a firm. In analysing this, it will be assumed that the entrepreneur is certain of the accuracy of the information at his disposal.

There are five main ways in which an entrepreneur can exploit commercial information:

1. He can license the information.
2. He can enter into bets with those who do not have the information and whose judgment as a result differs from his own.
3. He can buy up assets which, given his information, are currently undervalued, with a view to reselling later. Once the information becomes public, other transactors will revalue the assets and he will make a capital gain. This strategy relies upon other people coordinating the use of resources once the information becomes public. It also depends upon other entrepreneurs creating the market for the assets.
4. He can initiate the coordination himself. He can intermediate any additional transactions which the information indicates are required. He can also acquire control of any multi-purpose goods which need to be reallocated to another use.
5. He can act as coordinator, but as delegate rather than principal. He can offer his services as a delegate to someone who is liable to make the wrong decision – or whose existing delegate is inept – and rely upon the incentive system of his employer to reward a correct decision.

8.2   THE LICENSING OPTION

Consider an entrepreneur who believes that he has privileged information. He is absolutely convinced of its accuracy. He also believes that it is relevant to other people. If made available to them it will change their decisions and as a result improve their welfare. Under these conditions it seems perfectly reasonable to regard the item of information as a commodity which should command a positive price, and to market it as such. Given a perfect market in information, the entrepreneur should be able to sell his information for an amount equal to the capitalized value of its use.

However, information is not just like any other good and its market, far from being perfect, is in many cases prohibitively costly to organize. To sell any good it is necessary to be able to exclude people from it. Because information is a public good with practically infinite capacity it is difficult to enforce custody of it. Partly because of this difficulty, the law regards most information as being in common ownership. With the exception of certain items of information which are patentable, and others which are covered by the right to personal privacy, exclusion from information is not legally enforceable. Thus the problems of *de facto* exclusion are compounded by the absence of legal sanctions. In these circumstances the right of exclusion can only be upheld by secrecy.

It is an unfortunate fact that the very act of marketing information is likely to undermine its secrecy. The reason is that, where information is concerned, it is difficult to separate the product itself from its specification. As a result the information is given away as soon as the specification is announced. Separation of specification and product can be achieved in a few cases: newspaper vendors have developed the art of separating the description of news from the news itself. 'Famous film star dies' or 'Shock election result' describes what the news is about without describing precisely what it is. Even in these cases, though, people who have read the description may be able to make a reasonable guess at what the news item is. It follows that a vendor of information always runs a risk of giving his product away through the very act of specifying it to buyers. This in itself would not matter if information were not a satiation good. In some markets, sellers regularly give away samples of their product to stimulate future demand. But, because information is a satiation good, fulfilling demand just once destroys all subsequent demand from the same source.

If the seller decides to enforce exclusion by keeping the specification secret, then he creates uncertainty in the mind of the buyer. As a result the buyer cannot appraise the value of the information properly. His demand price will reflect a strong subjective probability that the information is worthless to him: he may know it already or it may simply be irrelevant to his needs. This makes it likely that the buyer will be unable to offer anything like what the seller believes the information to be worth. If the seller fails to recognize the buyer's uncertainty problem, then he may hold out for too a high price, and negotiations may break down.

Given the asymmetry in the perception of the situation between buyer and seller, it would be mutually advantageous for the seller to insure the value of the information to the buyer. The buyer would pay the seller only if the information was novel and relevant to him. The buyer would be willing to pay more if the payment were contingent upon the novelty and relevance of the information being proven, and the seller, being confident of this, would regard this payment as being just as assured as an unconditional payment. Unfortunately, this arrangement runs into the difficulties described in Section 7.3; for it is essentially a contingent contract, and one contingent upon factors (novelty and relevance) which are to some extent subjective. Unless the contract is very carefully specified, there will be ample opportunity for the buyer to default, by dishonestly claiming that he already had the information or that he could have done just as well without it. If in addition the information relates to a future state of the world, then the problem of default is magnified, for the contingent contract then becomes a forward contract too.

Information also poses severe problems of quality control. With most products a defect simply means that the buyer has wasted his payment. But with some products defects in quality can impose severe penalties on the buyer. Information typically comes into the latter category. This is because information is commonly used in decision making and mistaken decisions can result in severe losses due to resource misallocation. Just as correct information leads to coordination, so the use of incorrect information may lead to dislocation.

It has already been noted that the use of guarantees to insure the buyer is not usually reliable when severe losses are possible. Neither can the buyer satisfy himself of the quality by supervising the researching of the information, for this would destroy the seller's secrecy, and so eliminate the basis for the market. The best that can probably be hoped for is that the seller can offer to provide the buyer with corroborative evidence before the information is used. Effectively, this transforms the information from an experience good into an inspection good and so makes it easier for the buyer to control the risk that the information will actually prove a liability.

Finally, it is necessary to return to the problem of enforcing exclusion from a public good. It is apparent that, if two or more people already have access to a public good, then they are both in a weak position when selling access to a third party. If each can offer access, then neither can ensure exclusion unless they collude. Competition between them will drive down the price of access to zero. So far as information is concerned, this means that it normally has to be sold with restrictions upon resale by the buyer. If the buyer attempts to resell the information in competition with the original seller, then together they will bid away any reward from a subsequent sale. Restrictions on resale are notoriously difficult to police, and so the risk of default by the buyer is considerable. Furthermore, it is doubtful whether such restrictions would be enforceable in law. Given the widespread view that information is in common ownership, restrictions on resale are liable to be regarded as illegal restraints of trade. Thus, even if offenders could be detected, penalties could not be enforced in law.

8.3   THE BETTING OPTION

If an entrepreneur cannot sell his information to other people, then the obvious alternative is to exploit it himself. This is equivalent to internalizing the market for information. As exploiter of the information, he buys it from himself; as the possessor of the information, he sells it to himself.

In a world of perfect markets, betting would be the best way of exploiting information. The entrepreneur offers to bet with other people upon the event whose occurrence is uncertain, or upon the state of the world – or the aspect of it – which is in doubt.

Betting can operate in cases where licensing cannot. It can generate a private reward even to information which is quite irrelevant to personal welfare. All that is necessary for betting to succeed is that the parties with whom the entrepreneur seeks to bet are not totally risk-averse. Since the entrepreneur is by assumption convinced of the accuracy of his information he perceives no risk, and is therefore restricted in his bets mainly by the risk aversion of other parties. The other constraint is his wealth, which restricts the payments he can offer to make if he is wrong.

However, betting is not without its problems. One of them is that offering to bet with people may actually change their beliefs. This problem is particularly acute when betting upon events which are known to be irrelevant. If an event is irrelevant to the entrepreneur then his motive for betting cannot be insurance. It must be speculation. This signals to other people that the entrepreneur believes he has superior information. If he offers very large bets this suggests, furthermore, that he feels certain of his information. This in turn may persuade other people that he is probably right. The fact that the entrepreneur offers a bet may therefore change the mind of the people with whom he plans to bet. As a result, there may be nobody with whom he can bet on favourable terms.

Note that this problem is the reverse of the problem with licensing. Licensing rests upon the assumption that other people will believe the information when they are told it, and encounters problems because they may not. More precisely, licensing relies upon people believing the claims that are made for the information, and not challenging them once it has been supplied. Betting rests on the principle that people would not believe the information on which the entrepreneur acts even if they were told it. Indeed, the nature of the bet virtually tells them what it is the entrepreneur believes. Problems arise when other people actually believe that the entrepreneur's information is correct!

This problem with betting is somewhat reduced if the information relates to a relevant event or to a future one. When the entrepreneur bets upon a relevant event, it is conceivable that his motive is insurance. It is therefore possible that he does not have privileged information, and so it is less likely that other people will change their beliefs. Almost by definition, the entrepreneur cannot know the outcome of a future event, however strong his beliefs about it. Consequently, it is always possible that he is wrong. Furthermore, if the event lies in the future, it is more difficult for people to check the entrepreneur's information for themselves, and so there is less likelihood of his privileged access to it being eliminated. However, betting on a future event involves a forward contract and so incurs a risk of default. This implies, amongst other things, that the entrepreneur must have a reputation for integrity if his bets on future events are to prove acceptable to others.

Finally, betting shares a problem with licensing in respect of the multiplicity of markets that are required. Information is a very heterogeneous good, and so each item of information, and each bet, incurs its own market-making costs. Even if contact making, monitoring and enforcement costs can be shared between them, each item, and each bet, incurs its own specification and negotiation costs. The gains from exploiting some items of information may be sufficiently large to warrant the establishment of a special market, but generally this will not be so. On the whole, the market-making costs for information and bets are so high, and the possibilities of sharing them so limited, that it is uneconomic for specific items of information to be sold and specific bets to be placed.

8.4 PORTFOLIO SPECULATION

The problems of betting are largely overcome by portfolio speculation. Portfolio speculation, like licensing, applies only to the exploitation of information about relevant events. Also like licensing, it applies to information which will be believed once people gain access to it. The principle of portfolio speculation is that, because the information is relevant, resources will be reallocated once the information becomes public. In a market system this reallocation will be guided by prices. The entrepreneur can back his judgment by making spot purchases of assets which he believes will appreciate once prices change.

An asset is of course just a forward claim, or a bundle of such claims. It might be argued, therefore, that the method is similar to betting. However, there is one crucial difference, which is that portfolio speculation relies upon the revaluation of claims that already exist rather than upon the creation of purpose-made claims.

This has several advantages. First, there is the obvious advantage that no additional markets need to be created. The speculator enters markets that already exist for other purposes. The market-making costs incurred are marginal costs only: the fixed costs of market making are avoided altogether.

Secondly, the information upon which the entrepreneur is acting is masked by the remaining volume of trade in the market. This will be governed by other, possibly quite different, motives. Even in a purely speculative market there may be many people present, each speculating upon some different item of information. This makes it very difficult for those with whom the entrepreneur is trading to ascertain upon which event he is speculating, and to modify their own beliefs accordingly. Thus the confidentiality of the information is maintained by trading in a market where price is determined by other factors besides beliefs about the particular event concerned.

Finally, it is possible for the entrepreneur to trade in markets where forward claims are relatively secure. For example, it was noted earlier that durable goods may be regarded as an embodiment of forward claims on user services. Custody of a durable good – especially a private good – provides a very secure forward claim on a user service. If user services are liable to be revalued when the information becomes public, then an entrepreneur can take a speculative position in the spot market for durable goods. By working out which user services will become scarcer, he can determine which durables are liable to appreciate. If he concentrates his portfolio upon these, then he can anticipate a capital gain.

Of course, portfolio speculation has its disadvantages too. First it is necessary for the entrepreneur to think through the implications of the event concerned before he can speculate upon it. This means that he must have considerable background knowledge about the way the economy works. Unless he invests time and effort in analysing its implications, lack of background information, or simply faulty logic, may lead him to the wrong conclusion. Thus his information about the event may be right, but his speculative position wrong. Rather ironically, it is possible that in this situation two wrongs could make a right. If his information is misleading, and his interpretation of it incorrect, then his speculation may turn out successful. Obviously, though, it is impossible to rely upon such coincidence when undertaking speculation.

The main problem with portfolio speculation is that it relies upon other people responding to the information when it becomes public. It is other people that actually reallocate resources: the entrepreneur just sits back and takes a capital gain. If publication of the information is delayed, then coordination will be postponed and the potential reward from the information will be reduced. If information were costless to transmit there would be no problem. The entrepreneur would transmit the information right away, as soon as he had formed his speculative portfolio. Everyone would interpret the information in the same way as the entrepreneur, and his conjectures would be completely validated. Resources would be reallocated immediately.

But, in practice, information is costly to transmit, particularly if the message has to be forceful and clear. This is very important in the present instance because the entrepreneur is relying upon his conjectures about how other people will respond to the information to achieve his capital gain. If they misunderstand the message, or fail to recognize its implications, then coordination will be delayed and some of the value of the information lost. If the cost of reliable publication is very high, the only alternative is to rely upon the accidental rediscovery of the information by other people. For the entrepreneur this means uncertainty about exactly when, and by whom, implementation will be initiated. Under these circumstances portfolio speculation becomes a much less attractive option.

8.5 FORWARD INTEGRATION INTO COORDINATION

The problem of predicting other people's discovery of information, and their reaction to it, is avoided if the entrepreneur implements coordination himself. The entrepreneur still needs some background information to ensure that he does not miss any of the implications for coordination, but he does not need to make detailed predictions about other people's collective response to its announcement. Indeed, the boot is now very much on the other foot. Given his commitment to effect coordination himself, the entrepreneur desires protection against competition. He therefore wishes to inhibit the diffusion of information rather than to promote it.

The significance of the competitive threat depends upon whether there is a once-for-all opportunity for coordination, or a continuing one. Typically, a once-for-all opportunity involves stock adjustment, while a continuing opportunity involves the adjustment of flows (see Chapter 5). A once-for-all opportunity is easy to pre-empt simply by being the first in the field. The fact that the entrepreneur has a temporary lead in the implementation of the information guarantees his success.

Where a continuing opportunity is concerned, the entrepreneur must reconcile himself to the fact that eventually his successful exploitation of it will attract the attention of others. Even if they would not normally have discovered the information for themselves, they can do so now simply by studying his method of operation. There are two main strategies available to the entrepreneur for preventing the erosion of his profit. One is to use his temporary lead to invest in creating barriers to entry. This has already been analysed in detail in Section 5.8. The other is to supplement coordination with portfolio speculation. The principle underlying this strategy is as follows.

The entry of competitors will cause selling prices to be bid down and buying prices to be bid up as the entrepreneur's monopoly is destroyed. The benefits will accrue not to the competitors but to those with whom they trade. If, for example, the entrepreneur is buying user services which are in less than perfectly elastic supply, then the price of these services will be bid up. As a result the durable goods which generate them will appreciate in value. If the entrepreneur owns the durable goods whose services he uses, then, as an owner, he stands to gain from the entry of competitors. To exploit this opportunity fully, the entrepreneur will wish to own as many units of the durables as he can, and not just the units whose services he uses. In this way the entrepreneur can recover some of his losses by speculating upon the entry of his competitors.

Even if the entrepreneur does not anticipate competition, the ownership of inputs is a method of minimizing risk. It offers partial insurance not only against competition but against any other factor which could raise the price of inputs and reduce the gains from coordination. The principle applies most strongly to inputs which are in inelastic supply, since it is these inputs whose prices are most sensitive to disturbances.

It is apparent that forward integration into coordination is as much a complement to portfolio speculation as it is a substitute for it. Nevertheless, forward integration is not without its problems, the chief of which is that it requires a diversity of skills to be exercised by the entrepreneur.

The two main forms of coordination are production – in which choice of technique has to be coordinated with the state of nature – and the creation of trade, in which the plans of one individual have to be coordinated with the plans of another. Successful production requires not only privileged information about the state of nature, but detailed knowledge of how to implement the appropriate technique. Successful trade creation requires not only privileged information about transactors' willingness to trade, but also knowledge of market-making techniques. The entrepreneur must either have this know-how himself, or he must know where to hire it. But hiring know-how is difficult for the very reasons considered above. The same problems the entrepreneur encounters in selling his information to others will cause problems for an entrepreneur who wishes to buy information from others. If the entrepreneur cannot hire the know-how, he must supply it himself. It is this excessive demand upon the entrepreneur's knowledge and ability that constitutes the main disadvantage of forward integration.

8.6 FINANCING THE ENTREPRENEUR

The exploitation of information in the ways discussed above is liable to be constrained by the wealth of the entrepreneur. An exception may have to be made for licensing, but that option is usually excluded on other grounds. Betting is constrained by the entrepreneur's ability to pay up if he is proved wrong. Unless those who bet against him are irrational, they will not accept bets that could not be honoured. Portfolio speculation requires capital in order to buy up the appropriate assets. As noted above, forward integration into coordination is often an adjunct to portfolio speculation rather than an alternative to it. It also imposes its own capital requirements. Because of market-making costs, a producer may have to buy outright a producer durable whose services he would like to hire. For reasons explained in Chapter 9, to create trade efficiently, an entrepreneur may have to hold an inventory of the goods in which he trades, and an inventory of the means of payment to go with it. Furthermore, there are often economies of integrating production and market making, so that the entrepreneur is obliged to finance not only the purchase of producer durables but the creation of inventory as well.

It is tempting to suggest that if there were a perfect market in capital, then the wealth constraint would disappear and the entrepreneur could borrow as much as he wished at the prevailing rate of interest. But this is false, and only illustrates the dangers of carrying over the logic of perfect competition into the realm of the entrepreneur. Entrepreneurship has its own logic, which is equally simple.

The entrepreneur who believes that he has relevant information believes that other people have got the allocation of resources wrong. If he cannot license the information, then he exploits it by backing his own judgment against theirs. This entire policy rests on the fact that other people think differently to him. He cannot expect people who think differently to lend him money to back his judgment against theirs, when if their judgment is proved correct he will be unable to repay the loan.

It might appear that to lend any money to an entrepreneur is a denial of the logic of the situation. But this is an overstatement. Certainly, the lender perceives greater risks than does the entrepreneur. These risks would be reduced if the lender were better informed. To obtain a loan the entrepreneur must make his information available to the lender, together with any corroborative evidence that is available. The danger is that in doing so the entrepreneur builds up a competitor. Indeed, it is worse than that, for it is likely that the potential lender has far more capital than does the entrepreneur. The entrepreneur needs the lender, but once the lender has the information he no longer needs the entrepreneur. He can cut out the entrepreneur and exploit the opportunity himself.

Wherever there is an obstacle to trade, people will seek to develop market-making institutions to overcome it. That is the moral of entrepreneurship. Loans are a form of intertemporal trade, and the information asymmetry between borrower and lender is an obstacle to trade. The obstacle can be overcome if there is a market-making institution which has a reputation for integrity and confidentiality. The institution invites applications for loans and considers them in confidence using information supplied by the proposer (the entrepreneur). The institution voluntarily commits itself not to undertake on its own behalf projects of the kind for which loan applications are submitted. It also debars itself from approaching other people with proposals based upon those that have been submitted. It honours these commitments because it finds the loan business it can attract using its reputation for integrity is more valuable in the long term than any gains it could make in the short term by breaching this commitment. The type of institution which normally assumes this role is of course, the bank – in particular, the merchant bank.

This is in fact a special case of a more general phenomenon, namely the contribution that reputation makes to the creation of markets. An alternative to the bank's reputation for integrity is the entrepreneur's reputation for accuracy. If the entrepreneur has a record of successful judgment in similar projects, then the lender may be willing to accept that the entrepreneur is correct without knowing precisely what his information is. This preserves the entrepreneur's confidentiality while keeping down the lender's perception of risk. It provides privileged access to capital for the experienced and successful entrepreneur. But it does nothing to solve the strategic problems faced by the first-time entrepreneur.

Finally, it is important to consider the case in which there are several like-minded individuals, each of whom has insufficient wealth to exploit the information properly. If the individuals can establish contact with one another, then they can pool their resources. Effectively, they agree not to compete, but to collude, in backing their collective judgment against that of everyone else. The fact that each party has limited wealth affords security to the others that he will not drop out of the group and go it alone in competition with them. This concept of pooling entrepreneurial wealth is of course the basis of the joint-stock company. It is of particular importance when the implementation of coordination involves economies of scale.

8.7 REDUCING LENDER'S RISK

There are various ways in which a lender can reduce the risks involved in backing an entrepreneur. The first is to assess the entrepreneur's general knowledge and his basic business skills. If the entrepreneur is ignorant of even basic information, then it is likely that his difference of judgment emanates not from knowing more than others but from knowing less. If he does not possess basic business skills, then, whether or not his information is correct, he is unlikely to translate it successfully into profit. Other relevant attributes of the entrepreneur include his ability to reason, to communicate and to cross-check information. It has even been claimed that qualities such as imagination and foresight can be assessed by studying behaviour in the simulated situations which appear in business games. If this claim were entirely correct, then many of the problems characteristic of financing entre-preneurship could be easily solved. In practice, it is quite likely that entrepreneurs have more imagination than the people who devise the games. On the other hand, the potential reward to devising a successful method of screening for entrepreneurship is so great that continual improvement of technique is likely even if complete success cannot ever be attained.

Another method of controlling risk is to exploit the fact that the implemen-tation of any activity always generates information as a by-product. Where the activity is designed to exploit privileged information, the information thrown up by the activity can be used to validate the initial claim. The sooner the information becomes available, the sooner errors can be detected and corrective action taken. So far as the lender is concerned, full and accurate reporting of the information is crucial in minimizing the risk of loss.

A lender is not automatically entitled to information of this kind. Even if he were to contract to receive such information, he would still need to check that there was no concealment, or deliberate distortion. Nor can the lender rely upon the entrepreneur agreeing to the correction of errors in the way that he would desire. To check that the entrepreneur is not concealing informa-tion, the lender needs to be able to monitor the implementation of the activity himself. He must have unrestricted access to the premises where the activity is carried on. As new information becomes available he must have the right to consult the entrepreneur and, if things turn out badly, the right to overrule the entrepreneur in the interests of reducing the loss and protecting the repay-ment of his loan.

This suggests that the lender should participate in the project as one of its principals, with the entrepreneur assuming the role of delegate. Naturally, the arrangement must provide for the entrepreneur to be rewarded if his judg-ment is correct. This can be achieved by the entrepreneur acting as joint principal with the lender and receiving a fixed reward for his work as delegate, or by the entrepreneur acting as delegate under an incentive system which pays delegates by their results.

Finally, it is possible for the lender to use the fact that collateral for his loan may be available in the form of durable goods and inventory owned by the entrepreneur. Given the additional risks perceived by the lender it is unlikely that his valuation of the collateral will be as high as the entrepreneur's. Nevertheless, the lender can reduce his risk either by purchasing the assets himself and renting them on a long-term basis to the entrepreneur or by acquiring a first charge on the assets so that, should the project fail, the lender can obtain custody of them. If the assets can be mortgaged to the lender, then his potential loss is limited to the excess of the loan over a conservative, or pessimistic, valuation of the assets.

8.8   THE ENTREPRENEUR AS EMPLOYEE

The simplest way for the entrepreneur to act as delegate is to become an employee. The entrepreneur's principal provides him with the necessary finance. The entrepreneur continues to bear some of the risks because he is paid by results. But the risks that he cannot afford to bear are borne by somebody else.

Employment, however, is implicitly a long-term arrangement. Although an entrepreneur may become an employee in order to obtain financial backing for a project, can he continue as an entrepreneur and originate subsequent projects while remaining employed? This depends very much upon the nature of the post to which the entrepreneur is appointed.

Who would wish to hire an entrepreneur specifically to act in that capacity? The answer is another entrepreneur who believes that there is a gap in the market for entrepreneurship. An entrepreneur may believe that there is an entire field of economic activity in which there are many unexploited opportunities for coordination, and will continue to be so for some time. His judgment is that, if only the right people were directed to these areas, then very large profits could be made. He does not have the depth of information required to recognize and exploit these opportunities himself. What he does have is information which, if made available to people with more specialized knowledge, would enable them to exploit them.

Given the problems of licensing information of this sort, it is probably easier to advertise for prospective entrepreneurs to come forward. The entrepreneurs are screened for ability in the manner indicated above and offered employment under an incentive system. The incentive system may be a formal one in which each employee is constituted as a separate 'profit centre' and receives a proportion of his profits as salary. Or it may be an informal system in which the employees' decisions are monitored and those who are most successful relative to the others are promoted, while those who are least successful are demoted or fired.

The delegate entrepreneurs are provided with information by their employer. They may also be expected to pool information among themselves. Typically, each delegate is expected to put forward proposals for comments by the other delegates and, after suitable revision, for assessment by his employer. At each stage the proposal goes before a panel, or committee, in which the delegate advocates the implementation of his proposal. If he can persuade the others of its value, then it proceeds to the next stage. If he cannot persuade them, then his proposals will be vetoed. A proposal is implemented when it receives the final assent of the employer or, in the case of small proposals, the assent of those delegated to give approval.

The arrangement described above effectively makes a market in entrepreneurship itself. It is an entrepreneurial response to the problems of quality control in the market for entrepreneurs. In fact it has a dual role in improving quality and in checking it. It improves the quality of judgment by giving delegate entrepreneurs free access to the judgments and skills of other delegates as well as those of the employer. It checks quality both by assessing the delegate's personal qualities before he is hired and by probing the proposals he puts up from the many different angles adopted by his fellow-entrepreneurs. The logic of linking the improvement of quality to the checking of it is quite simple. It exploits the fact that information gained from investigating one proposal may be useful in developing some other proposal. Thus having one entrepreneur screen another entrepreneur's proposals allows information to be 'captured' and put to further use.

Another way of explaining this is to say that the employer–entrepreneur internalizes the capital market. He performs a function similar to the banks, and other 'honest brokers' in the capital market, in allocating funds between alternative risky projects. But he lends to his own delegates rather than to independent borrowers. Because he can supervise and if necessary overrule his delegates, the risk of large losses is reduced. Furthermore, because his reward is directly related to the performance of the projects, he has a strong incentive to provide his delegates with information that will not only help to avoid losses but will help to make large profits on their projects even larger.

The advantages of this system cannot really be questioned. The only question is how the employer–entrepreneur can get it to work. From whom does he get his own funds in the first place? How does he prevent his delegates from quitting once they have learnt their employer's secrets? How does he ensure that the different delegates cooperate with each other rather than compete?

The short answer is that the employer–entrepreneur can do these things only with difficulty. He must have an exceptional reputation in the capital market. He must be extremely good at organizing delegation. He can prevent delegates from learning too many of his secrets by compartmentalizing the system so that no delegate has access to all compartments at once. Thus at any one time each delegate may know a few secrets, but not sufficient to provide him with the overall perspective of the situation, which must remain unique to his employer. To retain his most able delegates, he must reward their judgment appropriately. This involves making a careful assessment of what they could expect to earn by exercising their judgment elsewhere. Finally, he must devise incentives which, while rewarding individual success, also reward cooperative contributions to the success of other people's projects, and penalize success which is achieved at their expense.

8.9   THE SIGNIFICANCE OF THE FIRM

The contractual arrangements discussed above between entrepreneurs and lenders, and between one entrepreneur and another, are typically institutionalized in the firm. The firm is a legal fiction. The firm can own resources on its own behalf, and is in turn owned by other people (or by other firms). The capital structure of the firm, together with its contracts with employees, determines the allocation of risk. In principle, the firm could issue many different kinds of contingent forward claims upon its output, and hold many different contingent forward claims upon its inputs. In practice, because of market-making costs, firms typically buy their inputs in spot markets and issue just two main kinds of forward claim. One is an unconditional claim, promising repayment of principal with interest, and the other is a residual claim on the profits of the firm. Within these two categories a number of variations occur. Some claims are transferable between lenders and some are not. Some claims are short-term, others long-term, and some perpetual. Some short-term claims may be renewable on demand, and some may not. Within the term of the loan, interest rates may be fixed or variable.

The most common forms of claim are equity, which is a transferable perpetual residual claim; debenture, which is a transferable long-term or perpetual fixed interest unconditional claim; a mortgage, which is a non-transferable long-term unconditional claim (normally at variable interest); and a bank loan, which is a non-transferable short-term unconditional claim, sometimes renewable on demand and normally at variable interest. Transferable claims are normally divided into shares so that each unit can be traded independently.

The existence of different types of claim enables lenders to specialize in insuring different types of risk. Holders of unconditional claims are exposed mainly to a risk of default, while holders of residual claims are exposed to the risk that profit will be less than the amount anticipated. By and large a more limited range of factors influence default than influence profitability, so that less judgment is involved in the valuation of unconditional claims than in the valuation of residual claims. Those who are best at assessing the factors which influence default will specialize in holding unconditional claims, while those who have the wider knowledge required to assess the factors which influence profit will specialize in holding residual claims. Similarly, lenders who believe themselves to be far-sighted will specialize in holding long-term non-transferable claims while those who are relatively near-sighted will specialize in holding short-term or transferable claims.

The holders of risk capital provide insurance to the employees. In particular, where an employee has discretion, the owners of capital will bear some of the loss incurred if the employee makes the wrong decision. The employee will bear some of the loss too, as he will be penalized by the incentive system. It does not follow, though, that the employee is necessarily seeking insurance. He may be risking as much through the incentive system as he could afford to risk if he were self-employed. In this case he chooses to be an employee only because the incentive system offers a bigger potential reward for the same degree of risk.

The existence of different types of firm whose risks are influenced by different factors facilitates both insurance and portfolio speculation. In the absence of markets in specific contingent claims, individual investors can substitute into markets for corporate equity. An individual insuring against, or speculating upon, a particular event can work out which types of corporate equity are most likely to appreciate relative to the others when the event occurs, and concentrate his portfolio upon them in the expectation of a capital gain.

Small-scale insurance and speculation is promoted by the availability of transferable shares in small denominations. It has already been established that share ownership allows like-minded entrepreneurs to cooperate in funding large-scale projects. As originally formulated, the argument does not depend upon the shares being transferable. But transferability and small denominations allow the principle to be applied more widely.

SUMMARY

This chapter has brought together a number of different strands of the preceding analysis to show that the entrepreneur who has gained privileged access to information must normally internalize its exploitation. For example, the entrepreneur may integrate forward into market making, or into production.

He may become the owner of a firm, or one of its employees. The internalization of the market for information explains why entrepreneurship is rarely observed in a completely pure form; it is usually integrated with other functions as well. If external trade in information were common, then the institutional structure of the economy would be quite different from what it is in practice. It is difficult to visualize an economy of this kind because the advantages of internalizing information are so overwhelming that almost every facet of economic organization takes this internalization for granted.

NOTES AND REFERENCES

The problems associated with external markets in information, and with the organization of the contingent contracts that would be required, are considered by Arrow (1975) and Radner (1968).

9. Speculative intermediation and the role of inventory management

9.1 FAILURE OF RECONTRACTING

In Chapter 6 recontracting was identified as one of the important characteristics of perfect competition. Recontracting means that buyers and sellers continue negotiating until their plans have been completely harmonized, and only then does trade proceed. However, negotiation takes time, and it is unreasonable to assume that the economy can remain in suspended animation following a disturbance until all trading plans have been renegotiated.

If trading continues after the disturbance and before renegotiation can be completed, then disequilibrium will ensue. Transactors on one side or other of the market will face quantity rationing; either buyers will be unable to purchase as much as they demand or sellers will be unable to dispose of all their supplies. Transactors' inability to fulfil trading plans in one market will force them to modify their plans in other markets. Indeed, because a rational individual formulates an integrated trading plan covering all markets, failure to fulfil the plan in one market is likely to have repurcussions in all other markets in which he is involved.

The consequences of continuing to trade without renegotiation are perfectly foreseeable. It is to be expected that an entrepreneurial response will be forthcoming. The obvious response is for a market-making firm to hold an inventory of the good in order to buffer fluctuations in demand and supply. An exogenous increase in demand, or a reduction in supply, is accommodated by running down the inventory. A reduction in demand or an increase in supply leads to a build-up of inventory.

While inventory is beneficial in buffering fluctuations in trade, it is not without its costs to the firm. These include the opportunity cost of the storage facilities required to keep the inventory in good condition and the additional cost incurred in moving the inventory to and from the store rather than directly from the buyer to the seller. These costs are likely to be higher the more perishable is the good and the more difficult it is to transport.

Another major component of cost is the opportunity cost of postponing demand. Inventory normally has to be kept idle because only then is it immediately available for supply. Putting a good into inventory therefore delays the use of it. This incurs a cost to buyers who are impatient to consume it and to people who could use it in the meantime to produce something of greater value. This is reflected in the interest cost of financing inventory.

As the size of inventory is increased, so the benefit conferred by the marginal unit of inventory diminishes and its cost increases; the point of equality between benefit and cost determines the optimal inventory level. Two kinds of inventory investment may now be distinguished. Unplanned inventory investment is the net investment undertaken to accommodate fluctuations in supply and demand. It is positive when supply unexpectedly exceeds demand and goods are taken into stock; it is negative when demand unexpectedly exceeds supply and the stock has to be run down. Planned inventory investment is the net investment undertaken to restore inventory to its target level. Planned investment is positive when inventory is too low and has to be augmented, and is negative when it is too high and has to be run down.

The fundamental law of inventory behaviour is that planned investment is undertaken in response to the unplanned investment that has occurred since the last planned investment decision was undertaken. Each time planned investment is undertaken, it is with the object of returning the inventory to its target level. If there are lags in implementing investment plans, then further unplanned investment may occur before the investment is effected, in which case the target level may not actually be realized. If there are no lags, then inventory will return to its target level and remain there until the next disturbance occurs.

Most models of inventory systems present a partial analysis of the wholesale and retail distribution of goods produced under constant costs. They emphasize the way that economies of lot size influence the frequency of inventory adjustment and the target level of inventory. Such models are inappropriate to a general analysis of the role of inventories in market making as a whole. The reason is that they fail to stress the interplay between inventory control and pricing policy.

Consider a market-making firm whose inventory has fallen below target level as a result of an unexpected shortfall in supply. It believes that, apart from price effects, fluctuations in demand and supply are uncorrelated and serially independent. It therefore regards the disturbance in supply as purely random, and so its expectations of demand and supply for the next period remain unchanged. Its planned inventory investment, however, now constitutes a component of the next period's demand. Its expectation of total demand has therefore increased relative to its expectation of supply. The only mechanism by which inventory plans can be realized is the attainment of a new equilibrium at a higher price. The market maker must therefore increase his buying price and his selling price. Higher prices increase expected supply and reduce expected demand, creating a gap which can be filled by inventory investment. This case illustrates the general proposition that, for a market-making firm, price adjustment is the instrument of inventory adjustment.

9.2 SPOT PRICE STABILITY

The previous section considered how the failure to recontract influences the provision of market-making services. This section considers the related issue of how the prohibitive cost of making some forward markets influences the quality of service in the corresponding spot markets.

It was argued above that recontracting was undesirable because it delayed the completion of transactions. The only way to avoid delay would be to speed up negotiations to the point where communication costs become prohibitive. It is apparent, therefore, that the time dimension in recontracting is crucial.

There is one situation in which there is ample time for renegotiation, and this is when transactors are trading forward claims. Since transactors are planning their trades well ahead, there is time to haggle over the price. Forward claims are useful to households because they are a method of ensuring future supplies of consumption and future demand for labour services. They benefit firms, too, for, given the lags in the production system, they enable current decisions to be made so that the future outputs of the different firms are compatible with each other and with household requirements. They are particularly useful in intermediate product markets, where they help to reconcile the output plans of the suppliers with the input plans of the users.

For reasons already discussed, forward markets are difficult to operate. Where the user services of durable goods are concerned, forward claims can be established by buying up durable goods in the spot market. Where long-term forward claims on other goods and services are concerned, the costs of making markets in individual claims mean that individuals are often obliged to follow a two-stage procedure. The procedure involves purchasing an asset in a spot market and reselling it later in exchange for a spot acquisition of the good they require. To reduce the administrative cost of resale, it is desirable to hold an asset in which there is a ready secondhand market. To reduce uncertainty about the future spot rate of exchange between the asset and the good, it is desirable to hold an asset whose value is relatively stable in terms of a representative good. The most suitable type of claim is usually corporate debenture: that is, long-term unconditional transferable corporate debt.

Neither of these strategies, however, is satisfactory in establishing short-term forward claims on newly produced or perishable goods. In the absence of any substitute for such claims, transactors would experience considerable uncertainty when planning ahead.

Where intermediate products are concerned, the problem can often be solved by internalization. The buying firm and the selling firm can be merged into a single firm and the problem of enforcing forward contracts largely eliminated. But this strategy is not so readily applicable to households wishing to procure supplies of final products from other households or firms. Nor does it apply to households selling factor services to other households or to firms. The household is not normally a large enough economic unit to warrant acquiring a firm outright just to provide employment for its factors, and certainly not just to secure supplies of one of its consumption goods. Economies of scale in production usually require firms to combine the factor services of several households and to sell their final products to a great many more.

The potential failure of markets in short-term claims for factor services and final products has generated an entrepreneurial response which is reflected in the way that spot markets are organized. Market-making firms have evolved a system of quoting spot prices which are fairly stable in the short term. This provides price certainty for transactors and so facilitates efficient forward planning.

However, the commitment to price stability reduces the market-maker's ability to adjust supply to demand through price adjustment. It should be apparent that it also nullifies the main instrument of inventory adjustment. The greater the price stability, the lower is the frequency of price adjustment and the more difficult it is to maintain inventory close to its target level. The market maker can respond in one of two ways. He can either increase the target inventory to accommodate wider fluctuations in inventory level or he can increase the risk that he will go out of stock.

9.3 PRIORITY UNDER RATIONING

Naturally, buyers would rather that a market maker did not go out of stock. If there is no other convenient source of supply, then their plans are frustrated and their welfare reduced. Even if other sources are available, they have wasted resources making contact with the particular market maker involved.

If the market maker is out of stock, then buyers will prefer the delay in service to be kept to a minimum. However, given the constraint on price revision, the overall excess demand cannot be controlled. Thus servicing one buyer quickly means more delay in servicing someone else.

Some demand will be transitory and if not fulfilled will disappear again. But permanent unfilled demands will cumulate, and the market maker must determine in what order he will fill these demands when supplies become available. The simplest strategy is for the market maker to allow the customers to decide for themselves by asking them to call back. If stock is available, then they will be served; otherwise, they must keep returning until they are successful. Those who call back most frequently stand the best chance of being served first.

This strategy means that the market maker must deal with many requests that he cannot fulfil, but it avoids the administrative cost of recording customers' wants. If he decides to record wants, however, he is in a position to establish priorities between customers. The simplest system of priorities is that the first to order is the first to be served. But this simple system is not necessarily the most efficient.

It must be recognized that some buyers' demands may be more urgent than others. These buyers will attach a high value to priority service. Where there are two distinct categories of demand, one urgent and the other not, it is to the market maker's advantage to distinguish between them if he can. The idea is to create two categories of customer: the priority customer and the stand-by customer. Whenever there is rationing, priority customers are served before stand-by customers. Priority will be bought by those whose demands are most urgent and who therefore value the risk of delay most highly. The proceeds of the sale of priority enhance the market maker's profits.

Priorities may be allocated either before or after rationing has occurred. To allocate priority in advance is equivalent to creating a forward market in quality of service. Given the market-making costs involved, it might seem preferable to allocate priority on the spot once rationing has occurred. It is possible, though, that many people may take offence at this improvisation of rationing arrangements. It may appear that the market maker is reneging on his original undertaking to supply at a fixed price. Indeed, he is increasing his price at the very time that his overall quality of service has deteriorated. As a result, buyers may withdraw their demand in protest. Although this may not affect the market maker in the short run, because by assumption there is excess demand, it may affect him quite severely in the long run, when buyers as a whole seek out an alternative market maker instead.

It appears, therefore, that if priorities are to be allocated, they should be allocated at the outset. To reduce the cost of creating the forward market, it is possible to use implicit contracts, which are informal understandings backed by social sanctions, rather than formal contracts backed by the law. In a typical case, the market maker announces that customers who trade with him regularly – and perhaps exclusively – can acquire priority over occasional customers. Those who demand priority are then obliged to trade regularly with the market maker. Regular trade is less costly for the market maker to administer than is occasional trade, because costs of contact making are incurred only once irrespective of how often trade is repeated. This saving is passed on to the regular customer not by discounting the price but by offering priority of service instead. It does not follow, of course, that all regular customers want priority of service, or that those who want priority make the most suitable regular customers. This is the price that has to be paid when priority is bartered for rather than sold outright.

9.4   RESPECT FOR SOCIAL CONVENTION

Trade is not a purely economic activity but a social one as well. Trade involves communication between two people: they must make contact, exchange information about product specification and negotiate a price.

Some people are more pleasant to communicate with than others. Communication can increase personal welfare as well as trade itself. A chat with a cheery pub landlord may be some compensation for a poor pint of beer. Because of this, the provision of personal service, and the selection of suitable people to provide it, is often a strong element in non-price competition between market makers.

Because trade is a social activity, social conventions restrict the way that it is conducted. Social convention is the aspect of a culture that relates to the behaviour of people towards each other. Social convention tends to be self-policing, in the sense that each individual feels personally responsible for punishing deviations from convention. If one of the parties conducts trade in a manner that flouts convention, then the other parties will punish him by breaking off trading relations with him. The pleasure that they obtain from punishing the offence outweighs any harm that they may do to themselves in the process.

Social convention affects the way in which trade is set up, the terms of the contract, and even the type of goods in which trade is permissible. In setting up a trade, convention may demand that the parties exchange small talk and gossip, and perhaps that one of them should offer hospitality to the other, which then has to be reciprocated. Convention lends structure to negotiations by indicating who should make the first offer, how many rounds of negotiations are allowed and what sort of threats it is acceptable to make in order to extract concessions from the other party. Convention may also restrict the terms of the contract. It may dictate that certain goods and services must be offered free, as it would be demeaning for the seller to charge for them, and for the buyer to pay for them. It may outlaw the offering of, or the soliciting of, certain services, whether or not payment is made for them.

Respect for convention is vital to the success of market making. The market maker is particularly vulnerable to social sanctions as his activities tend to be very public, and therefore easily scrutinized, and he earns his living exclusively by intermediating trade. It is also generally recognized that market makers are opportunists, and that there is not always a very close relation between the market maker's margin and the cost of setting up a trade. Competition from new entrants may establish a 'fair' margin in the long run but there is no guarantee of this in the short run.

There is no doubt that many cultures are opposed to opportunism, which is seen as making a profit out of the potential misfortunes of others. Opportunists are tolerated because of the services they provide. But opportunists who overstep the mark may have to be punished. Sometimes the punishment is confined to individual market makers: transactors simply switch to competing market makers instead. At other times market makers as a group are punished by the introduction of restrictive legislation, or special taxes, to outlaw, or to compensate for, alleged abuses of market power.

The need for the market maker to conform may be a factor motivating the provision of some of the market-making services discussed above. It must be recognized that people are by no means unanimous in supporting the use of price as an allocator of resources. They may concede that price adjustment is necessary in the long run to prevent serious bottlenecks and shortages, but may be hostile towards short-run price adjustments. These may be regarded as evidence of opportunism by the market-maker. If such attitudes are common, the prudent market maker may forgo short-run price adjustment in order to retain the goodwill of his customers.

Another sensitive area is the use of price to allocate priorities when goods are out of stock. It has already been shown how the market maker can to some extent disguise the use of price by giving priority to regular customers over occasional ones. The disguise works because of the similarity to the principle of looking after one's friends (that is, regular customers) first. While the use of price may be socially unacceptable, there is normally no objection to giving priority to one's friends.

In some cases, however, social convention may be very strict indeed. For example, 'queue-jumping' of any kind may simply not be tolerated, so that the prudent market maker has no option but to deal with all orders in strict rotation. Alternatively, the market maker may be expected to discriminate between orders on the basis of need. In the context of rationing, need is related to the urgency of demand. But the principle of need usually prohibits the use of price to reveal the urgency of demand. The market maker cannot sell priorities but must confer them freely, using his own assessment of the situation. He may have to do this, even though he knows his own assessments are quite arbitrary, merely to conform with convention.

9.5 CAPITAL REQUIREMENTS AS A BARRIER TO ENTRY INTO MARKET MAKING

It has been shown that, because of the difficulty of recontracting, market makers are obliged to hold inventory in order to intermediate transactions. The inventory enables the market maker to offer 'on demand' service to his customers. The market maker needs in fact to hold two inventories, one of the product and the other of payment. The inventory of the product is necessary to facilitate immediate supply of unforeseen orders. The inventory of the payment is necessary to take up unforeseen offers of supply.

The need for inventories increases the amount of risk capital required by the entrepreneur and thereby makes it more likely that market-making entrepreneurship will be constrained by personal wealth. Although the constraint can be relaxed by borrowing, the strategic problems involved in finding backers, described above, mean that capital requirements may be a substantial barrier to entry into market making when inventory requirements are large.

This situation may be contrasted with the analysis of intermediation in Chapter 3, which was based upon the implicit assumption that recontracting was possible. The intermediator C contracted separately with his partners A and B, but his contract with A was not confirmed until his negotiations with B were complete, and vice versa. Consequently, there was no risk that he would buy from A and then be unable to resell to B. Conversely, there was no risk that he would agree to sell to B and then be unable to obtain supplies from A. If recontracting had been ruled out, then the intermediator would have required an initial endowment of each commodity large enough to cover his proposed sale to each party. He would be exposed to the risk that, if one of the negotiations broke down, then his own consumption would become extremely unbalanced. He would be forced to consume the goods that he had bought from one party in the expectation of resale to the other, and would have to forgo consumption of the goods he expected to obtain from that party in exchange. Thus his initial endowments would constrain his ability to trade, while the risk that one of the transactions would break down and the other go through would reduce the incentive to intermediate in the first place.

9.6 SPECULATIVE BEHAVIOUR OF THE MARKET MAKER

The need for inventory emphasizes that market making is a speculative activity. The market maker's judgment is that there is a gap in the range of market-making services currently on offer to transactors. As a result, poten-

tial trades are not taking place. By providing additional market-making services, the obstacles to trade can be overcome, and a profit stream generated
from intermediating a series of trades.

Speculation occurs when resources are committed to backing one's judgment against that of others. If market-making costs were incurred as and
when intermediation is effected, then intermediation would not be speculative, but, in practice, many market-making costs are set-up costs which have
to be incurred before any trade can take place. This is certainly true of the
costs of market making identified in Chapter 6. Inventory costs are the most
obvious example of set-up costs, however. Quality of service depends upon
inventory being available before trade begins. The market maker therefore
has to back his judgment from the outset by investing in inventory. If his
judgment is incorrect and there is no market for the good, then his inventory
will almost certainly be worth less than he paid for it, and a capital loss will
be sustained.

Speculation is concerned not only with whether to invest in inventory of a
certain type, but also with how much to invest, and in particular with how
much to hold at any one time. If the market maker expects demand to move
towards a steady state, then the long-term level of inventory required is
determined by the quality of service he intends to offer. The larger the
inventory relative to the variability of demand, the lower the probability of
stock-out. Although transactors may not know precisely what the market
maker's level of inventory is, they should be able to assess from experience of
repeat-trading (or from his reputation) what the probability of stock-out is.

The market maker faces not only a demand for the product but also a
demand for each service that goes with it. Implicitly, there is a price for the
product itself and another price for availability from stock. If he can estimate
the intensities of these demands, then, given his cost of inventory and the
relation between inventory level and stock-out probability, the market maker
can deduce the profit-maximizing stock-out probability and the associated
long-term inventory level. This inventory level then informs his initial speculative investment in stock.

The market maker may anticipate that, in addition, there will be systematic
variations about the trend growth of demand, or about its subsequent steady-
state level. He can exploit systematic variations by varying the amount of
inventory held over from one period to the next. If, for example, he believes
that supplies will be very scarce in the following period, then current planned
inventory investment will be increased and at the same time planned inventory investment for the following period reduced. The market maker thereby
profits by buying cheap now in order to sell dear later. If the market maker's
expectations are correct, then price fluctuations will be smoothed out as a
result. On the other hand, if his expectations are incorrect, or if his own plans

are swamped by those of ill-informed imitators who drive the current price too high, then the price fluctuations will have been amplified instead.

It is interesting to note that the market maker's ability to exploit systematic variations in demand or supply may be constrained by his commitment to short-term price stability. As a market maker, one of his functions is to quote prices, and to retain goodwill he may have to adhere to these prices for some time. Since price adjustment is the main mechanism of inventory control, he cannot take up speculative positions with respect to price fluctuations within this period. Thus if, for example, prices can only be adjusted annually, then systematic fluctuations with a frequency of less than a year cannot be exploited for speculative purposes.

If there are systematic variations in the market, then the market maker may not be the only one to recognize them. Certainly, the market maker is in the best position to observe them, which is a point that will be developed later on. If he were to exploit them intelligently through short-term speculation, then it is possible that they would go unnoticed by other transactors. But if he is constrained in his speculative activity, then other transactors may recognize the symptoms of disequilibrium and decide to speculate instead. The symptom of disequilibrium is that the market maker goes out of stock. When this occurs, a speculator could sell his inventory at above the market maker's quoted price to those who are impatient for supplies. When there are systematic variations, the speculators can predict when the market maker is most likely to go out of stock. Shortly before this time they purchase stock, causing the market maker to go out of stock earlier than he would, as inventory is transferred from the market maker into speculative hands.

It is obvious that this situation is intolerable to the market maker. He can attempt to reduce the probability of stock-out by increasing his inventory to a level which is safe given any systematic variation of demand. This means that, if speculators do manage to buy up sufficient inventory to put him out of stock, their supplies will be so large compared to the frustrated demand that no premium can be charged. However, the cost of maintaining this level of inventory is likely to be very high. Under the circumstances, the market maker may be obliged to adjust price more frequently than convention suggests, notwithstanding the loss of goodwill involved.

It might be asked why the speculators themselves are not outlawed for flouting social convention. The short answer is that they are not established market makers, with a reputation to lose, but casual dealers exploiting an occasional opportunity. In fact, their activities are constrained by the fact that their market-making techniques are very primitive, as befits the small-scale casual nature of their trade. They are the fly-by-night operators, the wide boys, of the entrepreneurial world. They operate under the price umbrella of the established market maker. They can be tolerated by him so long as they do not disturb too greatly the fix-price equilibrium that he maintains by inventory adjustment. But if their activities become too great a nuisance, then the established market maker will have to change his operations in order to drive them out of the market.

SUMMARY

This chapter has shown that when recontracting is difficult, the market maker must respond by holding inventory. In calculating his target inventory the market maker must take account of constraints imposed by commitments on price stability made to customers and suppliers. He must also consider the disruption to customers' plans which results when he is out of stock, and the consequent loss of goodwill that he incurs. Loss of goodwill could in principle be reduced by operating an efficient system of priorities, though in practice an efficient system may actually lose more goodwill if it flouts social convention.

The constraints imposed by commitments to price stability and to inefficient priorities both imply that the target level of inventory must be increased. This inventory has to be financed somehow. Because of the judgmental nature of market making, financial backers may not value the inventory as highly as the market maker, and so the inventory may be regarded as poor security for a loan. It follows that, for market makers with little personal wealth, the financing of inventory may constitute a serious barrier to entry.

NOTES AND REFERENCES

On the role of inventories in market-making see Kotler (1976). The pure theory of speculative inventory is discussed in Goss and Yamey (1976). The relation between price adjustment and inventory adjustment is considered more formally in Casson (1981, ch. 11), while the significance of shortages is examined in detail by Kornai (1980). The role of priorities in queueing systems is considered by Jaiswal (1968).

10. Organizing the supply of market-making services

10.1 THE PACKAGING OF MARKET-MAKING SERVICES

In Chapter 6, six main market-making activities were distinguished. To these can now be added two more, which were identified in Chapter 9: inventory holding (to provide on-demand service) and the provision of personal attention, as demanded by social convention. This chapter considers why a single market maker would wish to undertake all of these activities himself. Why do different market makers not operate in the same market, each specializing in one of these particular activities? Why does a single market maker emerge who packages all of the services together?

The simplest answer is that a single entrepreneur has the initial idea of creating the market, and to protect his secret idea he will not want to involve other firms in any of the related activities. However, this only explains why one firm will package together all the activities at the outset. As the market expands, and competitors enter, the advantages of specialization may begin to reveal themselves. Some entrants may specialize in one market-making activity and others in another, allowing buyers to 'customize' their procurement of market-making services.

The obvious explanation of why market-making services are packaged on a recurrent basis is that packaging substantially reduces overall transaction costs. If the separate services were not packaged together, then each buyer and seller would have to negotiate individually for each of the specialist services. Without a packager, each buyer and seller would need to be paired up with a supplier of each of the services. With a packager, each buyer and seller is paired only with the packager, and the suppliers of the services are paired only with the packager too. A major component of market-making cost is associated simply with the pairing of transactors, and is independent of the number and size of the transactions which each pair subsequently effects. Thus, by reducing the number of different pairings, the packaging of market-making services offers potentially large savings in market-making costs.

10.2 THE PRICING OF MARKET-MAKING SERVICES

It is important to consider how the package of market-making services is priced. Experience suggests that, in many markets, buyers pay only for market-making services if the transaction is successful. The explanation lies in yet another service that the market maker supplies to his transactors. This is insurance against the risk that the transaction will break down. Essentially, the market maker insures the transactor against the risk that the payments he would normally have made for market-making services will be incurred in vain. The market maker is therefore supplying insurance against market entry risk: the risk that the transactor faces when he commits resources to entering a market in pursuit of a trade.

The natural explanation is that the market maker is relatively optimistic about the opportunities for creating trade, which is why he has taken a speculative position in entering, or even creating, the market. The customer has no particular reason to be optimistic, and so it is sensible for the market maker to bet with the customer about whether he will eventually make a trade. The market maker encourages the customer to enter the market and if he is correct then the customer will trade at a price which provides the intermediator with a margin that covers not only his market-making expenses but also a payment for winning the bet.

To increase his chances of winning the bet, the market maker needs to maximize his opportunity to persuade the customer to change his attitude to the product. This persuasion can be effected at the contact-making stage through the projection of an appropriate image of the market maker, at the product specification stage, by communicating an alluring description of the product's attributes, and at the negotiation stage by, for example, flattering the customer's ego in making him think that he has negotiated a bargain for himself.

This argument suggests that there may be a fairly close association between the provision of free market-making services and the potential for impulse buying of the product. The level of provision will of course reflect other factors too – in particular, the severity of the obstacles to trade that have to be overcome. The hypothesis is that the degree of overprovision of services relative to the obstacles involved will reflect the market maker's perceptions of buyer attitudes. The more buyers are believed to be vulnerable to persuasion, the greater will be the inducements offered to them to enter the market.

10.3 INTERNALIZATION OF MARKET-MAKING ACTIVITIES

Nine market-making activities have now been identified: they are shown in the left-hand column of Table 10.1. This section considers to what extent the markets in these services should be internalized by the market maker. The analysis focuses upon the market for a differentiated product which has to be distributed to buyers in different locations. The intermediator purchases the product from a producer who provides the technological know-how required for its production.

Table 10.1   Market-making activities and their most suitable contractual arrangements

Market-making activity	Appropriate contractual arrangement
Contact making	Delegate to retailer
Product specification	Integrate with producer
Negotiation	Internalize in hands of employees
Exchange of custody	Delegate to transport firms
Monitoring	Integrate quality control with producer
	Delegate monitoring of distribution to retailer
Enforcement	Delegate to legal firms and the state
Inventory holding	Delegate front-end inventory to retailer
	Integrate back-up inventory with producer
Personal attention	Delegate to retailer
Insurance of transactor	Delegate (where possible) to financial backers

It is assumed that the market maker has established a firm and is confident of his arrangements for delegating tasks to his own employees. The issue is whether the market-making services should be provided by his own firm or by other firms. The advantage of employing other firms is that they may have internal access to skills which his firm does not possess. The disadvantage is that there are costs of establishing arm's-length contracts with the other firms. Internalization is efficient only if the cost of establishing contracts exceeds the gains from specialization between firms.

There are some activities in which the case for internalization is practically overwhelming, and there is little point in analysing these in detail. It is extremely dangerous, for example, to delegate negotiation to someone else unless they can be maintained under the same close supervision as can an employee. The same applies to product specification and to monitoring.

There are other cases in which internalization is almost certainly undesirable. For example, the transport services required for exchange of custody are provided by the utilization of vehicles in which there are often major economies of scale. The existence of economies of scale creates a strong incentive to hire transport services from specialist firms.

The only case in which internalization of transport may be advantageous is if there is a large volume of regular trade with some particular customer (or neighbouring group of customers). Under these conditions it may be possible for the market maker to keep a large vehicle fully employed carrying only his own traffic. However, where only a small fleet of vehicles is involved, there remains the problem of coping with unforeseen breakdowns and so on and, where very small fleets are concerned, there may even be problems in replacing vehicles during their regular maintenance. It appears, therefore, that unless there is a large volume of regular trade between the intermediator and a geographically concentrated group of customers, internalization of transport services is unlikely to be efficient.

Another market that it is difficult to internalize is the market for enforcement services, that is the market for lawyers, bailiffs, policemen and so on. Services of this kind are highly specialized and it would need a large volume of trade to warrant full-time employment of specialist personnel. Indeed, unless the market maker is a specialist himself, he is unlikely to know whether a specialist is really necessary, and if so what kind of specialist is required and for how long he will need to be employed. Under these conditions it makes sense for the intermediator not to recruit the specialist as an employee, but to buy the specialist services from a market maker in these services, who will give a price quotation and guarantee the quality of the services supplied. In other words, it is efficient not to internalize the market, but to buy enforcement services at arm's length from specialist suppliers.

10.4   INTEGRATION OF PRODUCTION AND MARKET MAKING

So far it has been implicitly assumed that the producer and the market maker are two distinct people, connected by arm's-length trade in which the producer sells the product to the market maker, who assumes responsibility for its distribution to the final users. The rationale for this functional specialization is that the producer has technical skill but lacks a knowledge of the market, while the market maker has a knowledge of the market, but lacks the producer's technical skill.

In principle the arm's-length trade effects a separation of responsibilities, whereby the producer bears the risks associated with production and the market maker bears the risks associated with uncertain market prospects. But in practice the separation of risks is not quite so simple as this. There are at least two cases in which problems encountered in production may spill over to cause problems for the market maker. And there is at least one case in which the technical ignorance of the market maker may pose problems for the producer.

Each spillover is concerned with a particular market-making activity. To begin with, consider product specification. As noted earlier, the specification usually emphasizes the product's functions: claims are made for what the product will do. In the case of multi-purpose goods, considerable emphasis may be laid upon versatility in use. The market maker will wish to retain responsibility for communicating the product specification to the customers: it is after all a vital element in the contract of sale between them. But the specification reflects the design of the product. In many cases, in order to know what the product can do it is necessary to know how it was designed and made. This knowledge resides with the producer rather than the market maker. If the market maker's ignorance leads him to make exaggerated claims for the product, then the product may acquire an unjustifiably bad reputation. If, on the other hand, the market maker makes too modest claims for the product, then potential demand may remain unfilled. In either case, not only the market maker's sales will suffer, but the producer's too.

To minimize these risks, the producer needs to vet the specification that is communicated to the customers. He still needs the market maker's expertise to formulate a message that the customers can easily understand, and to ensure that it is broadcast to the right people, but he needs more control over the market maker than he can achieve simply through arm's-length sale of the product.

Another major spillover arises with quality control. Here the boot is on the other foot: the producer makes mistakes but it is the market maker that may suffer. When the customer buys from the market maker he demands an assurance of quality. Quality means that the product performs in accordance with specification, that is it is fit for the purposes intended. There are three aspects to the assurance: first, that the probability of being supplied with a defective item is small; secondly, that, should a defective item be supplied, a replacement will be readily available; and finally that compensation for damage caused by use of the faulty item will be forthcoming. The question of compensation will normally be covered in the contract of sale. Given the market maker's liability, the only questions concern his ability to meet his obligations and this depends mainly upon his wealth. His ability to supply replacements will be determined by his inventory policy, which is discussed later in this section.

So far as the first aspect of the assurance is concerned – the improbability of a defective item being supplied in the first place – the market maker is essentially underwriting the quality that has been attained by the producer. The market maker cannot afford to underwrite quality unless he is confident of it himself. Thus, wherever possible, he will wish to screen the supplies of the product for himself.

It must be recognized, however, that for many goods it is easier to check quality during production than it is once production is complete. Information about quality is a joint product of the production process itself. Monitoring the act of production itself often provides information which can only be obtained at the end by taking the product apart again. Efficient quality control implies that information from monitoring is used in the evaluation of quality. Since the producer almost certainly has information of this kind, it is important that this information is not wasted.

This analysis suggests that it is the producer, rather than the market maker, who should undertake quality control. But this depends upon the market maker having confidence in the producer. If he does not, he will need to check the producer's own quality controls, resulting in a wasteful duplication of effort. The alternative is for the market maker to monitor production. This implies that he has access to the producer's premises, and that he has sufficient technical know-how to understand what he should be looking for. This strategy is likely to work only for production by a widely-known technique. The fact that it is widely known means that the producer has no technical secrets to protect, and so is willing to admit an external monitor to his premises. It also means that a monitor employed by the market maker can readily acquire the skills needed for the job.

This suggests that, whenever production involves trade secrets, the producer will wish to assume quality control, and take over one of the market maker's functions for himself. Alternatively, the market maker will need to buy the trade secret from the producer in order to gain permission to monitor; in practice this means that the market maker will buy out the producer altogether.

A third area of spillover is concerned with inventory policy. One of the market maker's responsibilities is to provide quality of service by maintaining an adequate inventory. Once again this is a key function that he will be reluctant to contract out. The inventory level required for a given quality of service depends not only upon the variability of customers' demands, but also upon the producer's policy of supply. If supply is erratic owing to frequent breakdowns in production, for example, then the market maker is obliged to hold a larger inventory. If the producer reduces transport costs by bulking his deliveries to the market maker, then deliveries to the market maker become less frequent and once again the market maker's inventory requirement is increased. Finally, if the producer takes a long time to respond to orders placed by the market maker, then the market maker is exposed to a greater risk of stock-out from any given fluctuation in demand. Rather ironically, every time the producer's quality of service to the market maker deteriorates, the market maker's target inventory level has to be increased to maintain the safety margin in servicing demand, and so he has to place additional orders with the producer. Thus, in the short run at least, poorer service by the producer leads to higher sales to the market maker.

It is apparent that a straightforward arm's-length sale from producer to market maker does not encourage efficient distribution of the product. It discourages the producer from making his own inventory readily available to the market maker should the market maker's inventory be suddenly depleted. It also discourages the producer from rescheduling production should his own inventory, as well as that of the market maker, become depleted. He has some incentive to reschedule production, but not as great an incentive as the market maker would prefer.

In principle the problems of harmonizing production and inventory policies could be overcome using a spectrum of forward claims with different prices for claims of different maturities. In practice, these forward markets are best internalized by bringing production and inventory holding under common control. It has already been shown that problems of inventory control are most acute for products whose demand is highly variable, particularly those where the speculative element is strong. The problems of harmonizing inventory with production are particularly great when there are long lags in the production process, and where there are significant economies in bulk distribution. Thus there are strong grounds for internalizing product supply when the product has a variable or speculative demand, a long production lag and economies of bulk distribution.

10.5   THE SPATIAL DIMENSION OF DISTRIBUTION AND THE ROLE OF THE RETAILER

One of the major weaknesses of conventional economic theory is the scant attention it pays to the spatial dimension of economic activity. Indeed, the theory of entrepreneurship discussed above could be condemned on rather similar grounds. Some attention has been paid to the influence of transport costs on the economics of bulk trading, and consideration has been given to the spatial distribution of information sources, but that is about all. However, the spatial dimension is of crucial importance when analysing the internalization of contact making and inventory holding.

In a spaceless economy where all transactors were concentrated at a single point, the market maker would almost certainly wish to internalize contact making and inventory holding. Like most other market-making activities, they are so crucial to his enterprise that he would be reluctant to delegate them to anyone other than an employee. But many products have a world-wide market. The world is a big place, and it is asking a lot of a customer to make contact with a single worldwide sales point and to accept distribution from a single inventory store.

So far as the customer is concerned, quality of service is inversely related to distance. Where contact making is concerned, it is partly geographical distance and partly psychic distance that counts. Geographical distance matters because charges for the use of communication channels (post, telecommunications and so on) normally increase with distance, though not in direct proportion to it. This system of charges by the communications utilities makes economic sense, for in a communication network a long-distance communication not only uses up more energy but typically travels through more different nodes along its route and so incurs higher congestion costs.

Psychic distance is a measure of the difference between the language and culture of the place from which the message originates and the language and culture of the place in which the message is received. The greater the psychic distance, the greater the probability that the message will be misunderstood or, alternatively, the greater the cost of ensuring that it will be understood properly.

As noted earlier, market makers try to make contact as easy as possible for the customer, but the further away the customer is, the more difficult this becomes. Not only does the cost of contact making rise but the market maker's ability to subsidize the customer is reduced. For example, the market maker may be able to arrange with his local telephone company to offer toll-free dialling (that is, freephone facilities) but it may be difficult to extend this privilege to calls originating in other telephone companies' areas (for example, international calls). As a result the distant customer, who has to pay the higher charge, also gets a smaller subsidy.

It is not only ease of contact that deteriorates with distance – speed of supply does too. Assuming that inventory management is perfectly efficient, the speed of supply depends upon two things: how quickly the customer's order gets to the market maker, and how long it takes to transport the good to the customer. Both factors are related to distance, but since goods usually are slower to reach their destinations than messages, it is the time required for the delivery of the good that is crucial. Any movement of goods requires time for loading and unloading but, apart from that, the time required is likely to be proportional to the distance, and in this case to geographical distance alone.

To improve ease of contact and speed of service, it is desirable to decen-tralize contact making and inventory holding. This raises the question of precisely where to decentralize to. The basic principles are not difficult to establish. It is desirable to locate sales offices for contact making at key nodes on the world communications network, so that all major geographical concentrations of customers are close to one of the offices, where closeness is understood in terms of the cost structure of the network itself. It is desirable to locate inventory stores at key nodes on the world transport network so that as many customers as possible can be served quickly and cheaply from one of the stores. It is desirable that each sales office has easy communication with at least one of the stores. If each office can get in touch with several stores, then this will contribute to the flexibility of the system.

This discussion has implicitly assumed that the market maker will deliver the product to the customer, but in many cases it is more convenient for the customer to collect it. This imposes a further restriction on the location of the store. Because the customer is incurring a fixed cost of journeying to the store, he may wish to combine his trip with a visit to other stores. The other stores that he is most likely to be visiting are, first, stores of perishable essentials (for example, food) and other items which have to be bought regularly, and, secondly, stores of complementary goods. The goods may be technical complements, in the sense that they are required in order to utilize the product (or the product is required to utilize the complements) or they may be taste complements, in the sense that people who like the product usually like the other goods as well.

Even if the customer does not collect, he may wish to inspect the good before he sees it. Even if the good is delivered to the customer after purchase, it may still be more convenient for the customer to visit the good for inspection. In this case an inventory of inspection items must be made available at the point of contact, although the main store may be elsewhere. A sales office with inspection inventory is known as a showroom, and if the main store is adjacent to the showroom the premises as a whole are known as a shop.

The optimal location of a showroom or shop involves a complex of factors. Some of the factors have been outlined above, but a full treatment of them lies well beyond the scope of this book. An enormous diversity of knowledge is required to locate a shop efficiently. It is necessary to assess demand for a product, and relate it to the geographical residence of the probable customers. It is necessary to assess the habits of these customers – where they travel to and when – these habits being in turn a reflection of their underlying tastes. Having ascertained where they are likely to be at various times, it is possible to make contact with them in a reasonably selective manner. It is possible to locate inspection stock at a place which can be visited with only a small adjustment to their usual itinerary, and to keep opening hours which fit their daily schedule. To encourage them to visit, it may be necessary to display complementary items in the showroom, to offer staple items at discount prices, or even to provide callers with a free gift. Finally, the main store must be located so as to give easy access to the transport network which serves their place of residence.

It is apparent that the location of a retail outlet demands extensive local knowledge. It is unreasonable for a market maker in a worldwide market to imagine he has the geographical diversity of knowledge to site all his outlets efficiently. The simplest way of obtaining the benefits of this knowledge is to delegate the retail function.

But to whom should the function be delegated? Even at the local level, the diversity of knowledge required to appraise alternative sites means that opinions will differ about the best location. Who is the market maker to believe? The simplest solution is to determine who is willing to back their own judgment. The market maker should find a retail entrepreneur who is willing to put up his own finance and thereby insure the market maker against some of the costs of a mistaken location decision. Where several retail entrepreneurs are forthcoming, the most optimistic will select himself for the job by offering the most favourable terms. The actual site for the shop will therefore be chosen by the most optimistic retail entrepreneur.

The delegation of the retail function involves the delegation of contact making and of inventory holding. However, it is unnecessary, and indeed probably undesirable, to delegate all inventory holding to the retailer. The retailer will normally wish to hold his own inventory in order to provide prompt service, but there is no reason why all inventory should be allocated among the retailers. Indeed, if the retailers purchase inventory outright from the market maker, then they will be unwilling to accept inventory which they have not ordered. The market maker will therefore need to hold inventory of his own and, for reasons already discussed, it is normally efficient to integrate this inventory with that of the producer. Ideally, therefore, a two-stage inventory will be held: the front-end inventory will be held by the retailer and the back-up inventory by the market-maker and the producer. The front-end inventories will be topped up on demand using the back-up inventory, and the back-up inventory will be topped up by the producer. If the market maker and producer cannot integrate their inventories, then a three-stage inventory will have to be held, with the market maker owning a separate inventory which acts as a buffer between producer and retailer.

10.6   THE PRODUCER–ENTREPRENEUR AND THE RETAILER–ENTREPRENEUR

The implication of this discussion is that market makers will often integrate into production, but delegate distribution to independent retailers. In such cases the distribution channel is coordinated by cooperation between two distinct types of entrepreneur: the producer/market maker and the retailer. These may be termed the producer–entrepreneur and the retailer–entrepreneur. The producer–entrepreneur assumes responsibility for the product specification, quality control and the maintenance of a back-up inventory. The retailer–entrepreneur assumes responsibility for contact making and, where appropriate, for drawing people's attention to the product specification as well. This is a part of the personal service which the retailer is committed to provide. The retailer holds front-end inventory to provide customers with service on demand. Typically, both producer and retailer are responsible for hiring their own transport and enforcement services.

The retailer normally depends upon the producer's reputation for controlling the quality of the product. His own quality control is generally confined to selecting whose products he will stock. This still provides a service to the customer who does not himself know much about quality differentials between different brands of product.

The splitting up of the entrepreneurial function is not without its difficulties. These difficulties show up in the contractual relations between producer and retailer. It is extremely difficult to devise a simple contractual relationship which affords appropriate incentives to both parties. In practice the most common arrangement seems to be for retailers to purchase goods outright from the producer at a discount on the recommended retail price. The recommended retail price is fixed by the producer, and is the price announced by him in media advertising of the product specification.

The reason why the retailer purchases the product outright is fairly clear. He has physical custody of the product, and the producer will be reluctant to part with custody without receiving payment because of the risk of default. The discount principle, too, has a fairly simple rationale. It is a reasonable assumption that the retailer's efficiency in contact making and so on will be reflected in the volume of his sales. When delegating the retail function the producer will therefore wish to relate the retailer's reward to the volume of his sales. The simplest way of doing this is to offer the retailer a 'trade discount' on each unit sold.

The factors influencing the level of discount are more complex. In principle, the level of discount should reflect the amount of responsibility assumed by the retailer. For example, if the producer does little more than formulate the product specification and relies upon local publicity initiated by the retailer to promote product sales, then the retailer will expect a fairly generous discount to cover his advertising costs. If, on the other hand, the producer mounts a worldwide advertising campaign announcing the product specification, then the retailer's responsibility for generating sales is correspondingly diminished, and the discount should be lower. The discount should also be reduced if the producer offers certain privleges to the retailer, such as supply on a sale-or-return basis. It should be increased if the producer imposes constraints upon the retailer. One of the most common constraints used to be resale price maintenance, though this is now illegal in many countries.

Perhaps the most problematic influence on the discount is the quality of service the producer offers the retailer, in terms of the speed and reliability with which orders are fulfilled. Experience suggests that the adequacy of this service is perceived rather differently by producer and retailer. Producers feel that retailers should hold more inventory in order to reduce the incidence of rush orders, while retailers feel that producers should respond to rush orders more promptly. Because of their geographical separation, neither is in a good position to monitor the other's activities, and thereby acquire an understanding of the other's problems. It is mainly for this reason that conflicts arise in producer–retailer relations and make these relations the weakest link in the channel of distribution described above.

SUMMARY

This chapter has considered the contractual arrangements which prevail in the supply of market-making services to buyers and sellers. It is shown that these services will normally be packaged by a market maker and sold to the buyers and sellers on a 'no trade – no charge' basis. The provision of services on this basis helps to insure the buyers and sellers against the risk of incurring substantial costs in entering the market and then being unable to trade.

The market-making function is typically divided between a producer and a retailer. The producer determines the product specification using his technical knowledge, and guarantees the quality (on the grounds that the supervisor of production is in the best position to carry out quality control). The retailer is primarily responsible for contact making and for holding inventory, which is particularly important for inspection goods, and for goods which customers prefer to collect on the spot for themselves. Both producer and retailer retain their own responsibility for negotiation and delegate most of the remaining activities to specialists.

The discussion illustrates how very 'impure' the entrepreneurial function becomes in practice. Both producers and retailers are entrepreneurs, though they combine their entrepreneurial activities with many routine activities as well. The specialist suppliers of legal, transport and financial services are entrepreneurs too, in so far as they are making judgmental decisions about making a market in services to be supplied to other market makers.

NOTES AND REFERENCES

The topics discussed in this chapter are often placed under the heading 'business strategy'. For an interesting survey of the literature, integrating business strategy with the theory of the firm, see Moss (1981); this book also provides some instructive examples of strategic decisions. Other key references include Chandler (1962, 1977) and Williamson (1975).

The spatial dimension of the product market is analysed by Greenhut (1971), while the economic functions of the retailer are considered by Baumol (1967), Baumol and Ide (1956) and McClelland, W.G. (1967).

PART III

Synthesis

11. Growth and dynamics of the firm

11.1 NATURE OF THE FIRM

The firm is a unit of control. As such it is not very different from a household. Households control the uses of the goods they own in much the same way as do firms, albeit on a smaller scale. Why, then, are the activities of a firm not performed simply as an extension of the activities of a household? Why create a separate legal entity which can enter into contracts in its own right, quite apart from any contracts which have been entered into by the individuals who own the firm?

One obvious reason is that firms enjoy certain legal privileges which households do not. A person who buys in order to resell may register (or incorporate) himself as a firm and thereby become entitled to set expenditures against tax, limit his personal liability for commitments entered into in the course of trade, and so on. The actual privileges acquired depend upon the form of incorporation that is chosen. A firm does not need to buy exactly the same things that it sells in order to qualify for these privileges – it is sufficient that the expenditures are on inputs which are necessary in order to produce the output. It is worth noting, though, that members of a household must purchase inputs of food, shelter and so on, to maintain themselves in good health so that they can sell their labour services. However, the need for subsistence in order to maintain the stock of labour is not normally considered an adequate basis for the household to claim the privileges of a firm. Tax law normally provides for subsistence inputs by giving individuals a fixed personal allowance against tax liability. To qualify as a firm, the household must do more than look after the personal needs of its members; it must buy inputs with the express purpose of reselling them, or transforming them in some way, in order to meet the needs of others.

The other main reason why firms are distinguished from households is concerned with the capital structure of the firm. The capital structure allows different households to share in the ownership of the same firm. It also allows households to specialize in bearing the different kinds of risk incurred by the firm, by holding the different types of equity and debt it issues.

The risks incurred by the firm stem in part from production, but chiefly from market making. Production risk is incurred when the output generated by a given input is dependent upon an uncertain state of nature. A typical production risk is that bad weather will ruin a harvest, or that machinery will unexpectedly break down. Market-making risk arises because the firm insures the buyers of its output – and to some extent the sellers of its inputs too – against the costs of entering the market. It supplies market-making services which the transactor pays for only if trade is effected. In the absence of forward markets, the firm is constrained to buy and sell at quoted prices which are fixed in the short run. In the absence of recontracting, the firm must hold an inventory of output so that buyers can be supplied on demand, and an inventory of a means of payment so that supplies can be purchased on demand. If the entrepreneur's judgment of the market situation is wrong, then he may be left with considerable unsold product inventory which can only be disposed of at a capital loss.

11.2   THE SCOPE OF THE FIRM

As noted in the previous chapter, very few firms are pure producers. Most producers integrate forward into the marketing of their product. On the other hand, many firms are pure market makers in the sense that they intermediate markets without producing the goods themselves. As market makers, they normally integrate backwards into the production of some of the market-making services, though other services may be produced by subcontractors instead.

Typical of the pure market maker is the owner of a retail shop. The retailer shares responsibility with the producer's marketing department for making contact with customers and communicating the product specification to them. He negotiates a price with the customer, subject to constraints imposed by the producer. His reputation rests largely upon the quality of his stock, which is determined by his skill in choosing suppliers who produce quality goods. In this respect he acts as a middleman, screening for quality on his customer's behalf. He maintains an inventory so that he can supply his customers on demand, and when he is out of stock he rations goods in accordance with social convention.

The typical retailer is very flexible when deciding whether to internalize the provision of market-making services. Typically, he does most of his contact making through his own 'shop-window', does his own negotiation and owns the inventory in his shop. He may subcontract some contact making to the media and perhaps leave it to customers to arrange the delivery of the products to their place of residence. Alternatively, he may subcontract delivery to a transport firm; and in a few cases he will do it himself.

In orthodox economics, production is modelled on manufacturing. Manufacturing production involves transforming material inputs into material outputs through the utilization of multi-purpose durable goods. Labour is probably the most important example of a multi-purpose durable good. The production of market-making services does not normally involve the transformation of materials but, like manufacturing, it does involve the utilization of multi-purpose goods. Labour is probably more important in market making than it is in manufacturing, though it is primarily mental labour and not manual labour that is used. The labour intensity of market making is a feature that it shares with many other 'service' industries.

An important feature of the firm is that it brings multi-purpose goods under common control. Coordination of the use of these goods is effected through internal markets (or planning) instead of through arm's-length contracts in external markets. External markets are still needed, however, in order to set up the internal markets. External trade in general rights – that is, in the multi-purpose goods themselves – is necessary in order to allow the agglomerations of multi-purpose goods to be formed. Only once these agglomerations have been formed can the internal markets be used to determine which of the specific rights inherent in each general right is to be exercised – or, in other words, to determine the use to which each of the multi-purpose goods is to be put. Firms are legal entities which bid in the external markets for the multi-purpose goods, and so act as the instruments by which the agglomerations are formed. The capital structure of the firms allows individuals to specialize in bearing the risks involved in the utilization of these agglomerations of goods.

11.3 ALTERNATIVE FORMS OF CONTROL

The advantages of the internal market, as noted earlier, are that it avoids haggling over price and reduces the risk of default. It also facilitates the pooling of information among those involved in the market. It is possible to exercise control in an internal market using procedures which mimic the external market, by setting notional prices for internal transactions between profit centres. However, the free flow of information in the internal market allows the provision of information to be separated from the making of decisions, if desired.

This produces a radical change in the way that control is exercised. Coordination is no longer effected by harmonizing decisions through market procedures, that is by the adjustment of price, but by the transmission of information to a central unit of control (or to a satellite of this unit, where multi-level planning is concerned). The internal market now no longer resembles an external market, but involves a hierarchy instead. The hierarchy is best adapted to intra-plant control, while market procedures are best adapted to inter-plant control, though exceptions are possible in both cases. When discussing the organization of the firm, therefore, it is important to remember that both methods of control may be present in some degree.

Coordination within the plant is normally best achieved by centralized control. Because the goods are close together, the interactions between them are relatively complex, which makes market methods of coordination inappropriate. Furthermore, because everything is close together, it is easy to supervise the provision of information for control: thus the quality of information can be guaranteed without recourse to market incentives. If the control problem is very complex, then it may be advantageous to introduce multi-level planning. However, this tends to slow down response to change and makes it difficult to allocate responsibility when errors occur. The disadvantages of multi-level planning become more serious as the number of levels in the hierarchy is increased. This sets an effective limit on the efficient size of plant. Once this limit has been reached, it is better to increase output by increasing the number of plants of a given size rather than by increasing the size of a single plant.

In a multi-plant firm the geographical separation of the plants serves to buffer the interactions between them. Interactions occur only along channels designed specifically for the purpose. A typical interaction arises from the transport of an intermediate product from one plant to another. Control of interactions of this kind normally calls for internal market procedures. The small number of interactions involved means that the full benefit is obtained from the selectivity of the information used by market procedures. The spatial separation of plants makes it difficult to supervise the provision of information, so that market incentives are called for in order to ensure the accuracy of the information used for control. Efficiency therefore demands that each plant is constituted as a separate profit centre, with the management of each plant being rewarded with a share of its notional profit.

The costs of setting up internal markets limit the size of the firm. The efficient size of a firm is set at the margin where the costs of further internalization would just offset the benefits obtained. However the costs and benefits of internalization vary over time, and it is this variation, together with variation in the size of the market, that governs the dynamics of the growth of the firm. This chapter analyses the processes which underlie the growth, and eventual decline, of a representative firm. It is shown that the concepts developed above lead to a simple explanation of several well-known aspects of the life cycle of the firm.

11.4 THE FOUNDING OF A FIRM

The origins of a firm lie in the family – specifically, in the family of its founder. Admittedly, some firms begin life as fully-fledged joint stock companies with many shareholders. But the vast majority of firms are founded by just one individual, and their early development is very much tied up with the founder's family. Furthermore, although the successful firm will almost certainly outlive its founder, the managers who succeed the founder may well be influenced by the culture and ethos with which he has imbued the organization. Even if the firm is amalgamated with others this influence may still live on, either because the firm continues as an autonomous subsidiary or because it is sufficiently dominant to influence the other constituents of the group.

Typically, a firm is founded because someone opts for self-employment. By becoming self-employed, a person commits himself to making his own market for his labour services, or for a product derived from those services. He does not rely upon an employer to make a market for him. The distinction is important because it does not normally require a great deal of initiative to find a job (though it may require initiative to find a very good job). Employers advertise vacancies, stipulate wages and screen the quality of applicants; all the employee has to do is to apply for the vacancy. The self-employed person has to take over this initiative from the employer. He has to make contact with customers through advertising. He must stipulate a price to the customer instead of having the employer stipulate a wage to him. He must display samples of his work, or provide testimonials from satisfied customers, in order to build up a reputation for quality. He cannot rely upon his employer to supervise his work and guarantee its quality to the customers.

Why should anyone opt for self-employment? Perhaps the most obvious reason is that no employment is available. Self-employment is chosen because unemployment is the only alternative. If the wage rates negotiated by trade unions are too high in the light of the government's fiscal and monetary stance, then there will be an excess supply of employee labour. Although jobs may be available in the non-union sector, the glut of employees entering from the union sector will severely depress wages. The floor to the non-union wage is set by the subsistence wage, or the unemployment benefit rate, whichever is the higher. Under these circumstances self-employment may be seen as the only acceptable alternative to unemployment.

Secondly, the individual concerned may be reluctant to alienate control over his own labour. The individual may feel that his personal dignity is offended if his employer can order him about from one job to another. Employment will be particularly demeaning if the employer demands a deferential attitude as well.

Another reason for becoming self-employed is that the individual requires only part-time work, to be performed at his own convenience. Perhaps he already has a full-time job, or he simply enjoys the social aspect of the job and wishes to pursue it just as a hobby.

Probably the most important reason for becoming self-employed is that the individual feels that employment would give him insufficient scope to exploit his talents. He may believe himself to be an entrepreneur, possessed of privileged information, and so he will be looking for an employer who will encourage him to use his superior judgment in taking decisions on his behalf. The individual is looking for an employer who will channel financial resources and complementary expertise to him through internal markets. But employers may reject his claims to superior judgment. The employers' screening procedures may fail to detect the talent that the individual believes is there. Alternatively, they may recognize the talent but offer what the individual considers to be an inadequate reward.

Of the motives for self-employment discussed above, it is the last that augurs best for the success of the firm. The first three motives are essentially negative ones: the individual simply acts as his own 'employer of last resort'. An individual who finds it difficult to get a job in competition with others, or to hold down a job once it has been obtained, is unlikely to have the personal qualities required for business success. An individual who is averse to employment *per se is* unlikely to be good at employing others, and this will soon limit the potential for business growth. An individual who only wants to work at his own convenience is unlikely to provide his customers with the quality of service they require, and will therefore not survive for long.

The fourth motive, of course, does not guarantee success. It may be suggested, for example, that a self-employed person with no previous experience as an employee will be at a serious disadvantage. To be successful it is desirable for the entrepreneur to start out as an employee. Employees can 'learn the trade' from their employers before branching out on their own. Their experience as delegates may teach them how to delegate properly as their own business grows. As representatives of their employer, they may be able to make contacts which will prove useful later in locating customers or in securing financial backing. Perhaps the most important thing is that the information passing 'across their desk' as an employee may provide the stimulus for new ideas. It may be as a direct consequence of developing these ideas that the individual parts company with his employer. He may decide simply to 'steal' the idea. He may seek internal resources to pursue the idea and be turned down. He may feel that he has been overlooked for promotion and that this shows that his employer undervalues the idea. In any of these cases the employee may quit to pursue the idea on his own initiative. The internal market has failed him (and possibly his employer too). By becoming self-employed he opts for the external market instead.

11.5   EARLY CONSTRAINTS ON GROWTH

Suppose that the self-employed person has the makings of a successful entrepreneur. Not all self-employed people are entrepreneurs, as indicated above, and by no means all entrepreneurs are successful. The non-entrepreneurs may be able to survive in self-employment, earning an income roughly equivalent to what they would expect to earn doing the same sort of job as an employee. The unsuccessful entrepreneur is almost certainly backing faulty judgment, and he will go out of business when he is unable to sustain his losses. The greatest interest attaches to the way the entrepreneur with superior judgment overcomes the obstacles to success.

The first obstacle is the need for capital: a need shared by nearly everyone who is self-employed. The entrepreneur may need to build up an inventory before he can begin to trade. In order to trade he must advertise his whereabouts and communicate the product specification to interested parties. All these activities incur resource costs before any trade takes place.

If the entrepreneur has inherited wealth, then capital will not be a constraint, at least to begin with. But if he lacks capital, then he faces a serious strategic problem in obtaining it. Since he is, by assumption, an entrepreneur, he believes that his judgment differs from that of other people. To obtain a private reward from this superior judgment it is necessary to have a monopoly in exploiting it (see Chapter 4). But since other people's judgment differs from his, they will be reluctant to lend capital to him to back his judgment against theirs. But if he passes all his information over to them in an effort to convince them of the correctness of his judgment, then he runs the risk that they will compete against him in the exploitation of the information. Indeed, since they already have the capital and he does not, the question is not so much whether they will compete against him as whether he will be able to compete against them.

In developed countries, financial intermediaries – merchant banks, and to some extent the clearing banks as well – have evolved to ameliorate his problem. The bank debars itself from competing with its clients and guarantees confidentiality with respect to information supplied by borrowers in support of their requests for loans. The main alternative to the bank is the family. In developing countries where financial intermediation is not very sophisticated, the family may be the only feasible source of finance.

There are two factors which make the family an effective substitute for a bank. First, the family spans generations, and so can exploit the life-cycle

pattern of saving to allow the older generation to finance the younger generation. In effect, the older generation can allow the younger generation to
capitalize upon its prospective inheritance. Secondly, the lenders have good
information about the personal qualities of the borrowers. This information is
likely to be particularly good if the family has stayed together so that borrowers and lenders are still living together. Even if the lenders' information is not
as good as they think it is, it is likely to err on the favourable side, so that the
lender may be just as optimistic as the borrower about the risks involved.

There is, of course, no guarantee that the entrepreneur's family – or even
his friends – can supply the amount of capital that he requires. If he is obliged
to borrow from a bank, then it is very unlikely that the bank, though optimistic, will be as optimistic as the entrepreneur himself. The cost of bank capital
will therefore reflect a substantial risk premium.

Faced with a high cost of capital, the entrepreneur's rational response is to
work harder and save more. He forgoes current leisure and current consumption in order to provide additional funds for investment. This sacrifice in his
living standards is warranted because of the high rate of return he anticipates
from investment in his own business. When the return has been realized he
can convert it back into consumption – and into leisure too if he chooses to
reduce his hours of work. Thus the high cost of capital encourages the
entrepreneur to purchase a high future living standard at the expense of his
living standard in the present.

This behaviour of the capital-constrained entrepreneur appears to be typical
of certain kinds of self-employment. Proprietors of corner shops and newsa-
gents are often cited as examples. It should be pointed out, however, that
simply working long hours and tolerating a low standard of living does not
necessarily indicate that a self-employed person is an entrepreneur. It is perfectly consistent with non-entrepreneurial behaviour by people with little ability,
a strong aversion to conventional employment and little preference for leisure.
In other words, it may simply reflect a petit-bourgeois mentality which seeks to
purchase autonomy through increased hours of work. The distinction between
the entrepreneur and the non-entrepreneur becomes apparent only later when
the entrepreneur's business succeeds and his consumption and leisure increases,
while the non-entrepreneur remains in his rut, with static low levels of consumption and leisure.

The fact that the successful entrepreneur's leisure may increase later on
does not, however, mean that he will take more leisure than the typical non-
entrepreneur, merely that he will take more leisure than he did before. It is
easy to overstate the antithesis between work and leisure where entrepreneurs
are concerned. The entrepreneur may enjoy his work just as much, if not
more than his leisure. The greater autonomy conferred by self-employment
may reduce the irksomeness of work, though there is bound to come a point

where the hours of work are so long that leisure acquires a positive utility. But perhaps the main consideration is that the entrepreneur has something to prove to other people – namely that his judgment is correct – and that this gives him an enthusiasm for work which is missing in many other people. This suggests that, while the entrepreneur may reduce his hours of work as the capital constraint eases, he will continue to work more than most people until he is satisfied that he has 'proved' himself – not only to his financial backers, but to the world at large.

If no further investment opportunities present themselves, then the entrepreneur can consume the profits of his past success. If further opportunities do appear, then – given the entrepreneur's previous success – it will now be easier for him to borrow funds. Thus in either case the capital constraint is eased and so the entrepreneur can afford to increase consumption and, if he wishes, to reduce his hours of work too.

In the latter case, however, it is unlikely that the capital constraint will disappear at once. One success does not guarantee another, and so the capital constraint will ease only slowly as the entrepreneur's record of successes improves over time. In the meantime, the entrepreneur remains at least partially constrained, and therefore dependent upon internal sources of finance. The primary source is income generated by previous projects. This lends a characteristic dynamic to the growth of the firm, in which profits generated by previous projects constrain the current rate of growth of the firm.

11.6   THE SUPPLY OF LABOUR TO THE FIRM

It is often difficult for a self-employed person to start trading alone as a one-man business. Production may call for teamwork, or market making may call for a secretary to answer the phone and deal with queries while the entrepreneur is tied up in other work. The entrepreneur must therefore begin by hiring labour. As noted in Chapter 7, social and legal constraints prevent effective intermediation in the labour market. Since households are not accustomed to making a market in their own labour services, the entrepreneur must take the initiative in recruiting labour.

Labour is of variable quality as regards both integrity and ability. Poor-quality labour can impose heavy costs on the employer, and quality is difficult to screen for. Some job applicants come equipped with educational qualifications, certificates of training or apprenticeship, or references from a previous employer. However, the inexperienced employer may be uncertain as to what such certificates mean, and whether they are issued by a reputable institution. Under these circumstances the family comes into its own as an internal supplier of labour. The entrepreneur knows his family much better than he knows the rest of the labour market. Thus a man may have more confidence in teaming up with his own children than he would with other people. Again he may prefer to use his wife as a secretary than to recruit outside help. The advantages are particularly great if the labour of other family members would otherwise be underutilized because of the costs to those family members of gaining access to the external labour market.

As the business grows, the complexity of decision making may be such that the entrepreneur is obliged to delegate. If the business is growing fast, then it may be necessary to allow delegates considerable discretion, for the new opportunities may be missed unless quick decisions are made, and this strongly favours decentralized decision making by delegates who possess significant autonomy.

The problem of quality control in recruiting delegate decision makers is much greater than for the typical employee. It therefore appears to make sense for the entrepreneur to promote family members to decision-making posts and enter the external market initially for lower-quality labour. The problem with this strategy, however, is that the family members may not have the skills required. The internal market afforded by the family may be too limited a source from which to recruit decision makers. In this case the entrepreneur's ability to transcend the boundaries of his family may be crucial to the continued success of the firm.

Of course, it is possible that, because family members have similar genes and share the same environment as the entrepreneur, they have similar qualities to his own. On the other hand, if they are entrepreneurs in their own right, they may have ideas of their own, and so may not have either the time, or the financial resources for that matter, to support another entrepreneur in the same family.

It is apparent that the stage at which delegation becomes necessary is a critical one in the growth of the firm. The family is normally too small a pool from which to draw suitable labour. There is no substitute for having recourse to the external market. The entrepreneur must develop skills of his own in recruiting labour. He must not only screen applicants but also provide them with suitable incentives once they take up employment as decision makers. If the incentives are wrong, then the wrong sort of applicant will be attracted to the job. Even if the right sort of person is appointed, he is liable to quit once he has a good idea of his own if the internal rewards are too small. If the entrepreneur is not careful, the only able people who join the firm will be those seeking introductions to key customers and suppliers so that they can set up later in competition with their employer.

Similar problems occur in the recruitment of specialists. As the firm grows, the entrepreneur has the opportunity of internalizing markets in specialist services. The volume of trade becomes sufficient to warrant the full-time employment of technicians, designers, accountants and so on. Once the internal market has been established, the economies achieved by pooling the skills of different specialists within the firm may be quite substantial. But to set up the internal market the entrepreneur must first recruit the specialist. Unless the entrepreneur has at least a superficial knowledge of the specialism he may be unable to appraise the quality of job applicants. He must know enough about each subject to know, for example, what sort of questions to ask at interview and what sort of replies he can reasonably expect. Given the diversity of the different specialisms, the entrepreneur requires a very broad background knowledge to recruit effectively in each area. Without such knowledge the entrepreneur will not only be unable to recruit suitable specialists, but he will be unable to make effective use of them when they are employed.

The employment of specialists has important implications for the organizational structure of the firm. It is natural to give each specialist his own area of responsibility and this implies that any employee who makes a decision should take relevant specialist advice first. There is a danger, however, that each specialist will become too assertive and insist on being consulted about quite trivial matters which are nominally within his area. Demarcation disputes may arise as specialists 'invade' each other's territory. The disputes are stimulated because each specialist believes it is to his own advantage to overstate the importance of his own skills. For this reason, an entrepreneur may be reluctant to recruit specialists in case they attempt to take decisions out of his hands. If he does take them on, he may find himself continually having to adjudicate upon disputes concerning matters about which he himself has very little knowledge. To exploit internal economies of specialism successfully, the entrepreneur must therefore have sufficient general knowledge to keep each of his specialists in his place. Only if a specialist believes that he will be punished for overextending his influence will he avoid entering into disputes with other parties.

11.7 GROWTH OF THE PRODUCT MARKET

So far the analysis has focused upon constraints on growth stemming from the supply of labour and the availability of risk capital. Problems of supply response, however, appear only because of the pressure built up by growing demand for the firm's product. A major factor affecting the growth of demand is the spread of information about the product.

It is assumed that the firm has been created in order to market a new product. In this context the term 'product' must be interpreted very broadly. A new product could be anything from an entirely new design of, say, a multi-purpose good down to a minor differentiation of a personal service. It is assumed, simply, that the product has a unique specification.

It is often useful to think of information about a product spreading like an infection, though like all analogies there are important limitations to it. The infection is launched when the product is first announced, and can be actively spread by the firm through advertising. Alternatively, the firm may take a passive role and allow information networks in society to spread the message. These information networks are built around families, clubs, places of work – indeed any places where people meet to socialize – supplemented by purpose-designed news and entertainment media: newspapers, television and so on.

Display of a product is often important in promoting demand. A product which looks good may be advertised simply by placing it in a shop window. Furthermore, if the use of the product is itself conspicuous – for example, clothing or motor vehicles – the product may advertise itself even when it is out of the showroom and in the hands of its purchaser. In the case of conspicuous products the 'message' is mainly a visual one, and so it can be communicated through physical proximity, independently of verbal intercourse. Thus 'infection' with information about conspicuous goods is likely to spread faster than in other cases.

Not everyone who knows about the product will necessarily want to buy it. Pursuing the previous analogy, the information may be regarded as a virus and demand as a symptom of the illness that is caused. Not everyone is equally susceptible to the virus. The unsusceptible will not buy the product once they get to know of it – only the susceptible will do so. An individual's susceptibility is a function of his tastes, his income and the price of the product. The lower the price of the product, the more people will be susceptible to it and the more units each susceptible person will buy.

In a very simple infection process, the probability that an uninfected person will come into contact with the virus is proportional to the number of people who have already been infected. In economic terms this is consistent with people meeting at random to exchange information, when those who buy the product pass on the information about it, but those who have decided not to buy it do not. This model is particularly appropriate to a conspicuous good, where a new buyer normally obtains knowledge of the good by witnessing someone else's use of it. In an alternative version of the model, the probability of coming into contact with the virus is related, not to the number of people who have been infected, but to the number of people who have previously made contact with the virus even though they have not been infected. This model is appropriate to inconspicuous goods, where information spreads verbally and those who have not bought the good are just as likely as those who have to pass the information on. In the special case where

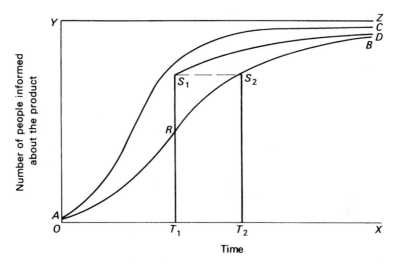

Figure 11.1   Diffusion curves with and without advertising

all individuals are susceptible, the two models give the same result: they describe a logistic process which leads first to an acceleration and then to a deceleration in the spread of the infection. The diffusion curve, showing the number of people infected at any one time, is illustrated in Figure 11.1 by the curve *AB*. The curve is sigmoid and is asymptotic to the horizontal line *YZ*, showing that eventually everyone becomes infected.

11.8   ADVERTISING AND MARKET GROWTH

At any stage of the diffusion process, the number of infected individuals can be increased through advertising. Advertising does not inform people who would otherwise never hear about the product: it simply means that they hear about it earlier than they otherwise would. In other words, advertising buys time. Advertising may be either a continuous process – as with a poster or shop window display which attracts casual passers-by – or it may be a one-shot affair – as when brochures are mailed out in bulk to a target sample of people.

The effect of continuous advertising may be modelled by assuming that one person – the entrepreneur – spreads infection faster than everyone else. The impact of continuous advertising is illustrated in Figure 11.1 by a switch to the new, steeper, diffusion curve *AC*. By contrast, the effect of one-shot advertising is to increase at a stroke the number of people who are informed about the product. Suppose, for example, that at time OT_1, an additional RS_1

people had been informed about the product. The state of information is now similar to what it would have been later, at time OT_2, if no advertising had occurred. Thus the subsequent spread of information continues from the base S_1T_1 instead of the base RT_1 as before. The new diffusion curve ORS_1D exhibits a discontinuity at time OT_1. The discontinuity arises because the segment S_2B of the original diffusion curve AB has been translated to the left through a distance T_1T_2 to form the segment S_1D of the new diffusion curve.

The analysis of one-shot advertising suggests that, the earlier the product is advertised, the more effective the advertising will be. If the product has a finite lifetime before it becomes obsolete, then the earlier the product is advertised, the longer is the period over which the advertising investment is paid back. Furthermore, if advertising is conducted at a time when almost no-one is infected, then the probability that those who are contacted already have the information is very small. If the advertising is conducted later, then many of the people contacted will already know of the product, so that part of the effort will be wasted. This explains why advertising is normally carried out at the time a product is launched, and is often only repeated later because the initial launch has failed.

This conclusion cannot remain unqualified however. The analysis above implicitly assumes that the population of buyers is fixed, whereas in fact the population is constantly turning over because of births and deaths. The obvious implication for advertising is that the population needs to be continually re-educated about the product. The initial effects of the one-shot advertisement will gradually wear off as the composition of the population changes.

It is important to recognize that the time path of infection – as represented by the diffusion curve – is not necessarily the same as the time path of demand. The two paths are the same (up to a constant of proportionality) only if each susceptible person repeats his purchases regularly in perpetuity. If, on the other hand, a purchase represents a once-for-all adjustment of the stock of a durable good, then the time path of demand will be governed by the marginal rate of diffusion: that is, at any time demand will be proportional to the slope of the diffusion curve. Assuming a logistic diffusion of information in a static population, and a constant degree of susceptibility in each person, the demand for a durable good will follow the time path DD' in Figure 11.2.

In practice, of course, few goods are perfectly durable. They wear out after a certain time and have to be replaced. Infrequent replacement leads to 'echo' effects in product demand. The early peak in initial demand reappears later when these early purchases need to be replaced. This leads to a cyclical pattern of replacement demand where the wavelength of the cycles is equal to the lifetime of the product.

Finally, it should be emphasized that the function of advertising is not merely to inform but to persuade. To put this another way, there are advan-

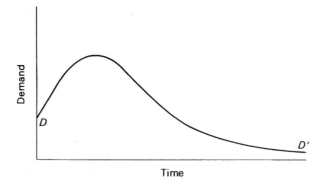

Figure 11.2   Dynamics of demand for a new durable product

tages to the producer in ensuring that the information conveyed about the product is highly selective. The information should emphasize the good points and play down the bad points. In particular, it should emphasize the product's advantages over its potential substitutes. This will not only increase demand at a given price but reduce the elasticity of demand as well. This will encourage the entrepreneur to capitalize on advertising not only through an increased volume of sales but also by setting a somewhat higher price.

11.9   IMPACT OF SOCIAL GROUPING ON PRODUCT DEMAND

The preceding discussion of diffusion – in particular the analysis based upon the logistic process – has implicitly assumed the absence of social barriers within the population. Each individual (except possibly the entrepreneur) has an equal probability of communicating with any other. Yet this is obviously not the case in practice. Communication takes place much more frequently within social institutions, such as families, clubs and firms, than it does between them. Information may move between two institutions only because some person is a member of both. But if the population is effectively segregated into different groups, and each institution typically draws its members from just one group, then members of the different groups may never overlap. Social segregation of this kind may restrict communication so much that information from any given source cannot diffuse throughout the population unless it is channelled through the news and entertainment media.

Each medium itself, however, has a selective audience. To communicate with the entire population the entrepreneur may have to use several different media. To reduce the costs of communication he will wish to use complementary media; that is, to use media whose audiences do not significantly overlap. In practice, though, he may not wish his coverage to be comprehensive. Because of differences in tastes and incomes, not everyone has the same susceptibility to the product. There is little point in communicating with people who are unlikely to express any demand. Suppose, for example, that taste for the product varies over the personal life cycle – say the product is demanded by people who are setting up home for the first time. People at this stage of their life cycle may constitute an identifiable social group. They may belong to one particular type of club and not to others. They may read particular types of magazine and visit particular kinds of places. The successful entrepreneur will exploit these social characteristics in making contact with his target audience. He may offer sponsorship to the clubs, advertise in the appropriate magazines and purchase display space in the places that members of the group visit. He may still rely upon the most alert members of the group to pass on the message to the others, though he must recognize that the message will normally be passed on only within the group. However, if his demand originates within just one group, then this constraint may be of little consequence.

Social factors exert a potentially strong influence on product demand. For many products, understanding social trends is the key to forecasting product demand. For example, in an affluent society, changing attitudes to housing may mean that all newly-married couples expect to live in a home of their own. The birth rate of the past determines how many young people are approaching marriageable age, and economic factors may influence the extent to which marriages are brought forward or postponed. Given suitable economic and demographic information and his knowledge of social trends, the entrepreneur can predict the probable size of his target market, and the best way of communicating with it. The extent to which the entrepreneur can synthesize all this information will determine the accuracy of his forecasts, and his subsequent success in matching supply to demand.

11.10   CAPITALIZING ON EXPERIENCE

Another reason for the entrepreneur to advertise continuously is that the quality of his product may change over time. Improvements in quality depend upon the exploitation of information; some of this information may be generated internally by production and marketing activities, while other information may be obtained externally – for example by observing other firms and 'borrowing' ideas from them. The flows of information involved in quality improvement are indicated schematically in Figure 11.3. The figure appears to suggest that quality improvement is a distinct activity carried out by

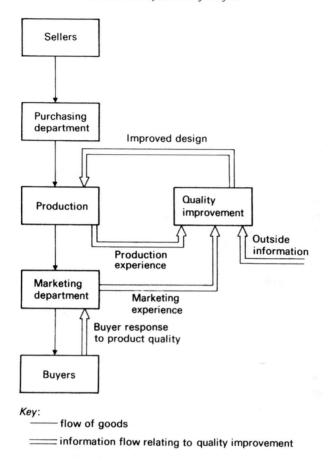

Figure 11.3   *Information feedbacks on product quality improvement: their internalization within the firm*

specialists, but of course this is not necessarily so. In a small firm quality improvement may be effected by the same person who produces the product and sells it. In such a case the information flows shown would be internal not only to the firm, but to the mind of the individual as well.

The use of internal information is an important influence on the dynamics of the firm. Internal information on production is generated by monitoring the activities of workers and machinery, and noting where slack exists and bottlenecks and errors occur. Internal information on marketing is generated by monitoring buyer reaction, and even more importantly by monitoring the reaction of people who inspect the product, appraise the price but decide not to buy. The amount of information generated in this way will be roughly proportional to the amount of output produced. Each unit produced generates additional experience in production. Each unit sold generates additional information on buyer reaction; and if each unit produced attracts a fixed number of appraisals, then experience of non-buyer reaction will be proportional to output as well. Consequently, the total stock of relevant information is roughly proportional to the cumulated output of the firm.

As more information is accumulated, so additional information becomes of smaller value, since much of it confirms what is already known, or suggests qualifications to existing knowledge which are of ever-diminishing practical significance. At any instant the rate of quality improvement is likely to be proportional to the rate of increase of the stock of knowledge, though perhaps with a lag due to the time required to put the new knowledge into practice. The factor of proportionality will decline as the stock of knowledge increases, because of the diminishing marginal returns to information noted above. Given that the stock of knowledge is directly proportional to cumulated output, the rate of quality improvement will be directly proportional to the level of output with a factor of proportionality which diminishes with respect to cumulated output. To put this another way, the quality of the product increases with respect to cumulated output, but at a diminishing rate.

Improvements in quality are often associated with either a redesign of the product or a change in production technique. Such changes may also increase efficiency and so reduce production cost. A change of this kind normally incurs a once-for-all set-up cost which is independent of the amount of output subsequently produced. The run-on cost of each subsequent unit is then reduced until some other change occurs. A redesign of the product or change of production technique may therefore be regarded as an investment which simultaneously improves product quality and reduces run-on cost. The feasibility of the investment is governed by the cumulated output of the firm. The return to the investment will depend crucially upon how effectively the improvement in product quality can be brought to the attention of potential buyers. In principle, the improvement in product quality should render substitutes less attractive. Normally, this increases demand for the product and renders it less price-elastic too. This would encourage the firm to increase the price, were it not for the simultaneous reduction in marginal cost. As it is, the direction of movement in price will depend upon whether or not the demand effect pulling the price up is sufficiently strong to outweigh the cost-reducing effect tending to pull the price down. With one or two exceptions, though, the output of the firm will definitely increase once the investment has been made.

Not all improvements in quality incur a set-up cost. The quality of output may be improved by an improvement in the quality of inputs. In particular, the quality of the labour input may be improved as employees gain on-the-job experience in production. This is the classic case of learning by doing, in which their cumulative experience gives the firm's employees a dynamic absolute and comparative advantage in production. It is most important to recognize, however, that the firm may encounter difficulties in capitalizing upon this advantage. Since the experience is a by-product of production it might appear to be the property of the firm. But in practice it may well be appropriated by the employee. The employee may threaten to quit unless he is rewarded for the experience he has gained at his employer's expense. If the employer does not pay up, then the employee may decide to set up in competition with his employer. If the employer decides to pay up, then he is redistributing his monopoly reward from himself to his employee.

It is not only on-the-job experience that the employer may have difficulty in capitalizing upon. Any employee through whom information is channelled within the firm may decide to use this information for himself instead of passing it on in the way he is supposed to. As experience within the firm increases, so the knowledgeability of the employees increases while the employer, if he is not careful, may get increasingly out of touch. Employees may decide that it is no longer necessary for their employer to intermediate between them and the customers. In the long run, therefore, potential rivals may be nurtured within the firm itself.

11.11 INDIVISIBILITIES AND THE DYNAMICS OF DIVERSIFICATION

Quality improvement and cost reduction are just two examples of the more general phenomenon of the capture and use of information generated within the firm. It has already been noted in discussing the growth of demand that social institutions such as the family and the club have an important role in promoting the flow of information between people. The firm is itself a social institution. It provides facilities for the exchange of information between employer and employee and between different employees. Since the firm is also a unit of production, information is generated on the spot as a by-product of its activities. The role of the firm as a social institution is to channel this information to the employees who can make the best use of it. The information may be used not only for quality improvement and cost reduction, but also for identifying new market opportunities. The new opportunities might relate to new market areas that the product has not yet penetrated, or to new products which could be developed – for example, complements in demand, for sale to existing customers, or complements in supply such as goods derived from by-products which previously went to waste. These new opportunities create a drive to diversify the firm both geographically and by product.

Diversification, unlike quality improvement, cannot normally be accomplished using only the resources already employed by the firm. It is necessary to hire new resources specifically for the purpose. Often there will be economies of scale in the use of these resources. The resources themselves may be indivisible or there may be economies in combining or agglomerating them. As a result a substantial volume of output may be required to utilize them fully.

Hiring the requisite bundle of additional resources imposes a recurrent fixed cost upon the firm. If the market into which the firm plans to diversify is relatively small, then the fixed costs can be spread over only a small volume of output. Diversification will be viable only if the firm can spread the fixed costs further by increasing the utilization of the new capacity. One possibility is to hire out user services but, as shown in Chapter 7, external markets in user services are often costly to operate. If the resources are multi-purpose goods, then the obvious alternative is to find some further market in which to diversify. The demand from this market will increase the demand for the services of the underutilized resources and allow their fixed costs to be spread further.

It must be recognized, however, that each additional market that is entered not only increases the utilization of existing resources, but creates demands for new ones. To keep these new resources fully utilized may require yet another market to be entered. Given the complexity of an efficient diversification strategy, it might be doubted whether a firm could ever successfully embark upon it. Certainly, it is doubtful if there is an entrepreneur anywhere sufficiently far-sighted to plan the diversification of his firm right from the outset. Because processing information in order to take complex decisions is a costly process, the entrepreneur will wish to plan each step in the diversification process separately. He will hope that the profit at each stage is sufficient to cover the additional fixed cost incurred, irrespective of whether or not the utilization of resources can be improved at a subsequent stage. Once each step has been accomplished he will look around for the next step. He will be guided in his search by a desire to increase the utilization of underutilized resources. Diversification therefore becomes a dynamic process in which investment made at one stage influences the search for investments to be made at a subsequent stage.

The search for opportunities for diversification has an opportunity cost in terms of the entrepreneur's own effort, or the efforts of those to whom the job is delegated. One way of reducing the opportunity cost is to employ underutilized administrative labour for this purpose. In particular, managers who have been hired to administer the most recent stage of diversification may be required to devote their spare time to investigating new opportunities. These opportunities, when exploited, will allow the manager's time to be more fully utilized on routine administrative work. In this way, the existence of managerial excess capacity helps to subsidize internally the search for new investment opportunities. This response to excess capacity depends, however, upon the cooperation of the managers concerned. An underutilized manager has no obvious incentive to increase his own work load, so long as he believes that the work he does is of sufficient value to make his job secure. An additional incentive must be given to managers who identify new investment opportunities, and the incentive must be greater the more the manager's own work load is likely to increase as a result.

As the firm gets larger and more diversified, so the problems posed by indivisibilities diminish in significance. This reduces the potential rewards to further growth. When all resources controlled by the firm can be fully utilized by sharing them out internally between different activities, then the firm is likely to have achieved an optimum size. In particular, managerial excess capacity will have been eliminated. This means that there is no pressing need to seek out additional markets, and also there are no spare managerial resources inside the firm to do so anyway. Only when existing markets contract will resources become underutilized and managers be freed to seek out ways of replacing a contracting market with another one.

In theory the large diversified firm could remain indefinitely in a homeostatic equilibrium, adjusting its 'portfolio' of market demands to match the fixed portfolio of resources which it has under its control. In practice, though, it may be difficult to administer the internal incentives required to maintain equilibrium. Sooner or later inadequate incentives may cause the most able decision makers to leave, and less able decision makers to be recruited in their place. The less able people will have more difficulty in administering internal incentives and so, as they come to predominate, pressure may build up for incentives to weaken. The ethos of the organization may gradually change from rewarding the able to protecting the inept. Needless to say, once this trend gathers momentum, the profitability of the firm will decline. Markets will be lost and not replaced, and so the size and diversity of the firm will diminish too. Eventually, the firm will be either taken over privately and reorganized, or taken over by the state and reorganized or subsidized, or go into liquidation.

11.12   THE DYNAMICS OF MARKET STRUCTURE

Market structure is usually discussed in the context of an 'industry'. In analysing entrepreneurship it is appropriate to work with a very narrow concept of an industry. Essentially the industry is identified with a single product. The product is in turn determined by its specification. If product specifications were defined narrowly enough, then it is possible that every firm would produce a slightly different product and so belong to a different industry. This is very close to the approach developed below, but with one important difference.

It is assumed that buyers may not know absolutely everything they would like to know about the product specification. As a result two products which are in reality different may appear indistinguishable. When a significant number of buyers are in this position, then the two products are said to belong to the same industry. If the buyers are aware that there are differences – though they do not know exactly what – then they will perceive a quality problem. Given the use of the product that they have in mind, one of the specifications may be more desirable than the other. The desirable product is said to be of higher quality than the less desirable one.

Using this approach it is possible to distinguish two types of industry: in one the product is homogeneous and in the other it is not. In the first case all producers are known to supply a product of similar quality while in the second case they are not: buyers believe that there are differences in quality, and it is assumed that they are correct in this belief. The question of homogeneity is closely related to the complexity and the versatility of the product. By and large the more complex the design, and the greater the variety of the uses to which it can be put, the more difficult it is for the buyer to assess the quality.

Homogeneous industries are much easier to analyse than inhomogeneous ones, and their market structures are already well understood. Unfortunately for the theory, however, homogeneous industries are far less common than inhomogeneous ones. On grounds of both originality and relevance, therefore, it is appropriate to restrict the following discussion to inhomogeneous industries.

Without loss of generality it may be assumed that there is just one firm which is the first to innovate the product and that over time other firms will then replicate it. If two or more firms innovate simultaneously, then it is just as though replication were immediate. If no other firms replicate, then it is just as though replication has been deferred indefinitely.

By definition, the innovator is a monopolist for as long as he remains the sole supplier. His degree of monopoly power depends upon the closeness of existing substitutes for his product. He can attempt to consolidate his monopoly by erecting barriers to entry (see Section 4.4). An obvious strategy is to disseminate information about the product to potential buyers as quickly as possible. Besides increasing the present value of the revenue stream, this reduces the latent unsatisfied demand which an entrant could seek to exploit. This is particularly important where demand is socially or geographically dispersed, for an obvious strategy for an entrant is to identify a segment of the market which news of the innovation has been slow to reach. Reducing unsatisfied demand may also discourage the entrant by raising his average cost of production. If there are increasing returns at the plant level, up to some minimum efficient scale, then the smaller the residual market the more difficult it is for the entrant to cover his average cost of production. If he cannot cover average cost, then he will not produce at all, and so the residual market will remain unexploited until the innovator himself gains access to it.

The entrant's ability to cover costs depends of course on the price at which he is able to sell. With a homogeneous product both innovator and entrant must sell at the same price. If the entrant's price expectations are based upon the innovator's current price, then the innovator can in principle deter entry by setting a 'limit price'. The limit price is set conditional upon the minimum efficient scale of plant (and other relevant parameters of production cost) so that, given production at this scale, no potential entrant could expect to make a profit.

However, if the quality of the entrant's product is liable to be different, then he may have to sell it at a discount on the innovator's price. There are two main reasons for this. First, the entrant may have to rely upon switching some demand from the innovator's product. However, the buyers concerned have already experienced the innovator's product and are therefore better informed about it. They perceive fewer risks in continuing to purchase the product they know than in switching to an untried alternative. To compensate for these risks the entrant must subsidize the buyer's experiment with the alternative product by discounting his price. The second reason is that the innovator can trade upon his greater experience of production and suggest to buyers that his greater experience enables him to offer a product of superior quality. This may persuade the uncommitted to opt for the 'old-established' product.

It may, however, be questioned whether the entrant's product really is inferior. If it is, then the discount at which it will have to be sold in perpetuity may indeed deter entry. If it is actually superior, buyers' scepticism will in the long run be overcome. There is still a barrier to entry, because the delay in penetration of the market will reduce the present value of entry. It may also lead to short-run losses being incurred in getting the product launched, so that the capital requirements may be increased. But, subject to these qualifications, entry may now seem worthwhile.

But how is it that the entrant can produce a product superior to the innovator's, given the innovator's greater experience? The answer lies in the appropriability of this experience to the firm. It is conceivable that an outside imitator could at least match the quality of the innovator's product by reverse-engineering the design (assuming patent protection was inadequate). A much more likely explanation, however, is that the entrant is an 'insider' who has previously worked for the innovating firm. The experience may have accrued to him as well as to his employer. Indeed, the experience may in the first instance have been his alone, and only a proportion of this experience may have been passed on to the employer. Thus, when the entrant appears from within the industry, the quality of the entrant's product may actually embody more of the innovator's experience than does the innovator's product itself.

Once entry occurs, the battle for customers is joined. The main controversy is over the quality of the rival products. Whichever product is perceived as inferior must be sold at a discount if its producer is to maintain his market share. The main battle, therefore, is over customers' perceptions of product quality. It is perceptions of quality which govern prices rather than prices which govern perceptions of quality. True, there may be some consumers who regard a low price as an admission by the producer of low quality in the product. This may actually discourage producers from engaging in price competition, as each may feel that undercutting his rival's price may damage the image of his product. Under these conditions the battle over product quality becomes not a war of prices but a war of words.

Each producer will formulate claims which put his product in the most favourable light. Some claims may be true but others may be false. The incentive to make false claims is greater the more difficult they are for the rival to refute. The incentive to falsehood is also normally much greater the more inferior the product is. There seems to be no guarantee, in the short run at least, that the superior product will actually be the successful one. Indeed, the battle may well be inconclusive, with the innovator and entrant achieving stable long-run market shares.

There is no reason, of course, why there should be just a single entrant to the industry. If the initial entry has been successful, then this may encourage other entrants to follow suit. Subsequent entries may be much easier because customers may have overcome their suspicion of alternative products, and some may even have come to identify a new product with improved quality. As the range of products increases, so customers may become more experienced at evaluating them. At the same time the movement of managerial and technical personnel between the producers may turn production know-how into a public good within the industry. As a result the industry may move in the long run towards a competitive market for a basically homogeneous product.

The main factor inhibiting this trend is economies of scale. Given the size of the market, there may be room for only a limited number of plants in the industry. This will not prevent the product becoming standardized, but it may terminate entry at a point where the industry still has an oligopolistic structure. Given that economies of scale constitute a barrier to entry, this provides an incentive for the oligopolistic firms to collude. Although each firm may have an incentive to cheat upon a collusive agreement, the small number of firms involved makes policing an agreement fairly straightforward. The collusion could be institutionalized by a merger, though given current social and political attitudes to monopoly this would probably not be advisable. A similar objection applies to a formal cartel. The most effective arrangement is probably an informal cartel of which no written records exist, for example the fixing of prices and/or quotas at meetings organized on some other pretext.

Collusion must not, of course, raise profits to a level which would attract further entrants. The incentive to collude is greatest when, owing to past miscalculations, industry capacity has been expanded to above the level at which long-run normal profits could be earned. This is particularly common in industries subject to an unforeseen contraction in demand due, for example, to a change in tastes or, more usually, to the innovation of a substitute product. Under these conditions collusion may be a success if it simply restores profits to their normal level. It therefore recommends itself very strongly to oligopolistic producers in a declining industry.

SUMMARY

This chapter has synthesized results from previous chapters in order to elucidate the factors which govern the rate of growth of the firm. The formation of a new firm is the consequence not only of the recognition of an entrepreneurial opportunity, but also of a belief that this opportunity is best exploited through self-employment. The founder of a firm is likely to find problems in both recruiting labour and acquiring capital; the family has a major role as an 'internal' source of both labour and capital.

The role of the family exhibits a crucial characteristic of any institution, namely that it facilitates communication and creates an internal pool of information which each member can use at will. The institution 'captures' information that is a by-product of one member's activities and makes it available to help others get started on new activities. In the context of the firm, it is the capture of production and marketing experience, its use in developing technical and quality improvements, and its feedback into production and marketing, which generate the main dynamic for the growth of the firm. This activity is supplemented by the scanning of external information sources for new ideas, and the selective dissemination of information through advertising to augment the word-of-mouth processes which are responsible for the growth of product demand.

Institutional adaptation becomes more difficult as the size of the firm increases; it may become difficult to retain key employees, who may quit in order to set up in competition with their former employer. This suggests the possibility, first, of a life cycle for the industry in which the firm is involved and, secondly, a life cycle for the firm itself.

NOTES AND REFERENCES

There is an extensive literature on the topics covered in this chapter and only a selection of the most useful references can be given.

The motives underlying the formation of new firms, and the constraints on their early growth, are considered by Boswell (1973), Cross, M. (1981), Davids (1963), Johnson and Cathcart (1979), Kaplan (1948) and Oxenfeldt (1943) . The financial problems of small firms are considered in detail by Bates (1964), Bolton (1971) and Coles (1973); see also Carstensen and Morris (1978). The role of families and 'groups' as a source of finance is discussed in a stimulating paper by Leff (1978); see also Strachan (1976). The significance of capital market 'imperfections' is considered from a theoretical point of view by Stigler (1967).

The role of information processes in the growth of firms is usually analysed in terms of the research and development function of the innovating firm: see Kay (1979), Mansfield (1964, 1968, 1969) and Mansfield, Rapoport, Schnee, Wagner and Hamburger (1971). The classic study of the feedback of information in the form of production experience is Arrow (1962b); for an integrated treatment of 'experience curves' and the growth of demand, see Bass (1980), where other references can be found.

There is a very extensive literature on the diffusion of information, though surprisingly little of it is concerned with specifically economic issues. For a survey of the subject, see Katz, Levin and Hamilton (1963), Robertson (1971), Rogers (1962) and Rogers and Shoemaker (1971). The role of diffusion in the context of social and economic processes as a whole is analysed in Roberts and Holdren (1972). The economic functions of information generally are considered by Machlup (1962a, 1980).

The social mechanism of diffusion – in particular, word-of-mouth processes – is considered by Bartholomew (1973), Boone (1970), Cancian (1979), Coughenour (1968), Katz (1957), Katz and Lazarsfeld (1955), Levitt (1965), Rapoport (1953) and Rashevsky (1953). The effects of mass communication, in contrast to word-of-mouth processes, are considered by Katz and Foulkes (1962) and Klapper (1960).

While the social aspects of diffusion are usually discussed from the point of view of the diffusion of demand for the product, the spatial aspects are more often concerned with the diffusion, and adoption, of new techniques of production. On the spatial aspects of diffusion, see Brown (1975), Hägerstrand

(1967) and Webber (1972, 1979). The international diffusion of an innovation is considered by Nabseth and Ray (1974), Sloan (1973) and Tilton (1971).

The diffusion of information between firms – and the nature of the competitive threat to the innovator – has been considered by Baldwin and Childs (1969), Mansfield (1961, 1963a, 1963b) and Romeo (1975, 1977).

The logistic curve and its variants are extensively used in the study of diffusion processes of all kinds; the mathematical theory is discussed by Bartholomew (1973); its empirical application is exemplified by Stoneman (1976). The impact of product durability on the relation between the diffusion curve and the time path of product demand is considered by Swan (1970). The modelling of the dynamics of product demand is considered as a whole by Massy, Montgomery and Morrison (1970).

The role of product quality – and non-price product characteristics in general – is considered by Abbott (1955), Heflebower (1967) and Kotler (1976), while Iremonger (1972) and Lancaster (1966, 1979) have developed an activity-analysis approach which integrates particularly well with the theory developed in this book. The problems posed by uncertainty about product quality are considered in detail by Akerlof (1970), Kihlstrom (1974a, 1974b) and Spence (1977). The distinction between inspection and experience goods is due to Nelson (1970), though a slightly different terminology is employed by him. The significance of product guarantees, and of producer liability in general, is considered in the symposium edited by McKean (1970).

The relation between advertising, consumer information and product quality is discussed by Albion and Farris (1981) and Reekie (1981). The relation between advertising and word-of-mouth processes is considered by Glaister (1974). Life cycles in firms are discussed by Mueller (1972) and Penrose (1959).

12. The market for entrepreneurs

12.1 INTRODUCTION

The market for entrepreneurs allocates judgmental decisions to entrepreneurs. It has, in fact, four main functions:

1. to identify decisions which are judgmental,
2. to identify entrepreneurs whose judgment is likely to be correct,
3. to match entrepreneurs to judgmental decisions so that wherever possible the right decision is made, and
4. to distribute rewards to the entrepreneurs.

It is sometimes denied that a market for entrepreneurs can exist. This is incorrect. It must be admitted, however, that the market for entrepreneurs has some unusual features which mean that it operates in a different way from most other markets.

12.2 IDENTIFYING JUDGMENTAL DECISIONS

One of the idiosyncrasies of the market for entrepreneurs is indicated by the first of the functions identified above. It is extremely difficult to determine precisely which decisions are judgmental. As a result it is difficult for anyone to identify a precise source of demand for an entrepreneur.

Consider the demand for entrepreneurs within the economy as a whole, and consider too a single period, prior to which the economy has been in operation for some considerable time. A system of property rights has been evolved; decision-making power is conferred by ownership of general rights – typically rights to determine the use of multi-purpose goods (see Chapter 7). Many of these rights are vested in institutions such as firms. Each institution has an organization comprising a set of posts filled by delegate decision makers. Delegate decision makers within the same organization coordinate their decisions through either an internal market or a hierarchy.

The economy is subject to continuous unforeseen exogenous disturbances due, for example, to changes in population and tastes. Typically, the source of information about any change is localized, and diffuses slowly through a network of social contacts. Key elements in this network are institutions such as clubs and firms. Firms in particular attempt to capture information about change and channel this information to the delegate decision makers who are most likely to use it to advantage. It is this system of property rights and social institutions which determine at any one time who is making the decisions about resource allocation, and what information is available to them.

The system described above determines not only who will make the decisions but also what form the decisions normally take. For example, if the system is based upon voluntary trade in property rights using a specialized medium of exchange, then decisions will be concerned not only with how to utilize goods that are already under the decision maker's control, but also with decisions on whether to sell these goods, or to buy goods which are at present under someone else's control. (The structure of a monetary market economy of this kind was discussed in Chapter 5.)

The identification of judgmental decisions within a monetary market economy is itself a judgmental activity. Basically, a judgmental decision is one where some relevant item of information has not diffused to everyone. Those who have the information would therefore decide one way and those without it would decide another way. It is assumed that those who have the relevant information will make the right decision, while those who do not will make the wrong decision. It is possible, of course, that there are other factors, which no-one knows about, which make the available information misleading. It is therefore conceivable that those without the information might make a better decision, though this possibility will be ignored.

Some kinds of decision are widely recognized as judgmental: for example, decisions about complex investment projects which have numerous spillover effects. Different people will have different information concerning the probable outcome of such projects. In recognition of this, such decisions are typically taken by the boards of large companies; the company's information network ensures that each board member is well briefed, whilst consideration at board level ensures that the information of the separate members can be pooled before a decision is made.

But for many small and apparently simple decisions there is unlikely to be a consensus upon whether the decision is judgmental. Consider, for example, a relatively minor repetitive decision which has to be made anew each period. For reasons explained in Chapter 2, most people making a repetitive decision will tacitly assume that circumstances have not changed from the previous occasion. The decision is not given active consideration; a 'no change' policy is followed automatically. Only those who recognize (or believe they recognize) that a change has occurred will believe the decision to be a judgmental one. They may not know exactly what the change is, but they know enough to know that the tacit assumption of the other decision makers is wrong. The other decision makers tacitly believe that the decision is not judgmental, while those who have recognized a change believe that it is. It follows that the recognition of a judgmental decision is, in many cases, itself a judgmental activity.

12.3   IDENTIFYING AN ENTREPRENEUR

The qualities required of an entrepreneur were discussed in Chapter 2. It was emphasized that some of these qualities are extremely difficult to screen for. There is no objective test of entrepreneurial ability which can guarantee a high degree of accuracy, and there is unlikely to be one in the foreseeable future. Opinions are therefore likely to differ about whether a given individual has entrepreneurial ability. Some people may overestimate a person's ability and others underestimate it. This means that the identification of an entrepreneur is itself a judgmental activity.

Various hypotheses can be made about the identification of entrepreneurs. The simplest of them may be called the law of self-esteem. It asserts, basically, that everyone has a higher opinion of his own judgment than anyone else does. This means that many people who believe themselves to be entrepreneurs will not be recognized as such by other people. On the other hand, it denies the possibility that a true entrepreneur may so underestimate himself that he declines to become an entrepreneur when he really should do so. Potential entrepreneurs may be excluded from entrepreneurship by lack of financial backing or by other barriers to entry, but do not exclude themselves by self-effacement.

A second, and much stronger, hypothesis is the law of arrogance: this asserts that no-one thinks anyone else has what it takes to be an entrepreneur. According to the second law, anyone who thinks that he is an entrepreneur can be sure that everyone else disagrees with him. The second law is somewhat extreme, however, as it ignores the fact that, in the long run at least, an entrepreneur can acquire a reputation for successful decision making and thereby acquire the confidence of others. It also ignores the fact that there are both formal and informal methods of screening people for entrepreneurial qualities. The formal methods include in-depth interviews and the assessment of performance in simulated business situations; the informal methods rely on continuous observation of the individual at 'close quarters' and are open mainly to family and friends. None of these methods is guaranteed to succeed, but they do allow favourable assessments of other people to be made, albeit only tentative ones. The following analysis therefore accepts only the first law and rejects the second. It recognizes that the identification of entrepreneurs is judgmental. The most favourable assessment of an individual is likely to be his own, followed (at some distance, possibly) by that of his family and friends. On the whole, the most sceptical assessments are likely to be made by those who have had no contact with the individual at all.

12.4   MATCHING DECISIONS TO ENTREPRENEURS

The matching of decisions to entrepreneurs exhibits another special feature of the market for entrepreneurs, namely the extreme heterogeneity of the commodity that is traded. The commodity is a decision-making service – in particular, a service which leads to the making of the right decision. The right decision in this context is the best decision that can be made given the information that is available within the economy. To simplify the analysis it is assumed that each judgmental decision occupies one entrepreneur full-time for one period.

To make the market for entrepreneurs like the representative market in neoclassical theory it would be necessary to assume that anyone identified as an entrepreneur could make any judgmental decision with equal success: in other words, that different decisions are perfectly substitutable. Likewise, it would be necessary to assume that any decision identified as judgmental could just as well be undertaken by any of the entrepreneurs: in other words, that different entrepreneurs are perfect substitutes in making any given decision. Under these conditions, market equilibrium would be achieved when the number of entrepreneurs was equal to the number of judgmental decisions that needed to be made.

Such a concept of equilibrium is, however, largely irrelevant to the market for entrepreneurs. The reason is that the substitution possibilities described above do not exist. The problem of the heterogeneity of the commodity cannot be eliminated simply by postulating perfect substitutability, as in neoclassical economics. An alternative approach is to deny the possibility of substitution altogether. This approach asserts that each entrepreneur has superior judgment in respect of just one decision, and that, conversely, for each decision there is just one entrepreneur who has the necessary judgment to decide correctly. In this case each individual entrepreneur must be assigned to a particular decision. Equilibrium requires not only that in aggregate the number of entrepreneurs be equal to the number of judgmental decisions: it also requires that each entrepreneur be matched to the right decision. Essentially, therefore, there is not just one market for entrepreneurs: there are as many different markets as there are judgmental decisions to be made.

In practice, this model is probably too restrictive: substitution possibilities do exist, though they are very limited. The equilibrium pairing of decisions and entrepreneurs is not unique, though the number of possible combinations is small. In either case the question arises as to how the matching is administered. In discussing this it is most important not to reinvent the market mechanisms dismissed earlier in Chapter 6. These mechanisms are no more relevant to the market for entrepreneurs than they are to other markets.

In analysing the market mechanism another peculiarity of the market for entrepreneurs becomes evident. This is the exceptional skill required for intermediation. As noted in Chapter 9, most markets rely upon intermediation to facilitate adjustment. One of the major roles of the market maker is to screen for quality, but, as noted above, screening for the quality of an entrepreneur is exceptionally difficult.

Intermediation in the market for entrepreneurs is normally conducted by what may be called the entrepreneurial firm. The entrepreneurial firm has an elaborate network of contacts which enables it to identify judgmental decisions. These decisions concern the appraisal of investment projects designed to exploit potential opportunities for coordination. The firm also has sophisticated screening procedures which enable it to identify entrepreneurial ability with a reasonable degree of success. It also has internal procedures to match individual entrepreneurs to particular decisions.

Normally, the entrepreneurs are hired as delegates; they are salaried employees who combine their individual responsibilities for relatively minor decisions with a responsibility for collaborating on major decisions. The matching of decisions and entrepreneurs is achieved by a two-stage process in which the entrepreneurial firm first enters the labour market to hire entrepreneurial employees, and subsequently makes internal assignments of entrepreneurs to particular decisions. The ability of the firm to supervise its employees enables it to improve its assessment of each entrepreneur in the light of each decision he makes. Information on the outcome of each decision is captured by the firm and used to determine the best subsequent assignment for the entrepreneur concerned. Thus the longer the entrepreneur remains with the firm the more efficient the assignments are likely to become.

Because of the inherent difficulties of screening, not everyone with entrepreneurial ability can be matched to the appropriate post in an entrepreneurial firm. For example, it is economic for firms to use state educational qualifications as a part of their screening criteria, which means that educationally disadvantaged entrepreneurs may be unable to find employment with a firm. This in turn means that they have to find their capital for themselves. Banks have evolved to intermediate between self-employed entrepreneurs and their lenders, but banks face somewhat similar problems in intermediation to the entrepreneurial firms. If the entrepreneur is personally wealthy, or has good social contacts, then obtaining finance may be no problem, but otherwise capital requirements may prove an insuperable barrier to entry into entrepreneurship.

Another consequence of inaccurate screening is that people without ability may decide to become entrepreneurs. They may be appointed to posts in entrepreneurial firms, in which case these firms bear most of the losses which arise when they make the wrong decision. Alternatively, they may go into business on their own account, in which case they bear the losses themselves (except for losses that are shifted onto their backers if and when they go bankrupt).

It is assumed, to begin with, that screening is perfectly efficient in preventing people without ability from becoming entrepreneurs; the only problem with screening procedures is that they also prevent some people with ability from becoming entrepreneurs. This simplifying assumption means that, in terms of the concepts introduced in Chapter 4, anyone who becomes an entrepreneur is a potential leader; followers and failures are eliminated before they can start. Another consequence of this assumption is that the risk of becoming an entrepreneur is understated, for anyone who becomes an entrepreneur is assured that they have the ability to succeed. Some of the consequences of relaxing this assumption are considered in Section 12.6.

A person who has entrepreneurial ability and access to capital in one form or another is said to be a qualified entrepreneur. Typically, a qualified entrepreneur is either educationally qualified, personally wealthy or has good social contacts. A person who has entrepreneurial ability but no access to capital is said to be unqualified; to all intents and purposes he may as well have no ability either, for whatever ability he has cannot be exploited.

12.5 THE ENTREPRENEUR'S REWARD IN THE SHORT AND LONG RUN

In the analysis below there are just two categories of people: the qualified entrepreneurs and the rest. The proportion of able entrepreneurs who are qualified is determined by the screening procedures of the market makers. To simplify the analysis further, it is assumed that each entrepreneur is responsible not only for taking decisions but for identifying these decisions for himself. The activities of the market makers do not extend to identifying decisions on his behalf. This assumption avoids having to analyse simultaneously the activities of two different categories of entrepreneur: the entrepreneur who takes judgmental decisions and the entrepreneur who identifies the judgmental decisions to which other entrepreneurs can be matched.

The analysis below is essentially concerned with an economy in which the entrepreneur is either a salaried manager or a self-employed businessman and the market maker is, respectively, a large firm or a bank. The market makers stop anyone without entrepreneurial ability from becoming an entrepreneur, but they also stop some people with entrepreneurial ability from becoming entrepreneurs. Thus the individual entrepreneur identifies and takes his own judgmental decision and the market makers decide, on the basis of his personal characteristics, whether he shall have 'permission to proceed'.

The nature of the reward to entrepreneurship was discussed in the earlier chapters of this book. When an entrepreneur takes a decision with which everyone else, either implicitly or explicitly, disagrees, he can, in a manner of speaking, 'bet' against other people. The 'bet' can take many forms, of which the conventional bet is an insignificant and fairly trivial case. Stock market speculation is more significant, but the most important types of bet concern the innovation of new technologies or new products. The entrepreneur anticipates that his superior judgment will be confirmed by the way that events turn out. His own beliefs will be proved correct and the beliefs of those who bet against him will be proved false. When the entrepreneur is proved correct his opponents will have to pay up; this payment is a reward to the entrepreneur's superior judgment.

A necessary condition for the entrepreneur to be able to bet on favourable terms is that no one else attempts to compete in making the same bet (or, if they do, the size of their bet is insignificant). The most important barrier to competitors is secrecy; the entrepreneur must keep to himself the information upon which he believes his superior judgment is based. No single item of information need be vital; it is the synthesis of information achieved by the entrepreneur that has to be unique.

Consider now the long-run factors influencing entry to, and exit from, the market for entrepreneurs. In the long run, people are attracted into entrepreneurship by the rewards they believe it offers. An important influence on these rewards will be the pace of change in the economy. If large unforeseen changes are continually occurring, and information about each of these changes is initially localized, the scope for judgmental decision taking is very great. There is ample opportunity for the entrepreneur to take a dissenting view of some situation, based upon privileged access to information.

The individual entrepreneur's share of these rewards will, however, depend crucially upon the number of other entrepreneurs in the economy. The more qualified entrepreneurs there are, the smaller is the chance of any one entrepreneur being the first to identify any given judgmental decision. Furthermore, the greater the number of qualified entrepreneurs, the greater is the chance that two entrepreneurs will simultaneously identify the same judgmental decision. If each knew that the other had identified it, they could collude, or one could withdraw to allow the other a free hand in making the decision and exploiting it. But if neither knows that the other has identified it, then they will unwittingly compete against each other, driving prices up or down against themselves and eliminating their entrepreneurial reward. With competition of this kind the gains from coordination will accrue exclusively to the parties with whom they trade. Even if identification of the judgmental decision is not simultaneous, the presence of many entrepreneurs will reduce the average lag before a competitor appears. This will reduce the duration of the entrepreneur's temporary monopoly and make it more difficult for him to erect a barrier to competition in the short time that is available.

It must be recognized, of course, that an increase in the number of entrepreneurs will increase the proportion of the judgmental decisions that can be identified in any given period. Thus one entrepreneur's identification of a judgmental decision is not necessarily at the expense of some other entrepreneur. When the number of entrepreneurs is small, and the proportion of judgmental decisions identified is low, then the main effect of the entry of an additional entrepreneur will be to increase the proportion of judgmental decisions that are identified and the probability of an overlap with an existing entrepreneur is small. But as the number of entrepreneurs increases, so the probability of overlap rises and the increase in the proportion of judgmental decisions identified diminishes. In effect, there is increasing congestion between entrepreneurs in identifying judgmental decisions. The expected reward to entrepreneurship diminishes, not only because the rewards have to be shared out between more entrepreneurs, but because the total reward available to entrepreneurs diminishes on account of competition between them in exploiting the opportunities they find.

An individual's decision upon whether to become an entrepreneur will be based on a comparison of the expected reward to entrepreneurship and the reward to the best alternative use of his time. The individual has a choice of three full-time occupations: entrepreneurship, non-entrepreneurial labour or leisure. Non-entrepreneurial labour receives a competitive wage. Two main kinds of non-entrepreneurial labour may be distinguished. The first is manual work and the second is non-judgmental decision making (or administration for short). To simplify the analysis it is assumed that all individuals are equally able at both. This implies that no-one has a comparative advantage in manual work rather than administration, so that the competitive wage is the same for both. It also implies that an individual's comparative advantage in entrepreneurship *vis-à-vis* non-entrepreneurial work entirely reflects his absolute advantage as an entrepreneur.

Consider first the qualified entrepreneurs who value their leisure at less than the prevailing wage. The best alternative to entrepreneurship for these people is other work – that is, manual work or administration. The supply of entrepreneurs from this group will be infinitely elastic at the prevailing real wage. On the other hand, those who value their leisure more highly than the wage will find leisure the best alternative to entrepreneurship. The supply of entrepreneurs from this group will begin only when the expected reward to entrepreneurship exceeds the real wage. Those who value their leisure least will be drawn into entrepreneurship first and as the expected reward increases so those who value their leisure more highly will be drawn in too. Thus there is an upward-sloping supply curve of entrepreneurs above the prevailing real wage.

In Figure 12.1 the schedule *DD'* shows how, conditional upon the expected rate of change, the expected reward per entrepreneur varies with the number of entrepreneurs. The schedule *DD' is* not a demand curve in the conventional sense, though the analogy with a demand curve is useful if it is employed with care. The supply of entrepreneurs is illustrated by the schedule *SS'*, which has an infinitely elastic portion at the prevailing real wage *OW*, and is upward-sloping thereafter. (The supply curve never becomes backward-slop-

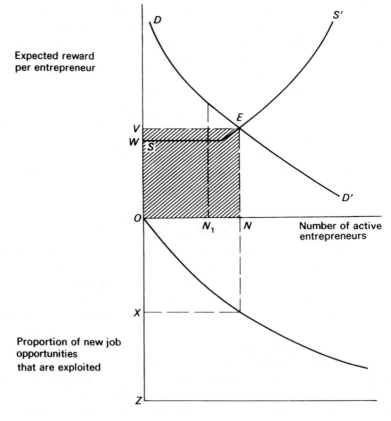

Figure 12.1   Steady state of the market for entrepreneurs

ing because each individual is committed to either full-time entrepreneurship or full-time leisure for the period concerned.) The schedules DD' and SS' intersect at E, corresponding to an expected reward OV accruing to each of ON entrepreneurs.

Suppose that initially the number of entrepreneurs was $ON_1 < ON$. At this point the expected reward to entrepreneurship would exceed the opportunity cost, and additional entrepreneurs would be drawn in. They would be drawn in first from non-entrepreneurial employment and then from leisure. As the number of entrepreneurs increased, so the expected reward to entrepreneurship would fall and the opportunity cost of entrepreneurship would increase. When the expected reward had fallen to OV, there would be no incentive to enter and the situation would stabilize. The expected total reward to entrepreneurship in the steady state is measured by the shaded area $OVEN$.

It is important to recognize that this mechanism of adjustment differs from the kind of market mechanism that is usually considered. The market is equilibrated by individuals' response to quantity signals and not price signals. The quantity signal is the number of entrepreneurs that are active. Each individual needs to know the total number of entrepreneurs already active in order to impute a 'price' to his entrepreneurial services. This imputed price governs his decision upon how to use his time. If the demand curve and supply curve remain sufficiently stable, then the market will adjust to a steady state over time. The condition that demand is stable is equivalent to a condition that there is a steady pace of change. The condition that the supply curve is stable is much more complex. In principle, there is little reason why individuals should change their valuations of leisure, and hence why the upward-sloping portion of the supply curve should change. However, the remaining portion of the supply curve is governed by the productivity of manual work and administration, which depend on a range of factors, some of which are quite volatile.

The implications of this simple model are quite straightforward. Although in the short run the reward of the entrepreneur is a monopoly reward to information, in the long run it is simply compensation for time and effort: namely, for the time and effort spent in identifying and making judgmental decisions. The equilibrium reward is greater, the greater is the demand for entrepreneurs and the smaller is their supply. The demand for entrepreneurs depends upon the pace of change in the economy. The faster change occurs, the greater will be the demand and the higher the reward to the entrepreneur. The relevant concept of supply is the supply of qualified entrepreneurs. The supply will be greater the greater is the stock of entrepreneurial ability among the population; the more effective are the screening procedures of the intermediaries in identifying entrepreneurial ability, the more likely it is that able entrepreneurs rejected by the screening procedures have personal wealth of their own, and that those without wealth have the social contacts necessary to procure finance elsewhere. In summary, therefore, the reward to entrepreneurship depends upon the pace of economic change, the distribution of personal wealth, and the social and institutional framework of the economic system as a whole.

12.6   RISK AND THE REWARD TO THE ENTREPRENEUR

So far it has been assumed that an individual's decision to become an entrepreneur is based solely upon the expected reward. This implies either that the individual perceives no risk in becoming an entrepreneur or that he is indifferent to risk. The only other possibility is that becoming an entrepreneur is neither more nor less risky than undertaking manual work. None of these conditions is likely to be satisfied in practice. Even a person with entrepreneurial ability cannot guarantee that his judgment will always turn out completely successfully.

Perhaps the greatest risk to an individual in becoming an entrepreneur, however, is uncertainty about whether he has the ability or not. An individual with ability is exposed to a much lower probability of loss than is one without it. As noted earlier, entrepreneurial ability is notoriously difficult to screen for; certainly, introspection is an unreliable guide. It is possible that some entrepreneurs may specialize in screening other entrepreneurs for ability, in which case an entrepreneur may be able to reduce his own uncertainty by undergoing screening by others. However, although the entrepreneurs who do the screening presumably have confidence in their own methods, this confidence may not be shared by others. In particular, those on whom the screeners reach a negative verdict may in turn reject the screeners' methods. This does not imply that those who reject the screeners' verdict are necessarily certain that they have ability. The validity of the screening procedures is to some extent a subjective issue about which opinions may rightly differ. Those who have been rejected may simply doubt whether the procedures are of any value – merely to preserve their self-esteem. In this case they remain subjectively just as uncertain as they were before about whether or not they have ability.

The only widely endorsed test of entrepreneurial ability is to try it out in practice. In principle, the trial could be conducted on a small scale, but there is a risk that, if the trial is on too small a scale, then technical diseconomies may bias the outcome towards failure. The existence of a minimum scale for a fair trial – and the consequent need for an irreducible amount of capital to be ventured – represents perhaps the major risk in becoming an entrepreneur. In comparing entrepreneurship with other activities, therefore, the expected reward to entrepreneurship must carry a premium to compensate for the unavoidable risk incurred in discovering whether or not the individual concerned has entrepreneurial ability. This premium must be added to the manual wage, or to the value of leisure (whichever is the higher) in measuring the opportunity cost of becoming an entrepreneur.

SUMMARY

This chapter has analysed how the number of entrepreneurs and their rewards are determined. In the short run the entrepreneur's reward is a temporary monopoly rent to superior judgment; this monopoly can sometimes be consolidated by erecting barriers to entry. In the long run the prospect of monopoly rents will attract entrepreneurs into searching for information; they hope to achieve superior judgment by synthesizing this information.

Some people are naturally better at synthesizing information than others. This ability, however, is difficult to recognize. People with ability may be unable to proceed with a search for information if other people are unwilling to give them financial backing. People with ability still need personal wealth, educational qualification or good social contracts in order to enter entrepreneurial activities. Likewise, people without ability may try their hand as entrepreneurs; if they do so, then either they or their backers may incur heavy losses.

The opportunity cost of becoming an entrepreneur is equal to the wage income forgone *plus* a premium for a risk incurred. 'Market equilibrium' is achieved at the point where the expected reward to the marginal entrepreneur is just equal to his opportunity cost. The demand for entrepreneurs is related to the pace of change in the economy, whilst the supply of entrepreneurs depends upon the amount of entrepreneurial ability and the system of screening for it; the latter reflects in turn the organization of education, the social structure and the personal distribution of wealth.

'Equilibrium' in the market for entrepreneurs is achieved not by contract but by conjecture. Because information is in common ownership, search cannot be coordinated through contractual arrangements. Entrepreneurs must conjecture the behaviour of other entrepreneurs, and only if these conjectures are mutually consistent will equilibrium be achieved.

13. Social mobility and the entrepreneur

13.1 INTRODUCTION

One of the main reasons why the entrepreneur has become a cultural hero of capitalism is that he is able to rise from humble origins to a position of power and status. His career reaffirms the ideal of an open society in which the underprivileged can achieve eminence on the basis of their personal merit alone. The personal qualities which are rewarded through entrepreneurship are imagination and foresight, and skill in organizing and delegating work.

The object of this chapter is to show that this heroic vision of the entrepreneur is, to a large extent, unfounded. Although there are, in most generations and in most societies, some people from humble origins who 'make it to the top', there are no grounds – in theory or in practice – for supposing that the probability of making it to the top through entrepreneurship is very high. There are major economic and social barriers to entrepreneurship which someone with potentially superior judgment may well be unable to overcome. The significance of entrepreneurship is not that it is an easy avenue of personal advancement, but that in comparison with other methods of personal advancement it may offer the best prospects to underprivileged people. In other words, an economically disadvantaged person who wishes to make it to the top may find it easier to do so through entrepreneurship than through other means. This means that entrepreneurship is of relative importance in social mobility, even if the absolute degree of mobility it affords is fairly limited.

13.2 ALTERNATIVE FORMS OF ENTREPRENEURSHIP

Before proceeding to the main discussion it is important to emphasize that entrepreneurship can take many different forms depending upon the economic system in which the entrepreneur is operating. The functional definition of entrepreneurship given in Chapter 2 is essentially institution-free: it describes a function which is, in principle, performed in all societies by people whose judgment differs from the norm.

Economic systems can be classified in many ways. There is an obvious distinction between a market economy, which relies upon coordination by voluntary exchange in external markets, and a command economy, which relies upon coordination by control within internal markets. The market economy depends to a large extent upon goods being in private ownership (and transferable ownership at that). The command economy can also function under private ownership: that, after all, is what the firm is, a command economy in a market environment. On the other hand, when all goods are in public ownership, the economy is perforce a command economy; there is no scope for markets because there is no-one else with whom the state can exchange goods. Finally, when all goods are in common ownership both markets and commands remain in abeyance: under common ownership coordination is possible only by conjecture.

Economic systems also differ in the way that ownership is acquired in the first place. Most systems provide for the intergenerational transfer of private property either at the discretion of the owner or through social convention (for example, the enforcement of primogeniture). Some systems provide for the private appropriation of newly discovered resources, while others do not. Most systems provide for the expropriation of private property by the state, though the constitutional constraints upon this differ considerably from one society to another.

Most societies employ a mixture of different economic systems. Typically, different systems are applied to the control of different types of resource. Each system affords some scope for entrepreneurship, though some systems afford much more scope than others. This means that in a typical society the entrepreneur has a choice of institutions within which to exercise his function. This in turn implies that entrepreneurship offers, not a single avenue of advancement, but a number of different avenues, reflecting the different kinds of institution available.

Consider, therefore, an individual living in a society which has a mixture of different economic institutions: the sort of mixture that prevails in most developed Western economies. The individual concerned is dissatisfied with the status and the standard of living that he currently enjoys. In the case of a young person he is dissatisfied with the prospects for a typical person with his kind of background. All sorts of people may come into this category. The individual may come from a very poor family and have a strong desire for conspicuous consumption. He may come from a middle-class family and dislike the prospect of being placed in a secure professional niche. He may be an achiever who has had high aspirations bred into him, or inculcated through his early upbringing. Or he may just be a rebel, perhaps someone who has such a high opinion of himself that nothing is ever good enough for him. In either case it is assumed that the person concerned is motivated to remedy the situation. He does not just aspire to success but has the determination to work for it too.

The various avenues of entrepreneurial advancement available to him are indicated in the left-hand column of Table 13.1. Self-employment and salaried management have already been discussed in detail (see Chapter 12). Both involve identifying opportunities for market making, or for designing and operating more efficient production plants, and so on. These opportunities are exploited by purchasing resources in order to control them more effectively. Financial speculation, on the other hand, involves purchasing resources without seeking to exercise control over them. The idea is to resell the resources later for a capital gain. The speculator relies upon the resources appreciating in value once the information upon which he is acting becomes known to the market as a whole.

Each of these types of entrepreneurship depends upon the voluntary exchange of private property rights; they are manifestations of 'private entrepreneurship'. The main alternative to private entrepreneurship is establishment entrepreneurship, which involves exercising judgment over resources owned by public and other non-profit-oriented organizations. The term 'establishment' is used to indicate that the organization enjoys considerable social status. Establishment organizations include the civil service, the armed forces, universities and the established church. It should be emphasized that not all decisions made within these bodies are concerned with the allocation of resources – at least not on a narrow definition of 'resource'. Within the terms of our definition, therefore, the exercise of judgment in such organizations is not always, strictly speaking, entrepreneurial.

A non-profit-oriented organization typically has a very elaborate and rigid hierarchical structure; indeed, this may be a direct consequence of the lack of profit criteria. As a result, the entrepreneur's objective is quite simply to get to the top of the hierarchy. He hopes that the exercise of his superior judgment will be rewarded by rapid promotion. It is not unreasonable, therefore, to describe the strategy of establishment entrepreneurship as 'pyramid climbing'. Salaried entrepreneurs, too, advance themselves by pyramid climbing, but because the pyramids in the private sector are less formal, and rewards are related not merely to position but to profit, the strategy is not so paramount as it is within the establishment.

Political entrepreneurship provides advancement through election to a governing office. The salaries associated with political posts are often relatively low, but the power and status afforded by the office may often be a reward in itself. Moreover, influence can often be exercised to obtain pecuniary rewards, ranging from consulting fees and remuneration for non-executive directorships to bribes.

The political entrepreneur needs to exercise judgment both before and after his election to office. The judgment exercised prior to his election is not dissimilar to the judgment exercised by a private entrepreneur. To secure

Table 13.1   Alternative forms of entrepreneurship

Type of entrepreneur	Status	Scope of judgment	Subject of judgment	Negotiation involved?	Control involved?
Private entrepreneur					
Self-employed owner of firm	Principal	Partial	Opportunities for making markets, building plants, etc		
Salaried manager	Delegate			Yes	Yes
Financial speculator	Principal	Partial	Valuation of resources	Yes	No
Establishment entrepreneur ('pyramid climber')	Delegate	General*	Means to achieve non-profit objectives		
Political entrepreneur	Representative	General		Some	
Revolutionary entrepreneur	Leader/Dictator	Partial	Opportunities for theft, extortion and racketeering		Yes
Criminal entrepreneur	Principal				

Note: * or partial coordination involving public goods.

203

adoption and then election it is normally necessary to present a personal manifesto. A manifesto is a package of policies, and is advertised by a set of promises (or claims) of varying degrees of sincerity. The political entrepreneur attempts to spot a gap in the market for manifestos, and to exploit it using a novel policy mix.

The analogy should not be overplayed, however. There are at least three important differences between the political and the private entrepreneur. First, the success of the manifesto is determined by a voting mechanism and not a price mechanism. Secondly, once elected, the political entrepreneur has to exercise further judgment in carrying out his policies. His 'product' is not actually delivered until his policies are implemented. Finally, the politician is normally elected for a fixed term of office, so that the electors cannot revise their purchasing arrangements whenever they like. This affords considerable protection to the politician who cannot deliver the promises he has made. These factors lead to important differences in the tactical behaviour of politicians and private entrepreneurs. They also have obvious implications for the quality of the product supplied to the consumers (the electorate).

Revolution and crime are both illegal forms of entrepreneurship (though inevitably a successful revolution acquires retrospective legality). Petty crime does not involve a significant element of judgment, only a willingness to contravene laws that most other people are willing to respect. It is normally only organized crime that qualifies as being entrepreneurial, as it involves the selection of targets that other criminals might well consider too risky or too difficult. Crime exemplifies coordination which is private but not social. The simplest crime is theft, which involves the involuntary redistribution of property. Extortion is somewhat more sophisticated, as it involves the sale of protection (often against theft). Extortion has the advantage that it avoids the perpetration of crimes which harm the victim more than they benefit the criminal; the criminal makes a market in protection and can appropriate the gains from trade with his potential victim. Extortion therefore involves social coordination with respect to the perpetration of the crime, though not, obviously, with respect to a situation in which the law is obeyed.

Perhaps the most entrepreneurial crime is racketeering, which involves the organization of an illegal market: for example, the market for alcoholic drinks under prohibition. Racketeering involves the same skills as any other form of intermediation, in particular skill in inventory management. It is riskier than conventional intermediation because of the possibility of detection and punishment. The racketeer will demand a higher rate of profit to compensate for the risk involved. The higher profit will be earned because the additional risk will deter potential competitors, and so enhance the racketeer's monopoly power. The racketeer may even apply additional deterrents of his own, for example the assassination of rivals; for when devising barriers to entry there is no reason why the racketeer should confine himself to legal means.

13.3 ALTERNATIVE AVENUES OF SOCIAL ADVANCEMENT

Entrepreneurship, of whatever kind, is not the only method of social advancement. Table 13.2 distinguishes three alternatives, though there are undoubtedly others. Competitive professionalism involves pursuing an activity which affords high rewards to people with exceptional ability. It is exemplified by the career of a professional entertainer or a sportsman. In many cases rivalry and

Table 13.2   Alternative methods of advancement and their requirements

| | | Requirement | | |
Method	Capital	Social contact with establishment	Formal qualifications	Personal ability
Entrepreneurship				
Private				
Self-employment	M	A		G
Salaried				
management		A	A	G
Financial				
speculation	L	A		G
Pyramid climbing		E	E	G
Political				
representation		A		G
Revolutionary				
activity				V
Crime				G
Non-entrepreneurial				
methods				
Competitive				
professionalism				V
Marriage		E	A	
Hard work and thrift				

Note: L = large, A = advantageous, G = good, M = modest, E = essential, V = very good.

excellence are key elements in the profession; exceptional ability is required because only being the best, or being first, will do. Competitive professionalism is risky in at least two ways. First, the career may end prematurely, if fashions change, injuries are sustained, and so on; even the most distinguished careers may be very short as a result. Secondly, it is often difficult for an individual entering a competitive profession to know whether or not he has the ability to succeed. A long time can be spent struggling for recognition which may never come. There is no completely reliable way of screening for the degree of excellence that is required in the competitive professions. It is necessary for an individual to work his way up from the bottom before he can discover whether he has what it takes to compete at the top.

The professional's success does not depend upon the continual exercise of superior judgment, but it does involve an initial act of judgment in assessing his own personal ability. Like the entrepreneur's qualities, the professional's qualities are difficult to screen for, so that he has to bear most of the risks himself. The professional must risk his own time and effort in getting his career under way, in the same way that the self-employed entrepreneur risks his capital in getting his business started. In both cases the individual makes an entrepreneurial assessment of whether the probability of success is sufficient to compensate for the cost of getting started.

Somewhat similar considerations apply to the second method of social advancement: marriage. In this context marriage represents any strategy of social advancement which seeks to exploit the system of inheritance, dowry or patronage. This system is, of course, a largely traditional and informal one, so that the financial prospects of a marriage may be insecure. Risks also arise because of the element of competition in the courting of particularly wealthy brides (and bridegrooms, too, for that matter). There is clearly some scope for entrepreneurial judgment in selecting suitable targets which other fortune hunters may have overlooked. Judgment is, however, probably only a small part of the competitive process; personal charm and social connections are probably the most important factors. It is on this basis that social advancement through marriage has been classified as a non-entrepreneurial activity.

The final method of advancement is hard work and thrift. In one sense this is decidedly non-entrepreneurial; taken by itself it is a dull and unimaginative strategy. On the other hand, many social historians have identified industry and thrift as key elements in the ethos of enterprising societies. The explanation offered below is that industry and thrift are useful adjuncts to entrepreneurial advancement because they allow the self-employed entrepreneur to accumulate sufficient wealth to get his business off the ground.

13.4 CONSTRAINTS ON ADVANCEMENT

When planning his social advancement, an individual must consider the requirements for the successful pursuit of each of the strategies outlined above. Four main requirements may be distinguished: capital (that is, personal wealth), social contact with the establishment, formal qualifications and personal ability. The kind of ability and the type of qualifications required will obviously depend upon the strategy involved.

Capital is absolutely essential for the financial speculator. Without capital he cannot purchase financial assets, for example equities, that he believes will appreciate in value. Capital requirements are to some extent reduced when an organized option market exists; they are also reduced if firms are highly geared. In either of these cases the speculator can purchase his gamble without contributing significantly to the overall funding of the firm. Even options and the equities of highly-geared firms have a positive value, however, and so, while the capital constraint is eased, it is not eliminated altogether.

Capital is also an important requirement for the self-employed entrepreneur. For example, a self-employed market maker may have to invest in advertising and in inventory before his trading can commence. It is difficult for him to borrow because potential lenders do not necessarily share his views, and so may regard the collateral provided by his inventory as rather poor.

The obvious way for the market maker to overcome the capital constraint is either to take employment as a manager (with a salary linked to his market-making performance) or to save up capital by taking routine work before commencing his entrepreneurial career. It is interesting to reflect that in most developed economies there has been a significant move away from the strategy of thrift towards the strategy of managerial employment. This change has been accompanied by a decline of the ethos of industry and thrift. It is not clear if there is any causal connection between these phenomena or, if there is, in what direction the causation works. It is possible, though, that both these phenomena are linked to a third phenomenon: the rise of formal procedures for screening entrepreneurial ability.

It has been repeatedly emphasized that it is impossible to screen perfectly for entrepreneurial ability; and the higher the level of ability is set, the less reliable screening procedures become. Nevertheless, there exist many organizations – especially the large conglomerate firms – which appear to specialize in screening entrepreneurs. A major instrument in the screening process is the qualification issued by a university, management school or professional association. People with suitable qualifications are taken on as probationary salaried entrepreneurs, and in this way can use their qualifications as an alternative to personal wealth in getting started on their entrepreneurial career. The development of high-level education and the sophisticated screening procedures associated with it may therefore explain the marked trend towards managerial entrepreneurship. The enhanced opportunities for managerial entrepreneurship may in turn account for the apparent atrophy of the ethos of industry and thrift.

The other main use of formal qualifications is in the 'establishment' sector of the economy. Here, it may be suggested, formal qualifications act as a substitute for social contact. Institutions which previously recruited from a very limited social group now recruit on the basis of formal qualifications instead. Aristocracy has given way to meritocracy: the social background of the establishment entrepreneurs may be more diverse as a result, but in some respects their educational background may be just as restricted. Indeed, the greater time in the 'formative years' that is now spent in academic and professional training may lead to a greater uniformity of outlook in the establishment than there was before.

Perhaps the most open avenue of advancement is competitive professionalism, where capital, social contacts and formal qualifications have only a relatively minor role. Competitive professionalism depends crucially on personal ability, though, and the development of ability depends in turn upon access to education and training. In the context of social mobility it is not just the overall level of educational provision that matters, but the way in which admission is regulated. The competitive professional from humble origins depends upon the free provision of facilities, not just of a basic kind, but up to a very advanced level. Since advanced facilities are often expensive, and access to them consequently very limited, he is also dependent upon a system of selective advancement by merit. Fortunately, experience suggests that most societies, whether totalitarian or democratic, encourage social advancement through sport and artistic excellence, and so on, and administer their facilities with these criteria in mind. Their motives, of course, may differ; some societies may support the system for providing 'equality of opportunity' while others may regard it as a means of maximizing the supply of talent for enhancing national status and prestige.

13.5   EDUCATION AND ENTREPRENEURSHIP

The educational system also has implications for the development of entrepreneurial abilities. Table 13.3 summarizes the various ways in which abilities may be acquired. Perhaps the most interesting point is that further education is shown as advantageous, but not essential, for the private entrepreneur. This reflects the view, first, that professional skills are not essential to the private entrepreneur provided that he knows how to delegate to professionals and to

Table 13.3   Personal abilities and the way they are acquired

Method of advancement for which ability is required	Innate ability	Requirements Academic eduction		Training
		Basic	Further	
Private entrepreneurship	E	E	A	
Pyramid climbing	A	E	E	
Political representation	A	E	A	
Revolutionary activity	E	E	A	
Crime				A
Competitive professionalism	E			E

Note: A = advantageous, E = essential.

motivate those that he employs. More significantly, however, it recognizes that in some respects further education may positively disadvantage the entrepreneur.

Formal education has an opportunity cost in terms of on-the-job training forgone; time spent in academic pursuits could have been spent 'learning the trade' as a delegate–entrepreneur. The training may, of course, follow on from the formal education, in which case the formal education merely delays the start of the entrepreneur's career. But in some cases formal education is used to obtain qualifications which give exemption from all or part of the practical training. This 'exchange' of formal education for practical training has two disadvantages. First, it means that the entrepreneur may begin his career in a post where he is delegating tasks which he has never had to perform himself, and as a result the motivation he can supply to his delegates and the quality of supervision he can offer may be very poor. Secondly, formal education may inculcate uniform attitudes among entrepreneurs and so destroy the individuality and diversity of their views. The essence of entrepreneurship is difference of opinion, while the emphasis of much formal education is on conformity of opinion instead. There is also a tendency in formal education to raise only the questions which can be answered precisely, and to avoid issues to which no definitive solution can be given. Entrepreneurship, on the other hand, is very much concerned with situations which cannot be easily defined – and often cannot even be categorized – because they are without precedent. In this context the concept of a precise solution is irrelevant; precision can only be obtained by introducing arbitrary assumptions, or by changing the question to another one. This highlights why it is that academic training, and the use of academic qualifications, has a very limited role in developing and screening entrepreneurs.

13.6   THE PERSONAL QUALITIES OF THE SELF-EMPLOYED ENTREPRENEUR

The preceding analysis generates a number of hypotheses about the sort of people who will opt for each particular strategy of social advancement. It suggests, to begin with, that advancement by entrepreneurship is most suitable for people who lack the exceptional abilities required for competitive professionalism. It is relatively easy to enter competitive professionalism, but very difficult to succeed. Exceptional ability is also required for social advancement by revolution: charismatic leadership, organizing ability and tactical awareness are all required if a revolution is to stand any chance of success.

It is natural for people with good, though not exceptional, ability to get their ability underwritten by some sort of professional qualification. However, as noted above, becoming qualified calls not only for ability but also for a willingness to conform. People who cannot conform, however superficially, are liable to find qualifications difficult to obtain. As a result, they will find it difficult to advance themselves as salaried managers or as pyramid climbers within the establishment.

Social contact with the establishment is an additional requirement for advancement through pyramid climbing. It is advantageous, though not essential, in most other methods of entrepreneurial advancement too. The main exception is organized crime. Although many people may be deterred by moral scruples, and by the risk of detection and punishment, it is apparent that people without social contact have a comparative advantage in pursuing a criminal entrepreneurial career.

Consider now an individual seeking advancement by entrepreneurship, who has adequate, though not exceptional, ability, a nonconformist attitude and a modicum of social contact with the establishment. The main avenues open to him are financial speculation, self-employment and political representation. The main difference between these methods lies in the amount of capital they require. Financial speculation typically requires a large amount of capital so that personal wealth is practically essential; it is a method by which those who are already wealthy can become much wealthier still. Self-employment requires a modest amount of capital, of the sort that could reasonably be accumulated through industry and thrift. It could also be obtained through marriage, though to marry wealth is difficult for someone who has only a modicum of social contact with the establishment. The entrepreneur would have to rely upon a two-stage procedure in which the wealth accumulated through industry and thrift is used to buy a way in to the establishment, and the opportunity is then exploited to make a favourable marriage.

Advancement through political representation may require only a small amount of capital, at least in launching a political career at local level. Essentially, the political entrepreneur solicits votes in the same way that the private entrepreneur solicits capital from financial backers: he 'sells' his policies to his supporters so that he can gain control of their resources – in the case of voters, the publicly owned resources that he controls in their name. The difference is that the political system provides a ready-made framework within which the political entrepreneur can operate, whereas the self-employed entrepreneur has to set up his own system in order to carry on trade or to produce his product.

If it is true that there is easy entry into a political career, then the question arises as to why so many people should opt for self-employment instead. Looking back at Table 13.1, there are three main differences in the role of the politician and the self-employed businessman. To begin with, the self-employed person has greater autonomy, since he is a principal whereas the politician is a representative. This autonomy is likely to be important to the 'rugged individualist': that is, to the person who is by temperament a non-conformist. If the politician is to exploit the institutional framework of a political party, then he needs to accept the constraints of, for example, the committee system by which both parties and governments operate. No such constraints limit the discretion of the self-employed.

Another, and very important, difference is that the self-employed business-man is concerned solely with effecting partial coordination, while the political entrepreneur is concerned with general coordination too (see Chapter 5). The general coordination may be effected at the local, national or international level. In either case the politician is dealing with much wider issues, and more far-reaching proposals for coordination, than is the businessman. The politician works on a broader canvas and pays correspondingly less attention to detail. The businessman seeks to exploit highly specific information within the existing economic order, while the politician uses more general and aggregative information to decide what the economic order should be.

Because of the broader issues with which he deals, it is difficult to devise precise criteria by which the politician's performance can be evaluated. Different members of the electorate have different objectives and so will evaluate the same outcome in different ways. Because he deals with narrower issues, and has only his own objectives to consider, the self-employed businessman can operate with a single precise criterion, namely profit. The businessman therefore exercises his judgment in a much more disciplined environment than does the politician. For this reason, politicians and businessmen, though both entrepreneurs, are in terms of their perceptions and attitudes, very different sorts of people.

It is interesting to consider the political economy of entrepreneurship in the context of this difference in outlook between politicians and self-employed entrepreneurs. Left-wing politicians, in particular, are often highly critical of the activities of self-employed entrepreneurs, and revolutionaries in capitalist economies, of course, take an extreme attitude on this. For their part, the self-employed often regard politicians and revolutionaries merely as incompetents who would be certain to fail in business.

It is possible to understand these attitudes in terms of the difference between partial and general coordination. It may be postulated that those who best understand how partial coordination works, and have the skill to effect it through market-making activities, cannot easily grasp the concept of general coordination as it relates to the reallocation of resources throughout the economy as a whole. They believe that, because it is impossible for any individual to reallocate resources for the entire economy in the same detail, and with the same precision, that they can be reallocated within an individual market, therefore the preparation of outline plans for economy-wide reallocation is a fruitless activity. Likewise, those who understand how general coordination can be achieved through a political process grossly underestimate the difficulty of achieving it in microcosm by the operation of an individual market.

This is not to say, of course, that the debate on the complex issue of alternative economic systems can be reduced to such a trivial level. But it does suggest a reason why sensible debate on this subject may be so difficult to achieve and why, as a result, popular criticism and support for the capitalist system is allowed to hinge upon a simple parody of the true entrepreneur. It is the selection mechanism, matching personal attitudes to different entrepreneurial roles, that in itself makes a common understanding of the nature of that mechanism so difficult to achieve.

13.7   RELIGIOUS AND ETHNIC FACTORS

So far nothing has been said about how religious and ethnic factors influence the method of social advancement. It is not at all clear that the economist has the professional competence to analyse such issues. It is, however, fairly obvious that in principle both factors affect the kind of person who becomes a self-employed entrepreneur.

First, religious views may influence entrepreneurial temperament (or vice versa). Roman Catholicism, for example, identifies personal salvation closely with membership of an institution – the church – and stresses conformity with this institution's outlook. Protestantism, on the other hand, denies the need for institutional intermediation between the individual and his God. The stress is on individuality rather than conformity and is therefore much more conducive to an entrepreneurial outlook.

Many religions emphasize self-denial, which is of course an inducement to thrift. They also emphasize stewardship, which favours maintaining control of assets that have been accumulated as a result of thrift. Some religions, notably Quakerism, discourage entry into certain fields of business and so encourage entrepreneurial activity to be concentrated on the remaining ones.

It is not only the religion itself, of course, which constrains the entrepreneur. The attitudes of society towards people with minority religious beliefs also impose constraints. The constraints on religious minorities are typically most severe in establishment institutions, in which there may be formal screening for religious affiliation. Social attitudes may also inhibit advancement through a political career, and through some of the professions too. Under these circumstances the 'anonymity' of the market place may provide the most attractive cover for personal advancement. As a result, religious minorities, particularly those whose religions emphasize nonconformity, may predominantly pursue social advancement through self-employment.

Religious and ethnic factors are often closely linked. Much of what has been said about religious outlook and attitudes towards religious minorities applies also to social and ethnic outlook, and to attitudes to ethnic minorities. The obvious conclusion is that ethnic minorities, as well as religious minorities, will pursue advancement through self-employment rather than through other means.

SUMMARY

This chapter has considered the alternative avenues of social advancement available to people who believe that they have superior judgment. It is suggested that self-employment is most attractive to people with good all-round ability rather than exceptional ability, with a modicum of social contact but an aversion to conformist institutions, a small amount of capital and a willingness to augment it by thrift, rather poor educational qualifications and a tendency to focus on the partial aspects of coordination, rather than the general aspects which are important in the political sphere.

NOTES AND REFERENCES

Social mobility has a major place in American folklore, as Sarachek (1978), Wohl (1953) and Wyllie (1954) emphasize. Probably as a result, considerable work has been done on the social origins of the US business elite: see Bendix and Howton (1959), Hughes (1966b), Mills (1945), Newcomer (1955), Redlich (1940–51) and Warner and Abegglen (1955a, 1955b). Much less work has been done on UK business elites, though see Copeman (1955), Erickson (1959), Lupton and Wilson (1959) and Sargent Florence (1961). Studies of business elites in other countries include Alexander (1964) (Greece), Marris and Somerset (1971) (Kenya), Nafziger (1978) (India), Papanek (1972) (Pakistan) and Sayigh (1962) (Lebanon). It is interesting that Frank Taussig, best known for his work on the theory of international trade, was sufficiently interested in social mobility and business elites to produce two studies on the subject. Unfortunately the first (Taussig, 1915) is rather cursory while the second (Taussig and Joslyn, 1932) provides a somewhat biased interpretation of the results (though his actual statistics are broadly in line with those reported by others).

At the other end of the spectrum there have been a number of interesting studies of the origins and attitudes of small businessmen. See, for example, Ahmed (1977), Davids (1963), Fogarty (1973), Lynn (1974) and Pelzel (1965).

Redlich has done some interesting work on the ability of establishment groups to switch into private entrepreneurship when their traditional status is assailed; see, for example, Redlich (1956, 1958).

Recent research on social mobility as a whole is critically reviewed by Kaelble (1981). There is a large and very diffuse literature on cultural aspects of entrepreneurship: see in particular Belshaw (1965), Bendix (1957), Cochran (1958, 1965a, 1965b), Fleming (1979), Gerschenkron (1953), Lamb (1952), Owens (1978) and Plum (1977). The classic studies of religion and entrepreneurship are Fanfani (1935), Sombart (1915) and Weber (1930). Of these, the Weber thesis has attracted the greatest interest; for a review of the debate, see Green (1959).

Smith, N.R. (1967) offers a simple classification of entrepreneurs according to their personal characteristics; the role of personality in entrepreneurship has also been considered by Collins and Moore (1964) and Jenks (1949, 1965). Criminal entrepreneurs have been studied by Blok (1974) and Smith, D.C. (1978), while Heyl (1978) considers entrepreneurship in prostitution.

14. Alternative theories of the entrepreneur

14.1 INTRODUCTION

This chapter critically reviews the leading economic theories of the entrepreneur: the X-efficiency theory of Leibenstein, the market process theory of Hayek and Kirzner, the risk-bearing theory of Knight and the innovation theory of Schumpeter. It also examines the relevance to entrepreneurship of the theories of the firm developed by Andrews and Penrose. It is suggested that the theory presented above is in many respects a synthesis and extension of these theories. Although there are a number of differences between the theories on specific aspects of entrepreneurship, on the whole their similarities are more significant than their differences. Each theory is valuable because it emphasizes some particular aspect of entrepreneurship. The theories are essentially complementary, both to each other and to the theory presented in this book.

14.2 LEIBENSTEIN'S X-EFFICIENCY THEORY

Leibenstein's X-efficiency theory, originally developed for other purposes, has been applied by him to analyse the role of the entrepreneur. Basically, X-efficiency is the degree of inefficiency in the use of resources within the firm: it measures the extent to which the firm fails to realize its productive potential. For a given set of inputs, productive potential is identified with a point on the neoclassical production frontier. X-efficiency arises either because the firm's resources are used in the wrong way, or because they are wasted – that is, they are not used at all.

X-efficiency is more than a concept, however; it is a new paradigm which, according to Leibenstein, contrasts starkly with the neoclassical paradigm. Where neoclassical theory assumes full rationality, in the sense that decision makers solve their problems using the calculus of maximization, X-efficiency theory assumes that there are psychological costs of being fully rational. These limit the extent to which individuals plan to exploit all the opportunities available, and to satisfy all the constraints to which they are subject. If *ex ante* plans only approximate to actual constraints then *ex post* the plans will turn out differently from what was expected. The more approximately an individual plans, the more likely it is that disequilibrium will result. The anticipation of disequilibrium leads to internally felt pressure. According to Leibenstein, individuals trade off 'constraint concern' for 'pressure'; different individuals have different attitudes, and hence exhibit different degrees of constraint concern and different degrees of neoclassical 'irrationality'.

Leibenstein identifies four other differences between X-efficiency theory and neoclassical theory. One is that contracts are incomplete: in particular, employment contracts do not specify jobs precisely, or quantify the amount of effort required. This in turn means, according to Leibenstein, that effort is discretionary: it is the employee himself, and not the employer, who decides how hard he will work. The employee will take this decision in pursuit of his own interests and not those of his employer. X-efficiency theory also asserts that effort is required in order to change the allocation of resources: it is unpleasant to have to break old habits, and it takes time to settle into a new routine. This creates a psychological inertia which discourages the individual from adjusting from one state to another. Inertia, like constraint, is a personality characteristic.

Finally, Leibenstein departs from simple neoclassical theory in regarding the firm as an organization of different individuals with no unanimity between them about objectives. The employer (or the shareholders, in the case of a joint-stock company) may be interested in maximizing profits, but the agents – who are the actual decision makers – are not. The agents pursue their own objectives, which are incompatible with maximum effort. The role of the organization is to apply pressure on the agents to maintain or increase their effort. The pressure is internal to the firm but external to the individual agent. The pressure increases the individual's constraint concern, raises his effort, and thereby moves the firm towards its neoclassical production frontier.

Leibenstein regards entrepreneurship as a creative response to X-efficiency. Other people's lack of effort, and the consequent inefficiency of the organizations that employ them, create opportunities for entrepreneurs. Entrepreneurial activities pose a competitive threat to an inefficient organization. This is translated into pressure on the agents which encourages them to maintain an adequate degree of constraint concern.

Leibenstein identifies two main roles for the entrepreneur. 'Input completion' involves making available inputs which improve the efficiency of existing production methods or facilitate the introduction of new ones. It is normally effected by intermediation in factor markets, in particular the markets for venture capital and management skills. The role of the entrepreneur is to improve the flow of information in these markets.

The second role, 'gap filling', is closely akin to the arbitrage function emphasized by Kirzner, and described below. Leibenstein provides a very vivid description of gap filling. He visualizes the economy as a net made up of nodes and pathways:

> The nodes represent industries or households that receive inputs (or consumer goods) along the pathway and send outputs (final goods and inputs for the other commodities) to the other nodes. The perfect competition model would be represented by a net that is complete: one that has pathways that are well marked and well defined, one that has well-marked and well-defined nodes, and one in which each element (that is firm or household) of each node deals with every other node along the pathways on equal terms for the same commodity. In the realistic model that we have in mind, there are holes and tears in the net, obstructions (knots) along the pathways, and some nodes and pathways, where they exist, are poorly defined and poorly marked or entirely unmarked from the viewpoint of elements of other nodes. We may refer to this net as impeded, incomplete, and 'dark' in contrast to the unimpeded and 'well lit' net that represents the competitive mode. (Leibenstein, 1978, p. 45)

Few people would probably now object to the gist of Leibenstein's argument, though there remain some doubts about his method of analysis. Leibenstein seems to believe that his psychologism is incompatible with the neoclassical view of rational economic man. Yet the main thrust of the neoclassical rationality postulate is simply to rule out inconsistent behaviour. In a world where information is costly and thought has an opportunity cost of time and effort, Leibenstein's individuals behave quite rationally. In operational terms their behaviour seems indistinguishable from rational individuals coping with the constraints imposed by limited information. For example, when information processing is costly, it is rational for an individual to apply the same decision rule habitually until a persistent disequilibrium is encountered and then, and only then, to modify it. Without some sort of rationality postulate it is difficult to predict what kind of decision rules will be used; but with a rationality postulate it is possible to identify optimal decision rules and to show how the optimal decision rule varies according to the circumstances. Thus, while the phenomena Leibenstein describes are real enough, his psychologism seems to hinder rather than help the explanation of them.

The absence of any substitute for the rationality postulate in Leibenstein's theory makes it compatible with a wide range of behaviour. It provides a framework of analysis which can accommodate practically anything. Unlike neoclassical theory, Leibenstein's theory can accommodate the entrepreneur. But without further assumptions it can say very little about the way that entrepreneurs behave. There is little or nothing in Leibenstein's theory which is incompatible with the theory presented in this book, but the present theory provides specific hypotheses about entrepreneurial behaviour which Leibenstein's theory cannot.

14.3   HAYEK AND KIRZNER ON THE MARKET PROCESS

Hayek's main contribution to the theory of the entrepreneur is to point out that the absence of entrepreneurs in neoclassical economics is intimately associated with the assumption of market equilibrium. According to Hayek the equilibrium postulate is equivalent to a postulate of full information; not full information in the sense of complete information about every conceivable thing, but full information in the sense that no further information is required in order to modify anyone's decisions.

> [Equilibrium] means only that the different plans which the individuals ... have made for action in time are mutually compatible. An equilibrium will continue, once it exists, so long as the external data correspond to the common expectations of all the members of the society. The continuance of a state of equilibrium in this sense is then not dependent on the objective data being constant in an absolute sense and is not necessarily confined to a stationary process ... It appears that the concept of equilibrium merely means that the foresight of the different members of the society is in a special sense correct. It must be correct in the sense that every person's plan is based on the expectation of just those actions of other people which those other people intend to perform and that all these plans are based on the expectation of the same set of external facts, so that under certain conditions nobody will have any reason to change his plans. Correct foresight is then not, as it has sometimes been understood, a precondition which must exist in order that equilibrium may be arrived at. It is rather a defining characteristic of a state of equilibrium. (Hayek, 1949, pp. 41–2)

According to Hayek, the empirical content of economics relates to the process of adjustment towards an equilibrium. This process involves the acquisition and communication of knowledge. The main hypothesis is that,

> under certain conditions, the knowledge and intentions of the different members of society are supposed to come more and more into agreement or, to put the same thing in less general and less exact but more concrete terms, the expectations of the people and particularly of the entrepreneurs will become more and more correct ... . The only trouble is that we are still pretty much in the dark about (a) the *conditions* under which this tendency is supposed to exist and (b) the nature of the *process* by which individual knowledge is changed. (Hayek, 1949, p. 45)

Hayek himself goes only a short way towards answering these two questions. His main contention is that a decentralized process of voluntary exchange, based upon the price system, is more efficient than a centralized process based upon bureaucratic organization.

> We must look at the price system as such a mechanism for communicating information if we want to understand its real function – a function which, of course, it fulfils less perfectly as prices grow more rigid. (Even when quoted

prices have become quite rigid, however, the forces which could operate through changes in price still operate to a considerable extent through changes in the other terms of the contract.) The most significant fact about this system is the economy of knowledge with which it operates, or how little the individual participants need to know in order to be able to take the right action. In abbreviated form, by a kind of symbol, only the most essential information is passed on only to those concerned. It is more than a metaphor to describe the price system as a kind of machinery for registering change, or a system of telecommunications which enables individual producers to watch merely the movement of a few pointers, as an engineer might watch the hands of a few dials, in order to adjust their activities to changes of which they may never know more than is reflected in the price movement. (Hayek, 1949, pp. 86–7)

By contrast, a centralized system effects a functional separation between those who acquire the information at first hand, and those who aggregate and act upon the information at second hand. The lack of incentive, the sluggish response and the bureaucratic costs of centralized organization are, to Hayek's mind, overwhelming arguments in favour of decentralization. Fellow-economists who advocate centralization undervalue the market because it has evolved by trial and error and improvisation: it is 'just one of those formations which man has learned to use ... after he had stumbled upon it without understanding it'. The market is not recognized as the 'marvel' that it is because it is not the 'result of deliberate human design'.

Hayek visualizes a world in which there is a continuous process of discovery: not usually major discoveries such as technological breakthroughs, but mostly minor discoveries about individual wants at particular times and places. These discoveries are localized, so that different people have access to different information; in particular, most people know much more about themselves than they do about others. Markets help people to communicate their discoveries to others and to learn of discoveries that other people have made. This enables individuals to coordinate their decisions and thereby move towards a state of equilibrium.

But Hayek stops short of modelling the process by which prices are set and by which they are adjusted towards an equilibrium. For Kirzner the adjustment of price is the main role of the entrepreneur. If the wrong price prevails in the market, then an opportunity for profit is created. Somewhere in the market is a frustrated buyer or seller who would be willing, respectively, to pay a higher price or accept a lower one. Then again, if different prices prevail in the same market, there is scope for profitable arbitrage between the two segments of the market. Or if the prices of inputs are out of line with the prices of outputs then there is scope for expanding production of some products at the expense of others.

According to Kirzner, alertness to disequilibrium is the distinguishing characteristic of the entrepreneur. Alertness enables some individuals to intervene in the market by changing the price while other individuals simply respond by changing their buying and selling plans in the light of the newly quoted price. Rather disappointingly, however, the introduction of the concept of alertness signals the end, rather than the beginning, of Kirzner's explanation of the market process:

> We do not clearly understand how entrepreneurs get their flashes of superior foresight. We cannot explain how some men discover what is around the corner before others do. We may certainly explain ... how men explore for oil by carefully weighing alternative ways of spending a limited amount of search resources, but we cannot explain how a prescient entrepreneur realizes before others do that a search for oil may be rewarding. As an empirical matter, however, opportunities do tend to be perceived and exploited. And it is on this observed tendency that our belief in a determinate market process is founded. (Kirzner, 1976, p. 121)

The reason for this abrupt termination of the analysis does not seem to be any technical difficulty, but rather a belief that further inquiry does not form part of a legitimate research agenda. As a disciple of von Mises, Kirzner maintains that the primary role of economic theory is to explain behaviour in terms of purposeful human action, and to consider to what extent purposeful human actions can interact to produce unexpected outcomes. To pursue the analysis of entrepreneurship further would be to go beyond the limits of this agenda. Worse than that, it would violate one of the tenets of Austrian subjectivism, namely that there is 'an indeterminacy and unpredictability inherent in human preferences, human expectations, and human knowledge'. It is of course, quite conceivable that the entrepreneur believes other people's actions to be predictable, and that that is why he intervenes in the market process. Conversely, anyone who believes that the entrepreneur is predictable has an incentive to intervene himself in the market process and so become an entrepreneur. To Kirzner this provides a satisfactory basis for asserting the inherent unpredictability of the entrepreneur. It suggests that no predictor can be anything but an entrepreneur himself, and so makes a predictive theory of entrepreneurship impossible.

14.4   KNIGHT ON THE ROLE OF UNCERTAINTY

Knight identifies the entrepreneur as a recipient of pure profit. Profit is the residual income available after all contractual payments have been deducted from the revenues of the enterprise. It is the reward to the entrepreneur for bearing the costs of uncertainty.

Knight identifies uncertainty with a situation where the probabilities of alternative outcomes cannot be determined either by *a priori* reasoning or by statistical inference. *A priori* reasoning is simply irrelevant to economic situations. Statistical inference is impossible because the situation involves a unique event. It does not belong to a larger population of identical events. In particular, there is no precedent for it, so that no assessment of probability can be made on the basis of relative frequency. This is the foundation for Knight's distinction between uncertainty and risk.

Uncertainty is a ubiquitous aspect of business decisions because production takes time. Decisions on inputs must be made now in order to create output for the future. Households, as factor owners, demand spot payment for their services. At the same time they are unwilling to commit themselves on future demand for the product, because they anticipate that unforseeable changes will occur.

> But the consumer does not even contract for his goods in advance, generally speaking. A part of the reason might be the consumer's uncertainty as to his ability to pay at the end of the period, but this does not seem to be important in fact. The main reason is that he does not know what he will want, and how much, and how badly; consequently he leaves it to producers to create goods and hold them ready for his decision when the time comes. The clue to the apparent paradox is, of course, in the 'law of large numbers', the consolidation of risks (or uncertainties). The consumer is, to himself, only one; to the producer he is a mere multitude in which individuality is lost. It turns out that an outsider can foresee the wants of a multitude with more ease and accuracy than an individual can attain with respect to his own. This phenomenon gives us the most fundamental feature of the economic system, production for a market. (Knight, 1921, p. 241)

Knight is mainly concerned to show how markets, together with institutions such as the large corporation, contribute to specializing uncertainty bearing in the hands of those best equipped to make decisions under uncertainty. The main quality required for making production decisions is foresight. Individuals differ in the amount of foresight they have, and competition ensures that individuals with the greatest degree of foresight (relative to other abilities) specialize in making production decisions.

However, it does not follow that individuals with foresight will become self-employed and make decisions on their own behalf. They may instead become managers of a large firm. Knight argues that business uncertainty can be reduced through 'consolidation'. Consolidation is to uncertainty what insurance is to risk: it is a method of reducing total uncertainty by pooling individual instances and allowing each individual to hold a share of the pool. It is widely recognized today that an individual's exposure to uncertainty can be reduced through portfolio diversification in the equity market. Knight recognizes this possibility, which he calls 'diffusion', but does not accord it much prominence as a vehicle for the reduction of uncertainty. He believes that uncertainty is reduced mainly through the pooling of uncertainties by the large firm.

The gains in uncertainty reduction from large-scale organization are, in Knight's view, quite considerable, so much so that the most important uncertainties relate, not to producing for a market itself, but to the selection of suitable managers to take production decisions. Once a person with foresight has been recruited by the firm, much of the uncertainty in producing for a market is eliminated. The crucial decisions made within the large firm are decisions about personnel recruitment. The pure profit generated by a large firm is compensation to people for bearing the uncertainty that they have delegated decisions to the wrong sort of person.

Knight does not seem to anticipate that there will be much difficulty in ensuring that managers with foresight exercise it properly on the stockholders' behalf. The moral hazard problem is negligible, presumably because close supervision of the manager is possible. Much greater moral hazard arises with the directors of the firm who recruit the managers and supervise them on the stockholders' behalf. The unavoidable moral hazard involved in delegating direction means that directors cannot possibly be fully insured against the consequences of their decisions. They must operate under profit-related incentives, and so effectively they must become stockholders in the firm. Thus directors who make decisions under uncertainty also bear the consequences of those decisions and are *ipso facto* recipients of pure profit.

Some people have good judgment of other people's abilities and others do not. But no-one can be certain of their own judgment of other people's abilities. As a result, confidence in his own judgment is perhaps the most important characteristic of the entrepreneur. This has to be coupled with a low aversion to risk, as reflected in a disposition to back up his judgment with his own capital. The elasticity of supply of self-confident people is, in Knight's view, the single most important determinant of the level of profit and of the number of entrepreneurs.

The income of *any particular entrepreneur* will in general tend to be larger (1) as he himself has ability, and good luck; but (2), perhaps more important, as there is in the society a scarcity of self-confidence combined with the power to make effective guarantees to employees. The abundance or scarcity of mere ability to manage business successfully exerts relatively little influence on profit: the main thing is the rashness or timidity of entrepreneurs (actual and potential) as a class in bidding up the prices of productive services. Entrepreneur income, being residual, is determined by the demand for these other services, which demand is a matter of the self-confidence of entrepreneurs as a class, rather than upon a demand for entrepreneur services in a direct sense. We must see at once that it is perfectly possible for entrepreneurs as a class to sustain a net loss, which would merely have to be made up out of their earnings in some other capacity. This would be the natural result in a population combining low ability with high 'courage'. On the other hand, if men generally judge their own abilities well, the general rate of profit will probably be low, whether ability itself is low or high, but much more variable and fluctuating for a low level of real capacity. The condition for large profits is a narrowly limited supply of high-grade ability with a low general level of initiative as well as ability. (Knight, 1921, pp. 283–4)

Knight's analysis exhibits very clearly the difficulties of theorizing about entrepreneurship, and in particular the problems of structuring the analysis in a coherent way. As a result, Knight's views have been widely misinterpreted in the past. Many parts of the present work are simply a reformulation of ideas first presented by Knight. The concepts of probability and judgment are slightly different, but the basic view of the way that the market system allocates judgmental decision making to entrepreneurs is the same in both cases.

14.5   SCHUMPETER ON INNOVATION

Schumpeter, perhaps more than any other writer, is very explicit about the economic function of the entrepreneur. The entrepreneur is the prime mover in economic development, and his function is to innovate, or to 'carry out new combinations'. Five types of innovation are distinguished: the introduction of a new good (or an improvement in the quality of an existing good), the introduction of a new method of production, the opening of a new market (in particular an export market in a new territory), the 'conquest of a new source of supply of raw-materials or half-manufactured goods' and the creation of a new type of industrial organization, in particular the formation of a trust or some other type of monopoly.

Anyone who performs this function is an entrepreneur, whether they are independent businessmen or the 'dependent' employees of a company such as managers or directors. Not all businessmen are entrepreneurs: the typical entrepreneur is the founder of a new firm rather than the manager of an established one.

Schumpeter is adamant that the entrepreneur is not a risk bearer. Risk bearing is the function of the capitalist who lends his funds to the entrepreneur. The entrepreneur bears risk only in so far as he acts as his own capitalist. Unlike Knight, Schumpeter does not perceive much problem of moral hazard for a capitalist lending to an entrepreneur.

Entrepreneurs spend a lot of their time doing non-entrepreneurial things:

> The entrepreneur of earlier times was not only as a rule the capitalist too, he was also often – as he still is today in the case of small concerns – his own technical expert, in so far as a professional specialist was not called in for special cases. Likewise he was (and is) often his own buying and selling agent, the head of his office, his own personnel manager, and sometimes, even though as a rule he of

course employed solicitors, his own legal adviser in current affairs. And it was performing some or all of these functions that regularly filled his days. The carrying out of new combinations can no more be a vocation than the making and execution of strategical decisions, although it is this function and not his routine work that characterizes the military leader. Therefore the entrepreneur's essential function must always appear mixed up with other kinds of activity, which as a rule must be much more conspicuous than the essential one. Hence the Marshallian definition of the entrepreneur, which simply treats the entrepreneurial function as 'management' in the widest meaning, will naturally appeal to most of us. We do not accept it, simply because it does not bring out what we consider to be the salient point and the only one which specifically distinguishes entrepreneurial from other activities. (Schumpeter, 1934, p. 77)

The climate most favourable to innovation is when the economy is approaching an equilibrium, for then the future seems relatively easy to foresee. The first innovations, made by the most talented entrepreneurs, prove successful, and this encourages less talented entrepreneurs to follow suit. Because they are adapting ideas which the pioneers have already tried out, the risks that the capitalists perceive in backing the less talented entrepreneurs are relatively low. A wave of innovation follows, which then, for a variety of reasons, quickly recedes.

Schumpeter believed that talented entrepreneurs were a very scarce breed. Their scarcity lies not so much in their alertness, or in their professionalism, as in their psychology. While entrepreneurs are rational economic men, their objective is not the pursuit of consumption in the usual sense of that word. The motivating factors are threefold:

First of all, there is the dream and the will to found a private kingdom, usually, though not necessarily, also a dynasty. The modern world really does not know any such positions, but what may be attained by industrial or commercial success is still the nearest approach to medieval lordship possible to modern man. Its fascination is specially strong for people who have no other chance of achieving social distinction.

Then there is the will to conquer the impulse to fight, to prove oneself superior to others, to succeed for the sake, not of the fruits of success, but of success itself. From this aspect economic action becomes akin to sport – there are financial races, or rather boxing matches.

Finally there is the joy of creating, of getting things done, or simply of exercising one's energy and ingenuity. ... Our type seeks out difficulties, changes in order to change, delights in ventures. This group of motives is the most distinctly anti-hedonist of the three. (Schumpeter, 1934, pp. 93–4)

The precursor to innovation is invention, which is a field of imaginative activity outside the province of the entrepreneur. The process of invention forms no part of Schumpeter's theory, but one of the attractive features of the theory is how easily the dynamics of invention can be grafted onto it. Schumpeter recognized that invention could be an endogenous process stimulated by the desire to alleviate pressing scarcities, but his attitude is basically to regard it as autonomous.

The possibility of grafting on a theory of invention may be illustrated as follows. It is often suggested that modern economic growth is related to the innovation of mass-market multi-purpose goods, such as the typical consumer durable. The innovation of these goods often depends critically upon the invention of components from which they can be made up. Innovation of a new multi-purpose good is possible only when the design of each of the constituent components has evolved sufficiently to provide the requisite standards of compactness, reliability and performance. If improvements in component design are generated by an autonomous random process of invention, then there will come a critical point at which mass production of the multi-purpose good becomes viable. This is the point at which each of the components has just evolved to the requisite standard. This may trigger off a major innovation – such as the railway or the motor car – whose repercussions are sufficiently widespread to stimulate a wave of subsidiary innovations. This wave of innovations uses up the outstanding stock of inventions which were pending adoption, and leads to a subsequent lull in innovation until the stock of inventions builds up again to a threshold level.

Schumpeter himself was very cautious about relying upon major innovations and their consequent economies and spin-offs as an explanation for the clustering of innovation observed during the business cycle. He regarded waves of innovation and their 'creative destruction' as a basic phenomenon of capitalist economic development. He recognized that the waves could take very different forms in different times and places: he was concerned to offer an analytical framework for the interpretation of varied historical experience rather than to formulate a narrow theory to which all historical experience was alleged to conform.

14.6   ANDREWS AND PENROSE ON THE ENTREPRENEURIAL FIRM

Andrews' theory is not concerned primarily with the entrepreneur, but with providing a realistic account of competition between firms at the industry level. His analysis is relevant to entrepreneurship because he analyses aspects of business strategy which are ignored by the neoclassical theory of the firm, but which are crucial to the success or failure of a business. The decisions which Andrews analyses are very much the decisions with which entrepreneurs are preoccupied in practice.

This is no accident. The primary requirement imposed by Andrews is that his theory should conform with the empirical regularities indicated by the fieldwork which he and his Oxford colleagues had conducted. Andrews maintains that the typical firm is in a state of disequilibrium – or at least incomplete equilibrium – but that firms in the same industry manage to maintain oligopolistic stability in the long run.

Competition within the industry maintains a fairly uniform price, with the market divided between the firms on the basis that each enjoys the goodwill of a certain group of customers. One aspect of goodwill is loyalty to the manufacturer's brand, as in Chamberlin's analysis of imperfect competition, but another aspect, on which considerable stress is laid, is the quality of service that the firm provides. Quality of service is achieved by maintaining the price stable and holding adequate inventory to meet all demand from stock. Firms do not adjust price and output to maximize short-run profit, but rather forgo short-run profit so as not to lose goodwill.

Most firms produce a range of different products, even though the products may all be within a fairly narrow industrial category. Firms are always prepared to enter others' markets; indeed, the typical entrant is not a new firm, which may be small and economically weak, but rather a large firm diversifying into a new product line. The threat of potential entry is normally strong, therefore, and this threat keeps the price level in each industry in line with average costs.

Andrews recognizes that the provision of quality of service to customers often has to be delegated by the manufacturer to the retailer. The main reason is spatial: to provide prompt and convenient service, stocks have to be located at all the major centres of demand. But to reach this demand effectively, and to maintain stability in market shares, it is necessary for the manufacturer to have influence – if not control – over the retailer's activities. It is necessary, for example, to ensure that the retailer holds adequate stocks to back up the demand created by the manufacturer's advertising. In Andrews' view such control may be quite legitimate, even if it involves restrictive business practices such as resale price maintenance.

Andrews develops his analysis using Marshallian techniques which do not seem very well suited to his purposes. It is possible that he was not radical enough in his theorizing and carried over equilibrium techniques to analyse disequilibrium situations. Thus, while the issues that Andrews identifies are also the issues which most businessmen (and indeed our own analysis, too) identify as important, his analysis of these issues does not provide entirely satisfactory answers.

Penrose, like Andrews, is concerned with injecting greater realism into the theory of the firm. Her analysis, though it does not involve formal technique, is in many respects much more tightly argued than Andrews'. She presents a truly dynamic theory of the firm, which explains how the creation and use of information governs the growth of the firm through a feedback mechanism. The starting point is an organizational theory of the firm:

> The business firm, as we have defined it, is both an administrative organization and a collection of productive resources; its general purpose is to organize the use of its 'own' resources together with other resources acquired from outside the firm for the production and sale of goods and services at a profit; its physical resources yield services essential for the execution of the plans of its personnel, whose activities are bound together by the administrative framework within which they are carried on. The administrative structure of the firm is the creation of the men who run it; the structure may have developed rather haphazardly in response to immediate needs as they arose in the past, or it may have been shaped largely by conscious attempts to achieve a 'rational' organization; it may consist of no more than one or two men who divide the task of management; or it may be so elaborate that its complete ramifications cannot even be depicted in the most extensive chart. In any event, there need be nothing 'fixed' about it; it can, in principle, always be adapted to the requirements of the firm – expanded, modified, and elaborated as the firm grows and changes.
>
> The productive activities of such a firm are governed by what we shall call its 'productive opportunity', which comprises all of the productive possibilities that its 'entrepreneurs' see and can take advantage of. A theory of the growth of firms is essentially an examination of the changing productive opportunity of firms; in order to find a limit to growth, or a restriction on the rate of growth, the productive opportunity of a firm must be shown to be limited in any period. (Penrose, 1959, pp. 31–2)

The personal qualities of the entrepreneur are an important influence on the growth of the firm. Versatility gives the entrepreneur a wider business horizon and encourages him to experiment with new products; he has 'the imaginative effort, the sense of timing, the instinctive recognition of what will catch on'. Fund-raising ingenuity is crucial, particularly for the owner of a small firm trying to get his business off the ground. Judgment, too, is important, for it is the accuracy of the entrepreneur's 'image' or perception of his environment that allows imagination to be exercised without too much risk of a mistake. Finally, there is the entrepreneur's ambition. Two different types of ambition are distinguished: the ambition of the 'product-minded' or 'workmanship-minded' entrepreneur who may be satisfied to maintain his firm at a fairly stable size, and the 'empire builder' who is interested in achieving dominance for his firm in its particular industry. Empire builders are often impatient for dominance, and are inclined to pursue growth through the fastest possible avenue, which is that of acquisition or merger.

A major influence on the firm's capacity to grow is the volume of managerial resources which are uncommitted to current projects. These managerial resources are available for investigating new avenues of growth. Excess managerial resources exist within the firm because it is normally efficient only to hire indivisible units of management – that is, full-time employees. Undertaking new projects expands the demand for routine managerial services and leads to an expansion of the management team. But the expansion is 'lumpy' and so unused managerial resources may persist, leading to further growth in the future. Provided the entrepreneur can adjust the organizational structure to accommodate additional managers, the limit to the size of the firm continually recedes. The ultimate limit on the rate of expansion is set by the ability of the entrepreneur and his existing management team to accommodate changes in the organization. New managers have to be recruited and have to be trained in organizational procedures. If the firm grows too fast, then the organization will become dislocated by excessive demands on managers, and disaster will ensue.

It is highly unlikely that large firms will be able to follow up all the openings that their current trading experience suggests are present. The very success of large firms may create 'interstices' that small firms can exploit. They may be able to supply complementary goods to the large firm's customers, to exploit spin-off from the large firm's production experience, or even to set up as specialist suppliers of one of the large firm's inputs. Although Penrose rejects biological analogy, it is not unreasonable to see this as a process by which the large mature firms, quite inadvertently, nurture small firms, some of which will eventually grow to maturity themselves. Where the analogy breaks down is that some of the large firms may continue to get larger, or at least maintain their size, so that not all the mature firms will necessarily eventually die off.

14.7   THE PRESENT THEORY AND ITS RELATION TO ITS PRECURSORS

Each of the theories reviewed above starts, to some extent, from where its predecessor leaves off. Leibenstein's theory describes the essential characteristics of the environment in which the entrepreneur operates. In the world of the entrepreneur it is inefficiency, not efficiency, which is the normal state of affairs. Economic success is of little interest when everyone is successful in making the best use of the resources at their disposal. Success only becomes interesting when failure is the norm. According to Leibenstein, the immediate cause of failure is lack of effort. Of course, if relaxation is a good and effort a bad then lack of effort is not difficult to explain. It does, however, raise the question as to whether relaxation *per se* can be regarded as an indication of inefficiency.

An alternative explanation of inefficiency is that the wrong decisions are made about the allocation of resources because the people who make the decisions either do not have all the relevant information at their disposal or do not interpret it properly. Possession of inadequate information may be a result of laziness, but it is more likely to reflect the fact that information sources are localized and that information is costly to transmit. The recognition of a wrong decision implies, of course, that someone else knows what the right decision is. This in turn means that there is someone who believes that they have better information, or better powers of interpretation, than the decision maker; in other words, that there is someone who believes they have superior judgment.

For Hayek, the essence of the efficiency problem is to channel information to the people who need it, and to channel it to them with maximum economy, using as sharp a signal as possible. According to Hayek, the best signalling system is the market. Improving the operations of markets is therefore the best way to improve allocative efficiency. As Kirzner explains, there is a continual incentive to improve market operations because of the profit opportunities that are created by market disequilibrium. Competition between entrepreneurs in exploiting these arbitrage opportunities causes price to adjust so that the signals reaching other transactors become more accurate indicators of scarcity. With the greater accuracy of the scarcity indicators, buyers and sellers form more realistic trading plans – that is, plans which are in equilibrium with each other.

But is there any guarantee that those who are attracted into arbitrage have the skills necessary to set the right prices rather than the wrong ones? If the arbitrager can recontract with buyers and sellers, then there is no risk that arbitrage can go wrong. But if recontracting is impossible, then the arbitrager has to buy from the seller before he can sell to the buyer, and if he misjudges the buyer's attitude then he may be left with unsold inventory.

This speculative nature of entrepreneurship was emphasized by Knight. He analysed speculation not so much in terms of intermediation but in terms of producing for a market. The combination of time lags in production, unforeseen changes in household circumstances, and the absence of forward markets in the product, exposes the producer to uncertainty about product demand. According to Knight, there exist people with sufficient foresight to reduce – if not eliminate – this uncertainty. The problem is that foresight is not a readily identifiable characteristic. Uncertainty is therefore translated into the context of the decision about whom to place in charge of production. In other words, uncertainty is a characteristic not so much of the product market as of the market in management.

Having isolated the main locus of uncertainty, Knight then examines how the bearing of uncertainty will be allocated in a market economy. In a sense, his analysis parallels our own, but his exposition is marred by an unfortunate definition of uncertainty. The crucially subjective nature of uncertainty does not lie, as Knight suggests, in the uniqueness of the business situation, but in the fact that opinions differ about what is the most appropriate policy in such a situation. The uniqueness of the situation clearly means that a difference of opinion is difficult to resolve by recourse to a precedent, but it does not, *per se,* make a difference of opinion inevitable. When there is a difference of opinion there are *ex ante* gains from betting. One person speculates upon the situation by offering the other insurance against the consequences of pursuing a particular policy. This is the mechanism of influence by which decisions are taken under uncertainty in Knight's world. If Knight's analysis is reformulated using a more appropriate concept of uncertainty, then his analysis appears as a prototype of the theory of speculative entrepreneurship developed in this book.

Schumpeter offers a much more radical view of entrepreneurship than any of the other theories do. The difference is particularly marked in respect of the Austrians. Hayek and Kirzner focus mainly upon how entrepreneurs function within a given set of markets, while Schumpeter views entrepreneurs operating on a much wider scale, by creating and destroying markets. Reading Kirzner, for example, it appears that the information to which entrepreneurs respond is mainly price information provided by the market itself. Schumpeter's entrepreneurs, on the other hand, cannot rely on price information to anything like the same extent because the markets in which they are seeking to operate do not yet exist. Schumpeter's entrepreneurs do not merely adjust markets, they make them and they destroy them. They are not just the mechanism, or the agents, through which the market system operates, they are the very creators of the system itself.

Schumpeter's analysis accords well with our concept of the market-making firm. Our analysis also recognizes the extent to which entrepreneurs make the system. Entrepreneurs themselves depend upon markets, notably markets for inputs of market-making services. These markets are in turn made by other entrepreneurs. The entrepreneurs who control large firms also create a market in delegate entrepreneurs, and it is even conceivable that there are professional company promoters who make a market in large firms themselves. This also ties in with Knight, who emphasized that the greatest entrepreneurial uncertainties arise in the market for the managers of large firms.

Schumpeter also recognizes the strategic aspects of entrepreneurship which are emphasized in this book. He recognizes implicitly that the information used by the entrepreneur is in common ownership and that the inability to appropriate the gains from exploiting it is a major disincentive to the entrepreneur. Schumpeter regards entrepreneurship as a very scarce talent, and supports any measures, such as patents and other restrictive business practices, which increase the appropriability of the potential monopoly rents. This point leads naturally into our own discussion of the strategic problems facing the entrepreneur: the problem of giving away information in the course of bargaining with customers or suppliers, or in the course of obtaining external finance. It also relates to our discussion of the competitive search for information and the problems of avoiding unintended duplication of search activity.

In Schumpeter's theory, the purely entrepreneurial act occupies the entrepreneur for only a small proportion of his time. There may indeed be only one quite ephemeral act, namely the creation of a new firm to effect an innovation. What the entrepreneur does the rest of the time is to manage the growth of his business by building up his organization and defending its strategic interests. The behaviour of the organization is the subject of the institutional theory of the firm – the theory of the firm as developed by Andrews and Penrose, amongst others. The subject of these theories is not entrepreneurship *per se,* but rather the skills that have to go with it: the ability to delegate, to provide internal incentives, to manage inventory, to contract out 'front-line' inventory to retailers, and so on. The integration of these functions with entrepreneurship makes it a multifaceted activity. The analysis of these relatively mundane functions is a key element in integrating the theory of the entrepreneur into mainstream economic theory. This integration is a two-sided process, involving a detailed analysis of entrepreneurial strategy, on the one hand, and the reconstruction of parts of orthodox economic theory, on the other. The objective of this book has been to advance the process of integration which began with the theories reviewed above.

SUMMARY

This chapter has reviewed the leading theories of entrepreneurship and shown how they can be placed in a logical sequence. The interface between these theories and orthodox theory is to be found in the institutional theory of the firm. The present theory synthesizes the main insights of these theories, and develops some of their implications.

NOTES AND REFERENCES

The main sources on the theories are, in order of appearance, Leibenstein (1966, 1968, 1969, 1976, 1978, 1979), Hayek (1937, 1945, 1949, 1960), Kirzner (1960, 1963, 1967, 1973, 1976, 1979a), Knight (1921, 1942), Schumpeter (1934, 1939, 1942), Andrews (1949, 1964), Andrews and Brunner (1975, chs 1 and 2) and Penrose (1959). For a rather ill-tempered critique of Leibenstein, see Stigler (1976). The relationship between X-efficiency theory and the Austrian school is examined carefully in Kirzner (1979b). Hayek's approach has recently been sympathetically reviewed by Shackle (1981). Many people have claimed to be building upon the work of Knight, but few have actually done so with much success. Schumpeter's work, on the other hand, has stimulated both interesting theoretical criticism and valuable historical investigation, see, for example, Gerschenkron (1968), Mason (1951, 1967), Nelson (1974), Nelson, Winter and Schuette (1977) and Solo (1951). An admirable summary of the Schumpeterian system is given by Clemence and Doody (1950); recent empirical work is reported in Hartman and Wheeler (1979). The connection between invention and innovation is considered by Machlup (1962b), MacLaurin (1953), Schmookler (1954, 1962, 1966) and Strassman (1959). The competitive role of product innovation is examined further by Reichardt (1962).

15. Conclusions

15.1 WELCOME BACK, JACK BRASH!

It is now time to return to the point at which we began, namely the biography of Jack Brash, entrepreneur. Jack Brash is to entrepreneurship what King Arthur is to chivalry: a legendary figure who personifies qualities which society believes to be important. The biography of Jack Brash can be seen in another light, however. In this chapter it is used to illustrate some of the main predictions of the theory of entrepreneurship. It cannot of course be used to test them, since, as we have seen, the 'rags to riches' career of Jack Brash is very much the exception rather than the rule.

Indeed, the predictions of the theory of entrepreneurship do not depend upon the identification of a particular individual, or group of individuals, as entrepreneurs. The predictions of the theory relate to all individuals, and specifically to the interactions between them. Entrepreneurship is about economic and social processes as a whole. It is about the interaction between one entrepreneur and another, between entrepreneurs and non-entrepreneurs, between leaders and followers, successes and failures, and so on. The case of Jack Brash can, however, be used to illustrate these economic and social processes: to show how they impinge upon one particular individual, and how certain key individuals can influence the way that the processes evolve.

15.2 ACCESS TO INFORMATION

This section presents three hypotheses about the role of information in stimulating entrepreneurial activity.

(i) *Information about profit opportunities needs to be synthesized from different sources.*

The story of Oskar, Jack's father, illustrates this, perhaps even better than the story of Jack himself. Oskar was an immigrant, and as such had knowledge of economic conditions in two different countries. He was therefore in a good position to identify opportunities for arbitrage. He exploited the opportunity to link the supply of Polish products to the demands of the immigrant Polish community; although other immigrants were in the same position, Oskar, as a seaman, had a greater knowledge of the shipping trade than most, and so was able to identify the most efficient means of transporting goods. This suggests two corollaries of the theory: first, that because migrants have a natural advantage in synthesizing information relevant to arbitrage they will be disposed to enter this particular line of entrepreneurial activity; secondly, that employment in the shipping trade may not only provide this kind of information itself, but allows this information to be synthesized with a practical knowledge of the transport system involved. Transport, and shipping in particular, is therefore a useful starting point from which an entrepreneur can move into merchandising and retailing. He may move out of transport as a result – subcontracting the provision of transport services – or he may retain his transport interests and integrate his merchandising activities with them.

Arbitrage involves a fairly simple form of information synthesis. A much more complex synthesis is required, for example, in product innovation. This is illustrated by Jack's innovation of the Flash Furniture range. On the demand side, Jack recognizes social and demographic factors which are increasing the demand for household furnishing. On the supply side, he is aware of new and cheaper furnishing fabrics which mean that new furniture need no longer be a luxury item. This suggests to Jack that there is a potential mass market for basic furnishing, and that such furnishing can be produced cheaply using new technology and by exploiting economies of scale.

(ii) *The family is a potentially valuable source of information. The nature and extent of his family's connections influence the opportunities that are available to an entrepreneur. Even the entrepreneur's knowledge of his own family may be turned to advantage by using the family as a source of labour. This strategy has its limitations, however, because the range of skills available within the family may be very small.*

Jack Brash is not at all well-connected. He is in a low stratum of society and his father, a potentially important source of contacts, has left home. This closes off many opportunities to Jack. For example, because he has no connection with the establishment, advancement by pyramid climbing is out of the question. Even getting a job when he has been made redundant poses problems, partly because his father is not there to provide tip-offs about jobs that may be going. In fact Jack becomes self-employed because, given the absence of family contacts and his lack of capital and educational qualifications, self-employment is the only alternative to unemployment. When he becomes self-employed he still relies upon his family even though only very meagre information is available. It is information about the marketing of his mother's outwork that gives him the idea for arbitraging between the East End and West End of London.

Most people so disadvantaged in information would never succeed as entrepreneurs. But Jack Brash is exceptional, and in the long run overcomes his disadvantage.

Jack Brash is not very good at delegating, and in particular he is very bad at recruiting managers to whom he can delegate. This gets him into serious difficulties on at least one occasion (see hypothesis (viii) below). At the start of his career there is really no-one in his family to whom he could reasonably delegate, but when his nephew grows up he begins to groom him as a senior manager and as his eventual successor. There is no reason, however, for believing that his nephew has the same abilities as Jack; and Jack's assessment of other people's abilities is known to be unreliable. The fact that the nephew is provided with a good education and first-class social contacts will certainly help him in acquiring information and making rational decisions, but whether he shares Jack's imagination and foresight must remain an open question. If he does, the business will go from strength to strength; if he does not, it may be a case of 'clogs to clogs' in just two generations.

(iii)   *The feedback of information from past activities is crucial to the long-run success of an enterprise.*

As noted above, Jack Brash starts with very little information. But information is generated continuously as a by-product of his trading activity, and Jack uses this information to the full. He learns from the deals that he makes, and he learns also from the deals that fall through. By analysing his experience he is able to turn adversity to advantage. Thus, when competitors move in on his field, he diversifies into a slightly different field. The diversification is successful because it relies upon information already gained in his original field, and simply puts it to a different use. It is only later on, when Jack integrates forward into a field about which he has very little knowledge, and in which he underestimates the risks, that he comes unstuck.

15.3   BARRIERS TO ENTRY INTO ENTREPRENEURSHIP

A great deal of entrepreneurial behaviour can be explained in terms of the existence of barriers to entry into entrepreneurship, and the strategies entrepreneurs use to overcome them. This section presents three hypotheses about entrepreneurial strategy.

(iv)   *Lack of personal wealth is a major constraint on the scale of entrepreneurial activity. Entrepreneurial strategy is strongly influenced by attempts to minimize the impact of this constraint. Informal contacts with family, friends and trading partners are important in obtaining capital, with financial intermediaries such as banks having only a limited role. The problems of obtaining external finance are most acute in the early years of an enterprise; during this period the rate of growth of the enterprise is much more strongly influenced by the profitability of its existing activities than by the entrepreneur's assessment of its future prospects.*

It goes without saying that Jack Brash is capital-constrained. No financial institution would lend to an unqualified lad from Stepney whose family is so poor that they can provide no collateral for a loan. Jack uses considerable ingenuity in obtaining the capital that he needs. He buys his first handcart on hire-purchase financed by the man he buys it from. The man has at least met Jack, has admired his determination, and is perhaps sufficiently naive to be persuaded by Jack to accept deferred payment. He knows, however, that Jack lives locally and that a handcart, in common with most other vehicles, is fairly easy to repossess.

Later on, Jack gets his customers to finance him by making prepayment for the reproduction frames they order. He borrows from his customers because they have dealt with him before and, being already established themselves, they have some capital to spare. Even so the cost of this finance is very high to Jack, for he has to offer an additional 5 per cent discount on the price of the frames to obtain it. This is still cheaper finance than he could obtain elsewhere, and the borrowing is warranted because of the high rate of profit he expects to earn.

Once Jack has got established, he buys his way into high society and acquires a small fortune through marriage. This provides him with sufficient capital to reverse his role and extend trade credit to others. If he is a good judge of the risk of default, then he can specialize in extending credit to entrepreneurs whom others are reluctant to finance. He can demand a high rate of interest because of the risks that other financiers perceive, and so operate in a highly profitable way as a banker to the trade.

Before his marriage, the expansion of Jack's firm was severely restricted by the need for hand-to-mouth trading. Each batch of new frames had to be financed by the reinvested profits of the previous batch, and this policy must have lost, or at least deferred, some of his sales. But as the batch size increased, so the profits increased, and the size of the batch could be increased again. Thus, once Jack's ideas had provided the motivation for growth, the rate of growth achieved was determined by the profit generated by the project itself.

Jack relies on his bank for finance at only one stage in his career. This is, however, a crucial stage in which the bank's role as 'honest broker' is absolutely vital. In seeking a loan, Jack divulges to his bank manager highly confidential information which would be very damaging if it were to reach his trade creditors. The bank acts as go-between for Jack, not only in the capital market, but in the market for professional services as well. It puts Jack in contact with specialists who can improve the organization of his business. The bank's reward comes from the high rate of interest it charges for the loan that, in conjunction with the professional services, puts the business back on its feet.

Finally, it is worth nothing that, in the very early stages of his career, Jack economized on his capital requirement by introducing an element of barter into his transactions. When buying from housewives he often offered part-payment in the form of a cheap replacement from his stock. This reduced the average cash balance he required in order to conduct his trade, at the expense of the inconvenience of having to carry part of his stock around with him.

(v) *Outside the family, clubs and societies are the most important non-profit institutions in which people can make contacts and acquire and disseminate information. Access to these institutions is often regulated by, for example, expensive subscriptions or by educational and professional qualifications. This means that the socially disadvantaged entrepreneur cannot easily gain access to the information and the capital he requires.*

Jack Brash does not gain acceptance by the establishment until quite late in his career. But he has one stroke of good fortune: the outbreak of war puts him into military service. At the time it seems an unfortunate interruption to a promising business career. But in the armed services Jack makes valuable contacts with people who, though they do not regard him as a social equal, acquire an obligation to him (perhaps reinforced by some polite blackmail on Jack's part). After the war Jack uses these contacts to obtain finance, to get tip-offs about invitations to tender for army surplus, and so on. As a result, Jack's second business starts under much more favourable conditions, and soon overtakes in size and profit anything that Jack's first business might have become.

(vi) *Educational qualifications are very important in reducing the constraints imposed by lack of personal wealth. Not only do they give entry to establishment institutions, they are also used as a screening device in recruiting managers. One way or another, therefore, they regulate the entrepreneur's access to other people's capital. People with ability may be prevented from gaining qualifications either because of restricted access to the educational system or because the system is biased in favour of conformity. The second factor is probably the greatest constraint on the underwriting of personal ability by the educational system.*

Jack Brash does not do well at school. The academic education provided does not tap the energy and enthusiasm that become apparent later in his business career. Had he done well at school, he could have won a scholarship and perhaps gone on to become a salaried manager. Opportunities for continued education were much more limited in the East End than elsewhere, of course, and in any case he might have felt unable to take them up because of the need to support his mother financially; but in the event the question did not arise.

It is interesting that later in his career Jack buys academic distinction by endowing universities. Ostensibly, this is charity, but it is possible to distinguish too an element of revenge. He places the academic establishment in the demeaning role of accepting patronage from someone who was previously rejected by it. He dictates that his bequests should be used to remedy defects in the system, and in particular to provide better educational opportunities for people like himself. Thus in bestowing funds he snubs the traditional type of university and favours the newer universities instead, which he identifies with a 'classless' meritocratic attitude to education.

15.4   THE SKILLS OF ENTREPRENEURSHIP

To exploit his superior judgment successfully the entrepreneur may have to call upon a variety of different skills. This section presents four hypotheses about entrepreneurial skills.

(vii)   *Negotiating tactics are an important element of entrepreneurial strategy.*

Jack Brash starts out as a dealer, buying and selling on doorsteps. The tactical problem facing a dealer is to explain to people simultaneously that he cannot afford to pay much for what they want to sell, but that he has to ask a lot for what it is they want to buy. Those who deal with him know that he is only in it for the margin. Notwithstanding this he must convince his trading partners that his offers cannot be improved, otherwise they are unlikely to agree to his terms. He must be skilled at influencing their expectations. The standard way of doing this is to give the initial offer careful thought, and then to stick to this offer using a hard-line strategy.

This policy is most likely to come unstuck when one entrepreneur employs it against another. Jack Brash discovers this to his cost when he starts bargaining with the buyer for a chain of high-street stores. The buyer dictates the terms and, in an attempt to extract concessions, Jack goes into competition on the retail front. But the buyer does not improve his terms and Jack's own efforts soon run into difficulties. He learns that, in bargaining with households, simple strategies may be consistently successful, but that it is not advisable to pursue the same approach against other entrepreneurs.

(viii)   *Organizational skills are important for the entrepreneur. There comes a point in the growth of any firm when the collection of information has to be delegated, and later on comes a point when decisions have to be delegated too. Some of the delegates may need to be specialists, who are difficult for the entrepreneur to recruit, and whose quality of work it is hard to check.*

These are critical points at which growth may falter, and the firm may even fail. At each point the entrepreneur must decide whether to delegate using rules, or to encourage delegates to use their own judgment instead. He must encourage delegates to check the accuracy of their information and to act upon it in their employer's interests. In many cases efficiency calls for decentralized organization in which the delegate who collects an item of information also acts upon it, and the consequences of that decision are reflected in a notional profit imputed to him. The establishment of such an organization may represent a considerable investment for the entrepreneur.

Jack Brash encounters considerable difficulty with delegation. One of the main reasons is that he has very little experience of working as a delegate himself. He gave up employment at an early age, since when he has always been his own boss. He has forgotten about the frustrations of being an employee. He has worked long hours making a success of his business and expects his employees to do the same even though their rewards are not directly linked to the firm's profitability. He wants to continue making all the key decisions but forgets to motivate his employees to provide him with accurate information.

His lack of education means that he cannot screen applicants for specialist posts. He tries to do without specialists when he needs them, and when he cannot do without them he appoints the wrong sort of person. It needs the advice of a specialist to hire a specialist, and eventually Jack is obliged to act on specialist advice by having professional nominees of the bank appointed to his board. The specialists help to 'turn round' the business, and free Jack's own time to get on with what he does best – developing new ideas.

(ix)   *Product innovation is probably the most important form of entrepreneurship, at least in a long-term perspective. A key element in many product innovations is the achievement of product versatility. Versatility is normally obtained using a multi-component design; versatility creates a mass market for the product – since the product substitutes for many different specialized goods – and thereby enables economies of scale to be exploited in the manufacture of individual components. To render the components compatible, it is normally necessary to standardize their design features and to guarantee precision in manufacture. The versatile good is essentially a concept for marketing a package of compatible components; because the product has many functions it is difficult to specify, and requires considerable skill to advertise.*

To illustrate product innovation in terms of Jack Brash's career, it is necessary to distinguish between two methods of achieving product versatility. The first involves the development of a multi-purpose good which combines different components in fixed proportion and allows different subsets of components to be activated to meet different uses. The second method involves providing a range of components that customers can combine in their own way to suit their own particular circumstances and tastes. The first method is most suitable when practically everyone has in mind a similar range of uses for the product. The second method is most suitable when different people have different uses in mind; it allows a degree of product differentiation to be introduced to the multi-purpose good at a minimal cost. The Flash Furniture range exemplifies the second kind of versatility. Jack recognizes that, when new homes are being furnished from scratch, the relevant marketing concept is not the individual furnishing item, but the furniture range. Homemakers are looking for a compatible set of furnishing components which can be permutated to meet their personal requirements within the space constraints of their home. The problem of explaining the concept to consumers is overcome, first, by devising a gimmick, the Adjustable Room Planner, and secondly by demonstrating the furniture arrangements in show-houses on the estates. To reduce the cost of communicating the product specification, the advertising is very carefully directed to the target group. Young people are identified as the main buyers and the furnishings are advertised in the kind of periodicals that they read. It is suggested that the Flash Furniture range is very different from the kind of furniture that might be offered by parents or bought secondhand. The estates chosen for furnished show-houses are those most likely to attract the first-time buyer.

(x)   *Market making does not call just for the obvious skills such as advertising and salesmanship. It calls too for less glamorous skills such as inventory management and quality control. Lack of attention to these factors can undermine an enterprise, and often does so just at the point where potential sales are about to increase dramatically.*

It is usually salesmanship that creates the dynamic for the growth of an enterprise. But if the product, or the quality of service associated with it, falls short of customers' expectations, then the enterprise may obtain a bad reputation which it is difficult to live down. Problems can arise if unexpected success in salesmanship causes demand to exceed supply. In these circumstances supply must be increased, not only to meet the backlog in demand, but to raise future stocks to a level which will guarantee that future orders are promptly filled. To increase supply at short notice it is tempting to relax quality control; lowering the rejection rate leads to a spontaneous increase in output, and may also facilitate the transfer of factory supervisors to other productive activities. But the reduction in product quality may be quickly perceived by consumers, and in the long run lead to more product resistance than would have been encountered had the quality of service remained poor instead.

Jack Brash's experience shows that there is no easy way of guaranteeing a plentiful supply of a high-quality product. At one stage, in an effort to improve retail service, he integrates forward into high-street outlets, but because of lax inventory management this creates more problems than it solves. The informal procedures he has relied upon as a dealer prove inadequate to cope with the day-to-day problems of retail sales through multiple outlets. Jack discovers that the management of a distribution channel calls for professional skills, and that, however good the product, without these skills the business cannot thrive.

15.5   TOWARDS A UNIFIED SOCIAL SCIENCE?

The hypotheses above are formulated in a very general way. They cannot easily be tested without the introduction of additional postulates. It is outside the scope of this book to provide these additional postulates; that is part of the research agenda for the future development of the theory of the entrepreneur. It is, however, possible to describe the nature of these additional postulates. Essentially, they are postulates about the relative costs of different sources of information and of different types of institution for structuring information flow. This cost structure in turn reflects both the technology of communication and the structure and the customs of society.

Of course, neither the technology of communication nor the social structure is static or autonomous. They are themselves influenced by the economic processes whose evolution they help to determine. This is the true significance of economic and social interdependence in a dynamic context.

The theory of the entrepreneur is, as noted earlier, really a special case of a general theory of economic and social process. A general theory of this kind has been the 'grand design' of social scientists for many years, although the formulation of a satisfactory theory of this kind is still a long way off. The development of the theory of the entrepreneur is, however, a step in this direction. As it stands, the theory is conditional upon the prevailing social structure. At the same time, there exist theories of social process which are conditional upon prevailing economic structure. At the moment, there is probably more to be gained by developing these two strands of theory separately; their integration might well be premature. If progress in these different fields can be sustained, however, it may eventually be possible to attain the social scientist's dream of the 'unified social science'.

It is relevant to inquire whether the redirection of economics towards an evolutionary perspective implies a radical break with orthodox theory. Certainly, it suggests a break with the tradition of emulating the physical sciences, and a move towards an 'economic biology' instead. It should be noted, however, that analogies of any kind, though they may be suggestive of new hypotheses, are unreliable when formulating the details of a theory, for there are almost invariably specific points upon which the analogy breaks down.

In this book a determined effort has been made to relate the theory of the entrepreneur to relevant areas of orthodox theory and to follow received techniques of analysis wherever these are appropriate. The theory involves a reformulation of orthodox models rather than a rejection of them. While the perspective of the theory is radically different, the technique of analysis is not. The reason is quite simply that the theory, like the neoclassical and Austrian theories, is based upon a rationality postulate. So long as this postulate is maintained, and the information available to the individual is properly specified, the theory rules out inconsistent behaviour and therefore acquires predictive power. Thus while individuals may, for example, follow decision rules to economize on information, their choice of a decision rule is always a rational one. It is the rationality postulate that explains why marginal analysis and its associated techniques hold the key to future developments in the theory of the entrepreneur.

SUMMARY

This chapter has summarized the main conclusions of the study and illustrated them using the biography of a stereotype entrepreneur. The conclusions are remarkable chiefly for the fact that the events and circumstances to which they refer are hardly ever mentioned in the neoclassical analysis of the market system. The theory of the entrepreneur offers a completely different perspective on the way that markets operate. It is dynamic rather than static, and evolutionary rather than mechanical. It is, however, still a predictive theory because it is based upon a rationality postulate. At some stage in the future it may be possible to combine the theory of the entrepreneur with a theory of rational social behaviour to provide a unified theory of economic and social process.

Bibliography

Abbott, L. (1955) *Quality and Competition: An Essay in Economic Theory*, New York: Columbia University Press.

Ahmed, M. (1977) 'Analysis of small-scale entrepreneurs in the Irish plastics industry', *Economic and Social Review*, 8, pp. 279–304.

Aitken, H.G.J. (1963) 'The future of entrepreneurial research', *Explorations in Entrepreneurial History* (Series 2), 1, pp. 3–9.

Akerlof, G.A. (1970) 'The market for "lemons": quality uncertainty and the market mechanism', *Quarterly Journal of Economics*, 84, pp. 488–500.

Albion, M.S. and Farris, P.W. (1981) *The Advertising Controversy: Evidence on the Economic Effects of Advertising*, Boston, Mass: Auburn House.

Alchian, A.A. (1950) 'Uncertainty, evolution and economic theory', *Journal of Political Economy*, 58, pp. 211–21.

Alchian, A.A. (1965) 'Some Economics of Property Rights', *Il Politico*, 30, pp. 816–29, reprinted in A.A. Alchian, *Economic Forces at Work*, Indianapolis: Liberty Press, 1977, pp. 127–49.

Alchian, A.A. (1969) 'Corporate management and property rights', in H. Manne (ed.), *Economic Policy and the Regulation of Corporate Securities*, Washington: American Enterprise Institute, reprinted in A.A. Alchian, *Economic Forces at Work*, Indianapolis: Liberty Press, 1977, pp. 227–57.

Alchian, A.A. and Demsetz, H. (1972) 'Production, information costs and economic organization', *American Economic Review*, 62, pp. 777–95.

Alexander, A.P. (1964) *Greek Industrialists: An Economic and Social Analysis*, Athens: Centre of Planning and Economic Research.

Andrews, P.W.S. (1949) *Manufacturing Business*, London: Macmillan.

Andrews, P.W.S. (1964) *On Competition in Economic Theory*, London: Macmillan.

Andrews, P.W.S. and Brunner, E. (1975) *Studies in Pricing*, London: Macmillan.

Armentano, D.T. (1972) *The Myths of Antitrust: Economic Theory and Legal Cases*, New Rochelle, N.Y: Arlington House.

Arrow, K.J. (1958) 'Utilities, attitudes, choices: a review note', *Econometrica*, 26, pp. 1–23.

Arrow, K.J. (1962a) 'Economic welfare and the allocation of resources for invention', in R.R. Nelson (ed.) *The Rate and Direction of Inventive Activity*, Princeton, NJ: Princeton University Press, pp. 609–26.

Arrow, K.J. (1962b) 'The economic implications of learning by doing', *Review of Economic Studies*, 29, pp. 155–73.

Arrow, K.J. (1970) *Essays in the Theory of Risk-Bearing*, Amsterdam: North-Holland.

Arrow, K.J. (1975) 'Vertical integration and communication', *Bell Journal of Economics*, 6, pp. 173–83.

Atkinson, J.W. (1957) 'Motivational determinants of risk-taking behaviour', *Psychological Review*, 64, pp. 359–72.

Bain, J.S. (1956) *Barriers to New Competition*, Cambridge, Mass: Harvard University Press.

Baldwin, W.L. and Childs, G.L. (1969) 'The fast second and rivalry in research and development', *Southern Economic Journal*, 36, pp. 18–24.

Bartholomew, D.J. (1973) *Stochastic Models for Social Processes*, 2nd edn, London: John Wiley and Sons.

Bartos, O.J. (1974) *Process and Outcome of Negotiations*, New York: Columbia University Press.

Basmann, R.L. (1965) 'The role of the economic historian in predictive testing of proffered "Economic Laws"', *Explorations in Entrepreneurial History* (Series 2), 2, pp. 159–86.

Bass, F.M. (1980) 'The relationship between diffusion rates, experience curves, and demand elasticities for consumer durable technological innovations', *Journal of Business*, 53, pp. 52–67.

Bates, J. (1964) *The Financing of Small Business*, London: Sweet and Maxwell.

Baumol, W.J. (1967) 'Optimal product and retailer characteristics: the abstract product approach', *Journal of Political Economy*, 75, pp. 674–85.

Baumol, W.J. (1968) 'Entrepreneurship in economic theory', *American Economic Review (Papers and Proceedings)*, 58, pp. 64–71.

Baumol, W.J. and Ide, E.A. (1956) 'Variety in retailing', *Management Science*, 3, pp. 93–101.

Becker, S.W. and Whisler, T.L. (1967), 'The innovative organisation: a selective view of current theory and research', *Journal of Business*, 40, pp. 462–9.

Belshaw, C.S. (1965) 'The cultural milieu of the entrepreneur', in H.G.J. Aitken (ed.), *Explorations in Enterprise*, Cambridge, Mass: Harvard University Press, pp. 139–62, reprinted in *Explorations in Entrepreneurial History* (Series 1), 7, pp. 146–63.

Bendix, R. (1957) 'A study of managerial ideologies', *Economic Development and Cultural Change*, 5, pp. 118–28.

Bendix, R. and Howton, F. (1959) 'Social mobility and the American business elite', in S.M. Lipset and R. Bendix (eds), *Social Mobility in Industrial Society*, London: Heinemann, pp. 114–43.

Bennett, W.B. (1943) *The American Patent System: An Economic Interpretation*, Baton Rouge: Louisiana State University Press.

Bernstein, P.L. (1953) 'Profit theory – where do we go from here?', *Quarterly Journal of Economics*, 67, pp. 407–22.

Bishop, R.L. (1964) 'A Zeuthen–Hicks model of bargaining', *Econometrica*, 32, pp. 410–17.

Blankart, C.B. (1975) 'Controversies on market failure in rewarding inventors', *Weltwirtschaftliches Archiv*, 111, pp. 760–69.

Blok, A. (1974) *Mafia of a Sicilian Village 1860–1960: Study of Violent Peasant Entrepreneurs*, New York: Harper and Row.

Bolton, J.E. (chairman) (1971) *Small Firms: Report of the Committee of Inquiry on Small Firms*, Cmnd 4811, London: HMSO.

Boone, L.E. (1970) 'The search for the consumer innovator', *Journal of Business*, 43, pp. 135–40.

Boswell, J. (1973) *The Rise and Decline of Small Firms*, London: Allen & Unwin.

Boulware, L.R. (1969) *The Truth about Boulwarism*, Washington, DC: Bureau of National Affairs.

Bowman, W.S., Jr (1973) *Patent and Antitrust Law: A Legal and Economic Appraisal*, Chicago: University of Chicago Press.

Broehl, W.G., Jr (1978) *The Village Entrepreneur: Change Agents in India's Rural Development*, Cambridge, Mass: Harvard University Press.

Brooks, J. (1963) *The Fate of the Edsel and Other Business Adventures*, New York: Harper and Row.

Brown, L.A. (1975) 'The market and infrastructure content of adoption: a spatial perspective on the diffusion of innovation', *Economic Geography*, 51, pp. 185–216.

Bruce, R. (1976) *The Entrepreneurs: Strategies, Motivations, Successes and Failures*, Bedford: Libertarian Books.

Buchanan, J.M. (1972) 'Notes on irrelevant externalities, enforcement costs and the atrophy of property rights', in G. Tullock (ed.), *Explorations in the Theory of Anarchy*, Blacksburg, Virginia: Centre for the Study of Public Choice, pp. 77–86.

Buchanan, J.M. (1973) 'LSE cost theory in retrospect', in J.M. Buchanan and G.F. Thirlby (eds), *LSE Essays on Cost*, London: Weidenfeld and Nicolson, pp. 1–16.

Buchanan, J.M. and Pierro, A.D. (1980) 'Cognition, choice and entrepreneurship', *Southern Economic Journal*, 46, pp. 693–701.

Buckley, P.J. and Casson, M.C. (1976) *The Future of the Multinational Enterprise*, London: Macmillan.

Bylinsky, G. (1976) *The Innovation Millionaires: How They Succeed*, New York: Charles Scribner's Sons.

Campbell, R.H. and Wilson, R.G. (eds) (1975) *Entrepreneurship in Britain 1750–1939*, London: A. and C. Black.

Cancian, F. (1979) *The Innovator's Situation: Upper-Middle-Class Conservatism in Agricultural Communities*, Stanford: Standford University Press.

Cantillon, R. (1755) *Essai sur la Nature du Commerce en Général* (ed. H. Higgs) London: Macmillan (1931).

Carstensen, F. and Morris, M. (1978) 'Credit, infrastructure and entrepreneurial opportunity in developing regions', *Journal of Economic History*, 38, pp. 262–5.

Carter, C.F. and Williams, B.R. (1957) *Industry and Technical Progress: Factors Governing the Speed of Application of Science*, London: Oxford University Press.

Carter, C.F. and Williams, B.R. (1959) 'The characteristics of technically progressive firms', *Journal of Industrial Economics*, 7, pp. 87–104.

Carter, E.C., Forster, R. and Moody, J.N. (1976) *Enterprise and Entrepreneurs in 19th and 20th Century France*, Baltimore: Johns Hopkins University Press.

Casson, M.C. (1979) *Alternatives to the Multinational Enterprise*, London: Macmillan.

Casson, M.C. (1981) *Unemployment: A Disequilibrium Approach*, Oxford: Martin Robertson.

Chamberlain, N.W. (1955) *A General Theory of Economic Process*, New York: Harper and Brothers.

Chamberlain, N.W. (1962) *The Firm: Micro-economic Planning and Action*, New York: McGraw-Hill.

Chamberlain, N.W. (1968), *Enterprise and Environment: The Firm in Time and Place*, New York: McGraw-Hill.

Chamberlin, E.H. (1962) *The Theory of Monopolistic Competition*, 8th edn, Cambridge, Mass: Harvard University Press.

Chandler, A.D., Jr (1962) *Strategy and Structure: Chapters in the History of the Industrial Enterprise*, Cambridge, Mass: MIT Press.

Chandler, A.D., Jr (1977) *The Visible Hand: The Managerial Revolution in American Business*, Cambridge, Mass: Harvard University Press.

Chandler, A.D. Jr and Daems, H. (eds) (1980) *Managerial Hierarchies: Comparative Perspectives on the Rise of the Modern Industrial Enterprise*, Cambridge, Mass: Harvard University Press.

Church, R.A. (1969) *Kenricks in Hardware: A Family Business, 1791*, Newton Abbot: David and Charles.

Clark, J.B. (1894) 'Insurance and profits', *Quarterly Journal of Economics*, 7, pp. 40–54.

Clark, J.M. (1942) 'Relations of history and theory', *The Tasks of Economic History: Supplement to Journal of Economic History*, 2, pp. 132–42.

Clark, J.M. (1955) 'Competition: static models and dynamic aspects', *American Economic Review*, 45, pp. 450–62.

Clark, J.M. (1961) *Competition as a Dynamic Process*, Washington, DC: Brookings Institution.

Clemence, R.V. and Doody, F.S. (1950) *The Schumpeterian System*, Cambridge, Mass: Addison-Wesley.

Clower, R.W. (1967) 'A reconsideration of the microfoundations of monetary theory', *Western Economic Journal*, 6, pp. 1–9.

Coase, R.H. (1937) 'The nature of the firm', *Economics* (N.S.), 4, pp. 386–405.

Cochran, R.C. (1958) 'The organization man in historic perspective', *Pennsylvania History*, 25, pp. 9–24.

Cochran, T.C. (1965a) 'Cultural factors in economic growth', in H.G.J. Aitken (ed.), *Explorations in Enterprise*, Cambridge, Mass: Harvard University Press, pp. 123–38, reprinted in *Journal of Economic History*, 20, pp. 515–30.

Cochran, T.C. (1965b), 'The entrepreneur in economic change', *Explorations in Entrepreneurial History* (Series 2), 3, pp. 25–38.

Cochran, T.C. (1968) 'Entrepreneurship', in D.L. Sills (ed.), *International Encyclopaedia of the Social Sciences*, Volume 5, New York: Macmillan, pp. 87–91.

Coddington, A. (1968) *Theories of the Bargaining Process*, London: Allen & Unwin.

Cole, A.H. (1942) 'Entrepreneurship as an area of research', *The Tasks of Economic History: Supplement to Journal of Economic History*, 2, pp. 118–26.

Cole, A.H. (1954) 'An appraisal of economic change: twentieth-century entrepreneurship in the United States and economic growth', *American Economic Review*, 40, pp. 35–50.

Cole, A.H. (1959) *Business Enterprise in its Social Setting*, Cambridge, Mass: Harvard University Press.

Cole, A.H. (1962) 'What is business history?', *Business History Review*, 36, pp. 98–106.

Cole, A.H. (1965a) 'Aggregative business history', *Business History Review*, 39, pp. 298–300.

Cole, A.H. (1965b) 'An approach to the study of entrepreneurship', in H.G.J. Aitken (ed.), *Explorations in Enterprise*, Cambridge, Mass: Harvard University Press, pp. 30–40.

Coles, F.A. (1973) 'Financial institutions and black entrepreneurship', *Journal of Black Studies*, 3, pp. 329–49.

Collins, O.F. and Moore, D.G. (1964) *The Enterprising Man*, East Lansing:

Bureau of Business and Economic Research, Graduate School of Business Administration, Michigan State University.

Copeman, G.H. (1955) *Leaders of British Industry: A Study of the Careers of more than a Thousand Public Company Directors*, London: Gee and Company (Publishers).

Coughenour, C.M. (1968) 'Some general problems in diffusion from the perspective of the theory of social action', *North Central Regional Research Bulletin*, 186, pp. 5–14.

Cross, J.G. (1965), 'A theory of the bargaining process', *American Economic Review*, 55, pp. 67–94.

Cross, M. (1981) *New Firm Formation and Regional Development*, Farnborough, Hants: Gower Press.

Cox, D.F. (ed.) (1967) *Risk Taking and Information Handling in Consumer Behavior*, Boston: Division of Research, Graduate School of Business Administration, Harvard University.

Dahmen, E. (1970) *Entrepreneurial Activity and the Development of Swedish Industry, 1919–1939* (trans. A. Leijonhufvud), Homewood, Illinois: Richard D. Irwin.

Davenport, H.J. (1913) *Economics of Enterprise*, New York: Macmillan.

Davids, L.E. (1963) *Characteristics of Small Business Founders in Texas and Georgia*, Washington, DC: Small Business Administration.

Debreu, G. (1959) *Theory of Value*, New Haven: Yale University Press.

Demsetz, H. (1968) 'The cost of transacting', *Quarterly Journal of Economics*, 82, pp. 33–53.

Denison, E.F. (1962) *The Sources of Economic Growth in the United States and the Alternatives Before Us*, New York: Committee for Economic Development.

Denison, E.F. (1967) *Why Growth Rates Differ: Postwar Experience in Nine Western Countries*, Washington, DC: Brookings Institution.

Durand, D. and Shea, D. (1974) 'Entrepreneurial activity as a function of achievement motivation and reinforcement control', *Journal of Psychology*, 88, pp. 57–63.

Erickson, C. (1959) *British Industrialists: Steel and Hosiery, 1850–1950*, Cambridge: Cambridge University Press.

Evans, G.H. Jr (1942) 'Theory of entrepreneurship', *The Tasks of Economic History: Supplement to Journal of Economic History*, 2, pp. 142–6.

Evans, G.H. Jr (1949) 'The entrepreneur and economic theory: a historical and analytical approach', *American Economic Review (Papers and Proceedings)*, 39, pp. 336–48.

Evans, G.H. Jr (1959) 'Business entrepreneurs: their major functions and related tenets', *Journal of Economic History*, 19, pp. 250–70.

Fanfani, A. (1935) *Catholicism, Protestantism and Capitalism*, London: Sheed and Ward.

Fleming, W.J. (1979) 'Cultural determinants of entrepreneurship and economic development: case study of Mendoza Province, Argentina, 1861–1914', *Journal of Economic History*, 39, pp. 211–24.

Fogarty, M.P. (1973) *Irish Entrepreneurs Speak for Themselves*, Dublin: Economic and Social Research Institute, Broadsheet 8.

Fox, H.G. (1947) *Monopolies and Patents: A Study of the History and Future of the Patent Monopoly*, Toronto: University of Toronto Press.

Freeman, C. (1974) *The Economics of Industrial Innovation*, Harmondsworth: Penguin Books.

Freeman, K.B. (1976) 'The significance of McClelland's achievement variable in the aggregate production function', *Economic Development and Cultural Change*, 24, pp. 815–24.

Galambos, L. (1966) 'Business history and the theory of the growth of the firm', *Explorations in Entrepreneurial History* (Series 2), 4, pp. 3–16.

Gerschenkron, A. (1953) 'Social attitudes, entrepreneurship and economic development', *Explorations in Entrepreneurial History* (Series 1), 5, pp. 1–19.

Gerschenkron, A. (1968) 'A Schumpeterian analysis of economic development', in A. Gerschenkron, *Continuity and Other Essays in History*, Cambridge, Mass: Harvard University Press.

Glade, W. (1967) 'Approaches to a theory of entrepreneurial formation', *Explorations in Entrepreneurial History* (Series 2), 4, pp. 245–59.

Glaister, S. (1974) 'Advertising policy and returns to scale in markets where information is passed between individuals', *Economica* (N.S.), 41, pp. 139–56.

Globe, S., Levy, W.G. and Schwartz, C.M. (1973) 'Key Factors and Events in the Innovation Process', *Research Management*, 16, pp. 8–15.

Goss, B.A. and Yamey, B.S. (eds) (1976) *The Economics of Futures Trading: Readings*, London: Macmillan.

Gough, J.W. (1969) *The Rise of the Entrepreneur*, London: Batsford.

Gould, J.P. (1974) 'Risk, stochastic preference and the value of information', *Journal of Economic Theory*, 8, pp. 64–84.

Grabowski, H.G. and Baxter, N.D. (1973) 'Rivalry in industrial research and development: an empirical study', *Journal of Industrial Economics*, 21, pp. 209–35.

Green, R.W. (ed.) (1959) *Protestantism and Capitalism: The Weber Thesis and Its Critics*, Boston: D.C. Heath.

Greenhut, M.L. (1971) *A Theory of the Firm in Economic Space*, Austin: Lone Star Publishers.

Gurzynski, Z.S.A. (1976) 'Entrepreneurship: true spring of human action', *South African Journal of Economics*, 44, pp. 1–26.

Hagen, E.E. (1962) *On the Theory of Social Change: How Economic Growth Begins*, Homewood, Illinois: Dorsey Press.

Hägerstrand, T. (1967) *Innovation Diffusion as a Spatial Process* (trans. A. Pred), Chicago: University of Chicago Press.

Harbison, F. (1956) 'Entrepreneurial Organisation as a Factor in Economic Development', *Journal of Political Economy*, 64, pp. 364–79.

Harris, J. (1973) 'Entrepreneurship and economic development', in L. Cain and P. Uselding (eds), *Business Enterprise and Economic Change: Essays in Honor of Harold F. Williamson*, Kent, Ohio: Kent State University Press, pp. 141–72.

Harsanyi, J.C. (1977) *Rational Behaviour and Bargaining Equilibrium in Games and Social Situations*, Cambridge: Cambridge University Press.

Hartman, R.S. and Wheeler, D.R. (1979) 'Schumpeterian waves of innovation and infrastructure development in Great Britain and the United States: the Kondratieff cycle revisited', *Research in Economic History*, 4 (Greenwich, Conn: Jai Press), 4, pp. 37–85.

Hawley, F.B. (1907) *Enterprise and the Productive Process*, New York: G.P. Putnam's Sons.

Hayek, F.A. (1937) 'Economics and knowledge', *Economica* (N.S.) 4, pp. 33–54, reprinted in F.A. Hayek, *Individualism and Economic Order*, London, Routledge and Kegan Paul, 1959, pp. 33–56.

Hayek, F.A. (1945) 'The use of knowledge in society', *American Economic Review*, 35, pp. 519–30, reprinted in F.A. Hayek, *Individualism and Economic Order*, London: Routledge and Kegan Paul, 1959, pp. 77–91.

Hayek, F.A. (1949) 'The meaning of competition', in F.A. Hayek, *Individualism and Economic Order*, London: Routledge and Kegan Paul, 1959, pp. 92–106.

Hayek, F.A. (1960) *The Constitution of Liberty*, Chicago: University of Chicago Press.

Heal, G.M. (1973) *The Theory of Economic Planning*, Amsterdam: North-Holland.

Heflebower, R.B. (1967) 'The theory and effects of non-price competition', in R.E. Kuenne (ed.), *Monopolistic Competition Theory: Studies in Impact*, New York: John Wiley and Sons.

Hey, J.D. (1979) *Uncertainty in Microeconomics*, Oxford: Martin Robertson.

Heyl, B.S. (1978) *The Madam as Entrepreneur: Career Management in House Prostitution*, Rutgers, New Brunswick: Transaction Books.

Hicks, J.R. (1963) *The Theory of Wages*, 2nd edn, London: Macmillan.

Hirschman, A.O. (1958) *The Strategy of Economic Development*, New Haven, Conn: Yale University Press.

Hirschman, A.O. (1970) *Exit, Voice and Loyalty: Responses to Decline in Firms, Organisations and States*, Cambridge, Mass: Harvard University Press.

Holmes, G. and Ruff, H. (1975) 'Perils of Entrepreneurial History', *Business History*, 17, pp. 26–43.

Hoselitz, B.F. (1951) 'The early history of entrepreneurial theory', *Explorations in Entrepreneurial History* (Series 1), 3, pp. 193–220.

Hughes, J.R.T. (1966a) 'Fact and theory in economic history', *Explorations in Entrepreneurial History* (Series 2), 3, pp. 75–100.

Hughes, J.R.T. (1966b) *The Vital Few: American Economic Progress and Its Protagonists*, Cambridge, Mass: Houghton Mifflin.

Hurwicz, L. (1969) 'On the concept and possibility of informational decentralisation', *American Economic Review (Papers and Proceedings)*, 59, pp. 513–24.

Hutt, W.H. (1939) *The Theory of Idle Resources*, London: Jonathan Cape.

Hyde, F.E. (1962) 'Economic theory and business history', *Business History*, 5, pp. 1–10.

Iremonger, D.S. (1972) *New Commodities and Consumer Behaviour*, Cambridge: Cambridge University Press.

Jaiswal, N.K. (1968) *Priority Queues*, New York: Academic Press.

Jenks, L.H. (1949) 'The role structure of entrepreneurial personality', in *Change and the Entrepreneur*, Cambridge, Mass: Harvard University Press, pp. 108–53.

Jenks, L.H. (1965) 'Approaches to entrepreneurial personality', in H.G.J. Aitken (ed.), *Explorations in Enterprise*, Cambridge, Mass: Harvard University Press, pp. 80–92.

Jensen, M.C. and Meckling, W.H. (1976) 'The theory of the firm: managerial behaviour, agency costs and ownership structure', *Journal of Financial Economics*, 3, pp. 305–60.

Jewkes, J., Sawers, D. and Stillerman, R. (1958) *The Sources of Invention*, London: Macmillan.

Johnson, P.S. (1975) *The Economics of Invention and Innovation: with a Case Study of the Development of the Hovercraft*, London: Martin Robertson.

Johnson, P.S. and Cathcart, D.G. (1979) 'New manufacturing firms and regional development: some evidence from the Northern region', *Regional Studies*, 13, pp. 269–80.

Kaelble, H. (1981) *Historical Research on Social Mobility: Western Europe and the USA in the Nineteenth and Twentieth Centuries* (trans. I. Noakes), London: Croom Helm.

Kalai, E. and Smorodinsky, M. (1975) 'Other solutions to Nash's bargaining problem', *Econometrica*, 43, pp. 513–18.

Kaldor, N. (1934) 'The equilibrium of the firm', *Economic Journal*, 44, pp. 60–76.

Kamien, M.I. and Schwartz, N.L. (1972) 'Timing of innovation under rivalry', *Econometrica*, 40, pp. 43–60.

Kamien, M.I. and Schwartz, N.L. (1974) 'Patent life and R&D rivalry', *American Economic Review*, 64, pp. 183–7.

Kamien, M.I. and Schwartz, N.L. (1975) 'Market structure and innovation: a survey', *Journal of Economic Literature*, 13, pp. 1–37.

Kamien, M.I. and Schwartz, N.L. (1978) 'Potential rivalry, monopoly profits, and the pace of inventive activity', *Review of Economic Studies*, 45, pp. 547–57.

Kaplan, A.D.H. (1948) *Small Business: Its Place and Problems*, New York: McGraw-Hill.

Katz, E. (1957) 'The two-step flow of communication: an up-to-date report on an hypothesis', *Public Opinion Quarterly*, 21, pp. 61–78.

Katz, E. and Foulkes, D. (1962) 'On the use of the mass media as "escape": clarification of a concept', *Public Opinion Quarterly*, 26, pp. 377–88.

Katz, E. and Lazarsfeld, P.F. (1955) *Personal Influence*, New York: Free Press.

Katz, E., Levin, M.L. and Hamilton, H. (1963) 'Traditions of research on the diffusion of innovations', *American Sociological Review*, 28, pp. 237–52.

Kay, N.M. (1979) *The Innovating Firm: A Behavioural Theory of Corporate R&D*, London: Macmillan.

Keller, S. (1953) 'The Social Origins and Career Lines of Three Generations of American Business Leaders', unpublished PhD dissertation, Columbia University, New York.

Kierulff, H.E. (1975) 'Can entrepreneurs be developed?', *MSU Business Topics*, 23, pp. 39–44.

Kierulff, H.E. (1979) 'Finding – and keeping: corporate entrepreneurs', *Business Horizons*, 22, pp. 6–15.

Kihlstrom, R.E. (1974a) 'A Bayesian model of demand for information about product quality', *International Economic Review*, 15, pp. 99–118.

Kihlstrom, R.E. (1974b) 'A general theory of demand for information about product quality', *Journal of Economic Theory*, 8, pp. 413–39.

Kihlstrom, R.E. and Laffont, J.J. (1979) 'A general equilibrium entrepreneurial theory of firm formation based on risk aversion', *Journal of Political Economy*, 87, pp. 719–48.

Kilbey, P. (1971) 'Hunting the heffalump', in P. Kilby (ed.), *Entrepreneurship and Economic Development*, New York: Free Press, pp. 1–40.

Kingston, W. (1977) *Innovation: The Creative Impulse in Human Progress*, London: John Calder.

Kirzner, I.M. (1960) *The Economic Point of View*, Princeton, NJ: D. Van Nostrand.

Kirzner, I.M. (1963) *Market Theory and the Price System*, Princeton, NJ: D. Van Nostrand.

Kirzner, I.M. (1967) 'Methodological individualism, market equilibrium, and market process', *Politico*, 1, 32, pp. 787–99.

Kirzner, I.M. (1973) *Competition and Entrepreneurship*, Chicago: University of Chicago Press.

Kirzner, I.M. (1976) 'Equilibrium versus market process', in E.G. Dolan (ed.), *The Foundations of Modern Austrian Economics*, Kansas City: Sheed and Ward, pp. 115–25.

Kirzner, I.M. (1979a) *Perception, Opportunity and Profit*, Chicago: University of Chicago Press.

Kirzner, I.M. (1979b) 'Comment: X-inefficiency, error and the scope for entrepreneurship', in M.J. Rizzo (ed.), *Time, Uncertainty and Disequilibrium*, Lexington, Mass: D.C. Heath, pp. 140–51.

Klapper, J.T. (1960) *The Effects of Mass Communication*, New York: Free Press.

Knight, F.H. (1921) *Risk, Uncertainty and Profit* (ed. G.J. Stigler), Chicago: University of Chicago Press, 1971.

Knight, F.H. (1942) 'Profit and entrepreneurial functions', *The Tasks of Economic History: Supplement to Journal of Economic History*, 2, pp. 126–32.

Kornai, J. (1959) *Overcentralisation in Economic Administration: A Critical Analysis based on Experience in Hungarian Light Industry* (trans. J. Knapp), London: Oxford University Press.

Kornai, J. (1971) *Anti-Equilibrium*, Amsterdam, North-Holland.

Kornai, J. (1980) *Economics of Shortage*, 2 vols, Amsterdam: North-Holland.

Kornai, J. and Liptak, T. (1965) 'Two-level planning', *Econometrica*, 33, pp. 141–69.

Körner, A. (1893) *Unternehmung und Unternehmergewinn*, Vienna.

Kotler, P. (1976) *Marketing Management: Analysis, Planning and Control*, 3rd edn, Englewood Cliffs, NJ: Prentice-Hall.

Koutsoyiannis, A. (1979) *Modern Microeconomics*, 2nd edn, London: Macmillan.

Lachmann, L.M. (1969) 'Methodological individualism and the market economy', in E. Streissler (ed.), *Roads to Freedom: Essays in Honour of Friedrich A. von Hayek*, London: Routledge and Kegan Paul, pp. 89–104.

Lachmann, L.M. (1976) 'From Mises to Shackle: an essay on Austrian economics and the Kaleidic Society', *Journal of Economic Literature*, 14, pp. 54–62.

Lamb, R.K. (1952) 'The entrepreneur and the community', in W. Miller (ed.), *Men in Business*, Cambridge, Mass: Harvard University Press.

Lamberton, D.M. (1965) *The Theory of Profit*, Oxford: Blackwell.

Lamberton, D.M. (1972) 'Information and profit', in C.F. Carter and J.L. Ford (eds), *Uncertainty and Expectations in Economics: Essays in Honour of G.L.S. Shackle*, Oxford: Blackwell, pp. 191–212.

Lancaster, K. (1966), 'A new approach to consumer theory', *Journal of Political Economy*, 74, pp. 132–57.

Lancaster, K. (1979) *Variety, Equity, and Efficiency*, Oxford: Basil Blackwell.

Leff, N.H. (1978) 'Industrial organization and entrepreneurship in the developing countries: the economic groups', *Economic Development and Cultural Change*, 26, pp. 661–75.

Leff, N.H. (1979) 'Entrepreneurship and economic development: the problem revisited', *Journal of Economic Literature*, 17, pp. 46–64.

Leibenstein, H. (1966) 'Allocative efficiency vs. "X-efficiency"', *American Economic Review*, 56, pp. 392–415.

Leibenstein, H. (1968) 'Entrepreneurship and development', *American Economic Review*, 58, pp. 72–83.

Leibenstein, H. (1969) 'Organizational or frictional equilibria, X-efficiency and the rate of innovation', *Quarterly Journal of Economics*, 83, pp. 600–623.

Leibenstein, H. (1976) *Beyond Economic Man: A New Foundation for Microeconomics*, Cambridge, Mass: Harvard University Press.

Leibenstein, H. (1978) *General X-efficiency Theory and Economic Development*, New York: Oxford University Press.

Leibenstein, H. (1979) 'The general X-efficiency paradigm and the role of the entrepreneur', in M.J. Rizzio (ed.), *Time, Uncertainty and Disequilibrium*, Lexington, Mass: D.C. Heath, pp. 127–39.

Lessner, M. and Knapp, R.R. (1974) 'Achievement orientation of small industrial entrepreneurs in the Philippines', *Human Organization*, 33, pp. 173–82.

Levitt, T. (1965) *Industrial Purchasing Behaviour: A Study in Communications Effects*, Boston: Division of Research, Graduate School of Business Administration, Harvard University.

Loasby, B.J. (1976) *Choice, Complexity and Ignorance*, Cambridge: Cambridge University Press.

Lupton, T. and Wilson, C.S. (1959) 'The social background of and connections of "top decision makers"', *Manchester School*, 27, pp. 30–51.

Lynn, R. (ed.) (1974) *The Entrepreneur: Eight Case Studies*, London: Allen & Unwin.

Machlup, F. (1962a) *The Production and Distribution of Knowledge in the United States*, Princeton, NJ: Princeton University Press.

Machlup, F. (1962b) 'The supply of inventors and inventions', in R.R. Nelson (ed.), *The Rate of Direction of Inventive Activity*, Princeton, NJ: Princeton University Press, pp. 143–67.

Machlup, F. (1980) *Knowledge: Its Creation, Distribution and Economic Significance, Volume 1: Knowledge and Knowledge Production*, Princeton, NJ: Princeton University Press.

MacLaurin, W.R. (1953) 'The Sequence from invention to innovation and its relation to economic growth', *Quarterly Journal of Economics*, 67, pp. 97–111.

Manne, H.G. (1966) *Insider Trading and the Stock Market*, New York: Free Press.

Mansfield, E. (1961) 'Technical change and the rate of imitation', *Econometrica*, 29, pp. 741–66.

Mansfield, E. (1963a) 'The speed of response of firms to new techniques', *Quarterly Journal of Economics*, 77, pp. 290–309.

Mansfield, E. (1963b) 'Intrafirm rates of diffusion of an innovation', *Review of Economics and Statistics*, 45, pp. 348–59.

Mansfield, E. (1964) 'Industrial research and development expenditures: determinants, prospects and relation to size of firm and inventive output', *Journal of Political Economy*, 72, pp. 319–40.

Mansfield, E. (1968) *Industrial Research and Technological Innovation: An Econometric Analysis*, New York: W.W. Norton.

Mansfield, E. (1969) *The Economics of Technological Change*, London: Longmans.

Mansfield, E., Rapoport, J., Schnee, J., Wagner, S. and Hamburger, M. (1971) *Research and Innovation in the Modern Corporation*, New York: W.W. Norton.

Marris, P. and Somerset, A. (1971) *African Businessmen: A Study of Entrepreneurship and Development in Kenya*, London: Routledge and Kegan Paul.

Marschak, J. (1968) 'Economics of inquiring, communicating, deciding', *American Economic Review*, 58, pp. 1–18.

Marschak, J. (1971) 'Economics and information systems, in M.D. Intriligator (ed.), *Frontiers of Quantitative Economics*, Amsterdam: North-Holland, pp. 32–107.

Marschak, J. (1972) 'Optimal systems for information and decision', in A.V. Balakrishnan (ed.), *Techniques of Optimisation*, New York: Academic Press, pp. 355–70.

Marschak, J. and Radner, R. (1972) *Economic Theory of Teams*, New Haven: Yale University Press.

Marshall, A. (1890) *Principles of Economics*, 8th edn (ed. G.W. Guilleband), 2 vols, London: Macmillan, 1961.

Martin, D.T. (1979) 'Alternative views of Mengerian entrepreneurship', *History of Political Economy*, 11, pp. 271–85.

Mason, E.S. (1951) 'Schumpeter on monopoly and the large firm', *Review of Economics and Statistics*, 33, pp. 139–44.

Mason, E.S. (1967) 'Monopolistic competition and the growth process in less developed countries: Chamberlin and the Schumpeterian dimension', in R.E. Kuenne (ed.), *Monopolistic Competition Theory: Studies in Impact; Essays in Honor of Edward H. Chamberlin*, New York: John Wiley and Sons.

Massy, W.F., Montgomery, D.B. and Morrison, D.G. (1970) *Stochastic Models of Buying Behaviour*, Cambridge, Mass: MIT Press.

McClelland, D.C. (1967) *The Achieving Society*, New York: Free Press.

McClelland, D.C. and Winter, D.G. (1969) *Motivating Economic Achievement*, New York: Free Press.

McClelland, W.G. (1967) *Costs and Competition in Retailing*, London: Macmillan.

McGaffey, T.N. and Christy, R. (1975) 'Information processing capability as a predictor of entrepreneurial effectiveness', *Academy of Management Journal*, 18, pp. 857–63.

McKean, R. *et al.* (1970) 'Symposium on product liability', *University of Chicago Law Review*, 38, pp. 1–141.

McNulty, P.J. (1967) 'A note on the history of perfect competition', *Journal of Political Economy*, 75, pp. 395–9.

McNulty, P.J. (1968) 'The meaning of competition', *Quarterly Journal of Economics*, 82, pp. 639–56.

Mill, J.S. (1848) *Principles of Political Economy*, new edn (ed. W.J. Ashley), London: Longmans, 1909.

Miller, W. (ed.) (1962) *Men in Business: Essays on the Historical Role of the Entrepreneur*, New York: Harper and Row.

Mills, C.W. (1945) 'The American business elite: a collective portrait', *The Tasks of Economic History, Supplement to Journal of Economic History*, 2, pp. 20–44.

Mises, L. von (1949) *Human Action: A Treatise on Economics*, London: William Hodge.

Montias, J.M. (1976) *The Structure of Economic Systems*, New Haven: Yale University Press.

Moss, S. (1981) *An Economic Theory of Business Strategy*, Oxford: Martin Robertson.

Mueller, D.C. (1972) 'A life cycle theory of the firm', *Journal of Industrial Economics*, 20, pp. 199–219.

Mueller, D.C. (1979) *Public Choice*, Cambridge: Cambridge University Press.

Nabseth, L. and Ray, G.F. (1974) *The Diffusion of New Industrial Processes: An International Study*, Cambridge: Cambridge University Press.

Nafziger, E.W. (1978) *Class, Caste, and Entrepreneurship: A Study of Indian Industrialists*, Honolulu: University Press of Hawaii.

Nash, J.F. (1950) 'The bargaining problem', *Econometrica*, 18, pp. 155–62.

Nelson, P. (1970) 'Information and consumer behaviour', *Journal of Political Economy*, 78, pp. 311–29.

Nelson, R. (1974) 'Neoclassical vs. evolutionary theories of growth', *Economic Journal*, 84, pp. 886–905.

Nelson, R., Winter, S. and Schuette, H. (1977) 'Technical change in an evolutionary model', *Quarterly Journal of Economics*, 90, pp. 90–118.

Newcomer, M. (1955) *The Big Business Executive*, New York: Columbia University Press.

Nicosia, F.M. (1966) *Consumer Decision Processes: Marketing and Advertising Implications*, Englewood Cliffs, NJ: Prentice-Hall.

Oi, W.Y. and Hurter, A.P. Jr (1965) *Economics of Private Truck Transportation*, Dubuque, Iowa: William C. Brown Co.; Chapter 2 reprinted as 'A theory of vertical integration in road transport services', in B.S. Yarney (ed.), *Economics of Industrial Structure*, Harmondsworth: Penguin Books, 1973, pp. 233–62.

Owens, R.L. (1978) 'Anthropological study of entrepreneurship', *Eastern Anthropologist*, 31, pp. 65–80.

Oxenfeldt, A.R. (1943) *New Firms and Free Enterprise: Prewar and Postwar Aspects*, Washington, DC: American Council on Public Affairs.

Pandey, J. and Tewary, N.B. (1979) 'Locus of control and achievement values of entrepreneurs', *Journal of Occupational Psychology*, 52, pp. 107–11.

Papandreou, A.G. (1952) 'Some basic problems in the theory of the firm', in B.F. Haley (ed.), *A Survey of Contemporary Economics*, vol. II, Homewood, Illinois: Richard D. Irwin, pp. 183–219.

Papanek, H. (1972) 'Pakistan's big businessmen', *Economic Development and Cultural Change*, 21, pp. 1–32.

Pelzel, J. (1965) 'The small industrialist in Japan', in H.G.J. Aitken (ed.),

Explorations in Enterprise, Cambridge, Mass: Harvard University Press, pp. 161–83, reprinted in *Explorations in Entrepreneurial History* (Series 2), 7, pp. 79–93.

Pen, J. (1952) 'A general theory of bargaining', *American Economic Review*, 42, pp. 24–42.

Penrose, E.T. (1959) *The Theory of the Growth of the Firm*, Oxford: Basil Blackwell.

Plum, W. (1977) *The Entrepreneur: Outsider in Industrial Society*, Bonn: Friedrich-Ebert-Stiftung.

Pollard, S. (1965) *The Genesis of Modern Management*, London: Edward Arnold.

Radner, R. (1968) 'Competitive equilibrium under uncertainty', *Econometrica*, 36, pp. 31–58.

Rapoport, A. (1953) 'Spread of information through a population with socio-cultural bias: I, assumption of transitivity', *Bulletin of Mathematical Biophysics*, 15, pp. 523–33.

Rashevsky, N. (1953) 'Imitative behaviour in nonuniformly spatially distributed populations', *Bulletin of Mathematical Biophysics*, 15, pp. 63–73.

Ravenshear, A. F. (1908) *The Industrial and Commercial Influence of the English Patent System*, London: T. Fisher Unwin.

Redlich, F. (1940–51) *History of American Business Leaders*, 2 vols, Ann Arbor, Michigan: Edwards Brothers.

Redlich, F. (1949) 'The origin of the concepts of "Entrepreneur" and "Creative Entrepreneur"', *Explorations in Entrepreneurial History* (Series 1), 1, pp. 1–7.

Redlich, F. (1956) 'The military enterpriser: a neglected area of research', *Explorations in Entrepreneurial History* (Series 1), 8, pp. 252–6.

Redlich, F. (1958) 'Business leadership: diverse origins and variant forms', *Economic Development and Cultural Change*, 6, pp. 177–90.

Redlich, F. (1959) 'Entrepreneurial typology', *Weltwirtschaftliches Archiv*, 82, pp. 150–68.

Redlich, F. (1963) 'Economic development, entrepreneurship and psychologism: a social scientist's critique of McClelland's "Achieving Society"', *Explorations in Entrepreneurial History* (Series 2), 1, pp. 10–35.

Reekie, W.D. (1979) *Industry, Prices and Markets*, Deddington, Oxford: Philip Allan.

Reekie, W.D. (1981) *The Economics of Advertising*, London: Macmillan.

Reichardt, R. (1962) 'Competition through the introduction of new products', *Zeitschrift für Nationalokonomie*, 22, pp. 41–84.

Richardson, G.B. (1960) *Information and Investment*, London: Oxford University Press.

Rizzo, M.J. (1979) 'Disequilibrium and all that: an introductory essay', in M.J. Rizzo (ed.), *Time, Uncertainty and Disequilibrium*, Lexington, Mass: D.C. Heath, pp. 1–18.

Roberts, B. (1971) 'Individual influence over group decisions', *Southern Economic Journal*, 37, pp. 434–44.

Roberts, B. and Holdren, B.R. (1972) *Theory of Social Process: An Economic Analysis*, Ames, Iowa: Iowa State University Press.

Robertson, A. (1974) *The Lessons of Failure: Cases and Comments on Consumer Product Innovation*, London: Macdonald.

Robertson, T.S. (1971) *Innovative Behaviour and Communication*, New York: Holt, Rinehart and Winston.

Robinson, E.A.G. (1934) 'The problem of management and the size of firms', *Economic Journal*, 44, pp. 240–54.

Rogers, E.M. (1962) *Diffusion of Innovations*, New York: Free Press.

Rogers, E.M. and Shoemaker, F.F. (1971) *Communication of Innovations*, New York: Free Press.

Romeo, A. (1975) 'Inter-industry and inter-firm differences in the rate of diffusion', *Review of Economics and Statistics*, 57, pp. 311–19.

Romeo, A. (1977) 'The rate of imitation of a capital-embodied process innovation', *Economica*, 44, pp. 63–70.

Rosenberg, N. (1976) *Perspectives on Technology*, Cambridge: Cambridge University Press.

Ross, N.S. (1952) 'Management and the size of the firm', *Review of EconomicStudies*, 19, pp. 148–54.

Rothbard, M.N. (1962) *Man, Economy and State*, New York: D. Van Nostrand.

Rothschild, M. (1973) 'Models of market organization with imperfect information: a survey', *Journal of Political Economy*, 81, pp. 283–308.

Rothwell, R. (1975) 'Intra-corporate entrepreneurs', *Management Decision*, 13, pp. 142–54.

Routh, G. (1975) *The Origin of Economic Ideas*, London: Macmillan.

Sarachek, B. (1978) 'American Entrepreneurs and the Horatio Alger Myth', *Journal of Economic History*, 38, pp. 439–56.

Sargent Florence, P. (1961) *Ownership, Control and Success of Large Companies*, London: Sweet and Maxwell.

Sawyer, J.E. (1951) 'Entrepreneurial error and economic growth', *Explorations in Entrepreneurial History* (Series 1), 4, pp. 199–204.

Say, J.B. (1803) *A Treatise on Political Economy: Or, the Production, Distribution and Consumption of Wealth*, New York: Augustus M. Kelley, 1964.

Sayigh, Y.A. (1962) *Entrepreneurs of Lebanon: The Role of the Business Leader in a Developing Economy*, Cambridge, Mass: Harvard University Press.

Schelling, T.C. (1960) *The Strategy of Conflict*, Cambridge, Mass: Harvard University Press.

Schelling, T.C. (1978) *Micromotives and Macrobehavior*, New York: W.W. Norton.

Scherer, F.M. (1965) 'Firm size, market structure, opportunity and the output of patent inventions', *American Economic Review*, 55, pp. 1097–123.

Scherer, F.M. (1967) 'Research and development resource allocation under rivalry', *Quarterly Journal of Economics*, 81, pp. 359–94.

Schiff, E. (1971) *Industrialization without National Patents: The Netherlands, 1869–1912; Switzerland, 1850–1907*, Princeton, NJ: Princeton University Press.

Schmookler, J. (1954) 'The level of inventive activity', *Review of Economics and Statistics*, 36, pp. 183–90.

Schmookler, J. (1962) 'Economic sources of inventive activity', *Journal of Economic History*, 22, pp. 1–20.

Schmookler, J. (1966) *Invention and Economic Growth*, Cambridge, Mass: Harvard University Press.

Schotter, A. (1981) *The Economic Theory of Social Institutions*, Cambridge: Cambridge University Press.

Schreier, J.W. and Komives, J.L. (1973) *The Entrepreneur and New Enterprise Formation*, Milwaukee, Wisconsin: Center for Venture Management.

Schultz, T.W. (1975) 'The value of the ability to deal with disequilibria', *Journal of Economic Literature*, 13, pp. 827–46.

Schumpeter, J.A. (1934) *The Theory of Economic Development*, Cambridge, Mass: Harvard University Press.

Schumpeter, J.A. (1939) *Business Cycles: A Theoretical, Historical and Statistical Analysis of the Capitalist Process*, 2 vols, New York: McGraw-Hill.

Schumpeter, J.A. (1942) *Capitalism, Socialism and Democracy*, 5th edn (ed. T. Bottomore), London: Allen & Unwin, 1976.

Schumpeter, J.A. (1965) 'Economic theory and entrepreneurial history', in H.G.J. Aitken (ed.), *Explorations in Enterprise*, Cambridge, Mass: Harvard University Press, pp. 45–64.

Shackle, G.L.S. (1957) 'The nature of the bargaining process', in J.T. Dunlop (ed.), *The Theory of Wage Determination*, London: Macmillan, pp. 292–314.

Shackle, G.L.S. (1961) *Decision, Order and Time in Human Affairs*, Cambridge: Cambridge University Press.

Shackle, G.L.S. (1970) *Expectation, Enterprise and Profit: The Theory of the Firm*, London: Allen & Unwin.

Shackle, G.L.S. (1979) *Imagination and the Nature of Choice*, Edinburgh: Edinburgh University Press.

Shackle, G.L.S. (1981) 'F.A. Hayek, 1899–', in D.P. O'Brien and J.R. Presley (eds), *Pioneers of Modern Economics in Britain*, London: Macmillan, pp. 234–61.

Shils, E.B. and Zucker, W. (1979) 'Developing a model for internal corporate entrepreneurship', *Social Science*, 54, pp. 195–203.

Shubik, M. (1959) *Strategy and Market Structure*, New York: John Wiley and Sons.

Simon, H.A. (1959) 'Theories of decision-making in economics and behavioural science', *American Economic Review*, 49, pp. 253–83.

Simon, H.A. (1976) *Administrative Behaviour*, 3rd edn, New York: Free Press.

Simon, H.A. (1980) *Models of Thought*, New Haven: Yale University Press.

Sloan, P. (1973) 'The international diffusion of an innovation', *Journal of Industrial Economics*, 22, pp. 61–9.

Smith, C.W. (1981) *The Mind of the Market*, London: Croom Helm.

Smith, D.C. (1978) 'Organized crime and entrepreneurship', *International Journal of Criminology and Penology*, 6, pp. 161–77.

Smith, N.R. (1967) *The Entrepreneur and His Firm: The Relationship between Type of Man and Type of Company*, East Lansing: Bureau of Business and Economic Research, Graduate School of Business Administration, Michigan State University.

Solo, C.S. (1951) 'Innovation in the capitalist process: a critique of the Schumpeterian theory', *Quarterly Journal of Economics*, 65, pp. 417–28.

Soltow, J.H. (1968) 'The entrepreneur in economic history' *American Economic Review (Papers and Proceedings)*, 58, pp. 84–92.

Sombart, W. (1915) *The Quintessence of Capitalism: A Study of the History and Psychology of the Modern Business Man* (trans. M. Epstein), London: T. Fisher Unwin.

Spence, M. (1977) 'Consumer misperceptions, product failure and producer liability', *Review of Economic Studies*, 44, pp. 561–72.

Stevens, C.M. (1963) *Strategy and Collective Bargaining Negotiation*, Cambridge, Mass: Harvard University Press.

Stewart, I.M.T. (1970) *Information in the Cereals Market*, London: Hutchinson.

Stigler, G.J. (1957) 'Perfect competition historically contemplated', *Journal of Political Economy*, 65, reprinted in G.J. Stigler, *Essays in the History of Economics*, Chicago: University of Chicago Press, 1965, pp. 234–67.

Stigler, G.J. (1961) 'The economics of information', *Journal of Political Economy*, 69, pp. 213–25.

Stigler, G.J. (1967) 'Imperfections in the capital market', *Journal of Political Economy*, 75, pp. 287–92.

Stigler, G.J. (1976) 'The Xistence of X-efficiency', *American Economic Review*, 66, pp. 213–16.

Stoneman, P.L. (1976) *Technological Diffusion and the Computer Revolution: The UK Experience*, Cambridge: Cambridge University Press.

Strachan, H.W. (1976) *Family and Other Business Groups in Economic Development: The Case of Nicaragua*, New York: Praeger.

Strassmann, W.P. (1959) *Risk and Technological Innovation: American Manufacturing Methods during the Nineteenth Century*, Ithaca, NY: Cornell University Press.

Swan, P.L. (1970) 'Durability of consumption goods', *American Economic Review*, 60, pp. 884–94.

Taussig, F.W. (1915) *Inventors and Moneymakers*, New York: Macmillan.

Taussig, F.W. and Joslyn, C.S. (1932) *American Business Leaders: A Study in Social Origins and Social Stratification*, New York: Macmillan.

Thirlby, G.F. (1946) 'The subjective theory of value and accounting "cost"', *Economica*, N.S. 13, reprinted in J.M. Buchanan and G.F. Thirlby (eds), *LSE Essays on Cost*, London: Weidenfeld and Nicolson, 1973, pp. 43–68.

Thirlby, G.F. (1952) 'The economist's description of business behaviour', *Economica*, N.S. 19, reprinted in J.M. Buchanan and G.F. Thirlby (eds), *LSE Essays on Cost*, London: Weidenfeld and Nicolson, 1973, pp. 201–24.

Tilton, J.E. (1971) *International Diffusion of Technology: The Case of Semiconductors*, Washington, DC: Brookings Institution.

Tucker, K.A. (1972) 'Business history: some proposals for aims and methodology', *Business History*, 14, pp. 1–16.

Tversky, A. and Kahneman, D. (1974) 'Judgments under uncertainty: heuristics and biases', *Science*, 185, pp. 1124–31.

Vanneman, R.D. (1973) 'Dominance and achievement in entrepreneurial personalities, in E.B. Ayal (ed.), *Micro Aspects of Development*, New York: Praeger, pp. 122–45.

Veblen, T.B. (1904) *The Theory of Business Enterprise*, New York: Charles Scribner's Sons.

Warner, W.L. and Abegglen, J.C. (1955a) *Big Business Leaders in America*, New York: Harper and Brothers.

Warner, W.L. and Abegglen, J.C. (1955b) *Occupational Mobility in American Business and Industry:* Minneapolis: University of Minnesota Press.

Webber, M.J. (1972) *Impact of Uncertainty on Location*, Cambridge, Mass: MIT Press.

Webber, M.J. (1979) *Information Theory and Urban Spatial Structure*, London: Croom Helm.

Weber, M. (1930) *The Protestant Ethic and the Spirit of Capitalism* (trans. T. Parsons), London: Allen & Unwin.

Weston, J.F. (1949) 'Enterprise and profit', *Journal of Business*, 22, pp. 141–59.

Weston, J.F. (1950) 'A generalised uncertainty theory of profit', *American Economic Review*, 40, pp. 40–60.

Weston, J.F. (1954) 'The profit concept of theory: a restatement', *Journal of Political Economy*, 62, pp. 152–70.

Willett, A.H. (1901) *The Economic Theory of Risk and Insurance*, New York: Columbia University Press.

Williamson, O.E. (1964) *The Economics of Discretionary Behaviour: Managerial Objectives in a Theory of the Firm*, Englewood Cliffs, NJ: Prentice-Hall.

Williamson, O.E. (1967) 'Hierarchical control and optimum firm size', *Journal of Political Economy*, 75, pp. 123–38.

Williamson, O.E. (1970) *Corporate Control and Business Behaviour*, Englewood Cliffs, NJ: Prentice-Hall.

Williamson, O.E. (1971) 'The vertical integration of production: market failure considerations', *American Economic Review*, 61, pp. 112–23.

Williamson, O.E. (1975) *Markets and Hierarchies: Analysis and Antitrust Implications*, New York: Free Press.

Wiseman, J. (1953) 'Uncertainty, costs and collectivist economic planning', *Economica*, N.S. 20, reprinted in J.M. Buchanan and G.F. Thirlby (eds), *LSE Essays on Cost*, London: Weidenfeld and Nicolson, 1973, pp. 227–43.

Wiseman, J. (1957) 'The theory of public utility price – an empty box', *Oxford Economic Papers*, 9, reprinted in J.M. Buchanan and G.F. Thirlby (eds), *LSE Essays on Cost*, London: Weidenfeld and Nicholson, 1973, pp. 245–71.

Wohl, R.R. (1949) 'An historical context for entrepreneurship', *Explorations in Entrepreneurial History* (Series 1), 1, pp. 8–16.

Wohl, R.R. (1953), 'The "rags to riches story": an episode in secular idealism', in R. Bendix and S.M. Lipset (eds), *Class, Status and Power*, New York: Free Press, pp. 388–95.

Wohl, R.R. (1954) 'The significance of business history', *Business History Review*, 28, pp. 128–40.

Wyllie, I.G. (1954) *The Self-made Man in America: the Myth of Rags to Riches*, New Brunswick, NJ: Rutgers University Press.

Index